How to Be Happy

Liz Hoggard

BBC BOOKS

About the author

Liz Hoggard writes about film, art and design for national newspapers including the *Observer, Guardian* and *Independent.* As a freelance broadcaster she has worked on *Woman's Hour, Night Waves, The Brian Morton Show,* Channel 4's *100 Sexy Moments at the Movies* and *Friends: The Last Ever Episode.*

Published by BBC Books
BBC Worldwide Limited
Woodlands
80 Wood Lane
London W12 0TT

First published 2005 to accompany the Optomen Television series produced for BBC TV.

ISBN 0 563 49320 8

Commissioning Editor: Nicky Ross
Project Editor: Charlotte Lochhead
Copy Editor: Patricia Burgess
Designer: DW Design
Production Controller: Kenneth McKay

Set in Futura and Spumoni
Printed and bound in Italy by LEGO SpA

For more information about this and other BBC books, please call 08700 777 001 or visit our website at www.bbcshop.co.uk

Contents

Introduction   6
Meet the Team of Experts   9
Happiness Manifesto   12

PART 1: THE THEORY

1   What Is Happiness?   15
2   Are You Happy?   23
3   The Science of Happiness   35

PART 2: THE PRACTICALITIES

4   The Friends Maintenance Programme   50
5   Can't Buy Me Happiness   63
6   Happy at Work?   72
7   Love Makes the World Go Round   90
8   Sexual Happiness   103
9   Happier Families   112
10 How to Make Happy Children   118
11 Eat Yourself Happy   128
12 Being Happy Makes You Healthy   143
13 Exercise: Why a Pedometer Beats a Vibrator   155
14 Happiness Is Pet-shaped   162
15 Happy Holidays   166
16 Happiness and Community   171
17 Smile and Feel Better   181
18 Laughter: the Sound of Happiness   185
19 Spiritual Happiness   190
20 Happy Ageing   198

PART 3: WHAT NEXT?

Further Help   206
Useful Addresses   211
Sources and Notes   213
Slough Facts, Figures and Short History   217
Appendix   220
Index   222

Introduction

'A lifetime of happiness! No man alive could bear it:
it would be hell on earth.'
George Bernard Shaw, author and playwright

What's so great about being happy? Pretty much everything. People who are happy perceive the world as safer, make decisions more easily, are more cooperative, and live healthier and more energized lives. Relationships, self-image and hopes for the future also seem more promising. Best of all, happy people are perceived as more attractive and more popular.

It's good news, then, that we can all learn to be more joyful. Scientific research increasingly suggests that happiness is a skill that can be learnt, like playing the violin or riding a bike. Everything we experience – joy, pain, curiosity, boredom – is represented in the mind as information. If we are able to control this information, we can decide what our lives will be like. So the exciting thing is that we really can learn to change the way the brain works and thus influence how happy we feel.

In fact you may be pleasantly surprised by what actually makes us happy. Today's social scientists agree that it's not success at work, pots of money, power or fame that guarantee a happy life. Instead bliss is to be found in simpler pleasures – family, community, sex with someone you love, pleasant surroundings, trust in fellow human beings, a less stressful commute to work.

There is no universal, one-fits-all solution for happiness, but there is a lot you can do to raise your capacity for joy. Start by looking at what you like to think about and do with your own free time. Then make sure you do more of it! No one is more expert on this topic than you are.

How to Be Happy is a book that will change the world – or at least one very important bit of the world: your bit. Take this book to work, read it on the bus, keep it in your handbag or briefcase, dip into it when you're feeling down or, more importantly, when you are having a really good time so that you can remember what exactly makes you feel good.

Chapters 1–3 explain the theory behind the fascinating new 'science of happiness', which combines the latest research in psychology, medicine and social science. In the past the goal was to bring us from a negative, depressed state to a neutral normal state. Now psychologists believe that they can take us from this neutral normal 'zero' state to plus five, which means that they (and we) can actually increase our happiness.

Chapters 4–20 offer you the practical details about how to change your life, looking at every aspect of well-being, from love and sex to health and travel. Here you can find out such things as the best mood-enhancing foods to eat, the number of sexual partners you should have to be happy, and ways of feeling more positive about exercise without actually going to the gym.

Of course, we wanted to back up our findings with genuine social experiment, so in May 2005 six experts in happiness spent three months working with a group of volunteers in and around Slough – a Berkshire town about 25 miles from London. The aim was to see whether the new science of happiness was effective or not.

We chose Slough for three main reasons: first because Slough's unemployment level (around 3 per cent) is amongst the lowest in the country and it's bristling with businesses (there are nearly 4000 in the town). So the factor that the scientists would be able to do least about – unemployment and income – was minimized. Second, Slough has a very diverse population, with a good mix of old and young, single people and couples, from a wide variety of ethnic and religious backgrounds, which meant we would be able to assess whether our interventions could work for everyone. The third reason that made Slough particularly attractive is that it is a town of fairly normal happiness levels: the people living there were no more (and no less) happy than anywhere else in the country. (See pages 217–19 for the facts, figures and history of Slough.)

Our happiness experts, who combine theoretical knowledge with hands-on expertise, created a programme of experiments and community-based activities tailored to the specific needs of Slough. Could they, for example, persuade the volunteers to cut their TV viewing by half, have a good laugh at least once a day, or count their blessings?

The result of their endeavours was the BBC series *Making Slough Happy*. This concentrated on four key aspects of happiness – the self, relationships, work, community – and was filmed chronologically, following the team of experts' progress.

As our experiment on happiness in Slough came to a climax, the experts and volunteers joined forces to convert the people of Slough to the happiness cause in one final celebration. In the town centre some of their newly learnt new tools of happiness were put into action. Slough residents found themselves unleashing their inhibitions as they created a human chain and talked to strangers. They even opened their vocal cords in an extraordinary primal scream! And eventually they found themselves hugging strangers along the High Street. Communities came together, infected by the spirit of happiness, to applaud the musical talents of fellow Slough residents.

Volunteers who had pushed themselves hard throughout the summer to learn to sing took to the stage to perform Slough's happiness anthem 'We're Going to Change the World'. Then the experts and volunteers took to the streets to persuade residents to keep Slough happy and sign up to the Happiness Manifesto (see page 12). And finally an enormous picture of a smiling face made from 2000 photographs of Slough taken by local residents, was unveiled by the people themselves. The picture represented how, through the summer of 2005, Slough had willingly succumbed to the new science of happiness and become a happier place. The picture remains in Slough today as a legacy of the town's happiness experiment.

This book not only explores and charts the new science of happiness, with statistics and evidence for a better understanding of how to be happy, but it also records many of the Slough exercises and testimonials from the volunteers who participated in the experiment. Their experiences are described, their words quoted, their changing attitude to life clearly revealed. By reading this book, tackling the exercises and following the tips you too can change the way you think and feel. The power to make your own life happier is in your hands.

'I wondered today, as I often do, if I need to change my life, move, find an easier job, or run away from life's responsibilities, even though I have so much. I need and want to provide a loving home for my family, but I just wish it could be a little easier…'
Slough volunteer at the start of the project

Remember, happiness is good for you, so don't be embarrassed about making it a priority. But finding it is not a competition. Authentic happiness derives from raising the bar for yourself, not rating yourself against others. A joyful life is an individual creation that cannot be copied from a recipe.

Read on to learn how you can increase your own happiness, and find out how you can help make your friends and family happier too.

How to Be Happy

Meet the Team of Experts

Richard Stevens

'Be happy to be alive' is the manifesto of Dr Richard Stevens, the team's psychologist. He is chair of the social psychology course and former head of the psychology department at the Open University, responsible for 11,000 students each year.

One of the most experienced and knowledgeable psychologists in the UK, Richard has been chair of the Association of Humanistic Psychology and was co-founder of the Consciousness and Experiential Section of the British Psychological Society. He was also on the team that organized the first European conference in positive psychology (the science of happiness). Revered among his students for his ability to link high-level psychological theorizing to issues of everyday living, he is also the author of several well-received books. Before becoming a psychologist, he directed several TV series, including episodes of *Dr Finlay's Casebook* and *Z Cars*.

Richard has a long-standing interest in understanding what makes us happy. Bold, articulate and passionate, he worked intensively with the Slough volunteers in regular all-day workshops designed to increase their happiness levels, and on exercises to develop the 'tools of happiness'. In addition, he set up away-days for the volunteers, including camping in the New Forest, visiting a health spa, a gratitude party and even a spot of graveyard therapy.

Brett Kahr

'I'm the traditional old-school nineteenth-century Freudian of the project,' says Brett, one of Britain's most distinguished psychotherapists, having worked in the mental health field for over 25 years. He is senior clinical research fellow in psychotherapy and mental health at the Centre for Child Mental Health in London, and visiting clinician at the Tavistock Centre for Couple Relationships.

Award-winning author of several books on psychoanalysis, he is also the resident psychotherapist on BBC Radio 2 and spokesperson for the BBC initiative 'Life II Live'. He has worked extensively as a consultant to many television programmes, including *Fame Academy* and *Operatunity*, and is also an accomplished musician and composer, who has worked widely in the West End.

Brett was responsible for holding group sessions with participants and putting together a 'happiness choir' that was designed to spread happiness through the joy of music and performance. The choir gave its first performance at the final celebration in Slough town centre.

Richard Reeves

Richard Reeves was the series' happiness evangelist, taking to the streets of Slough with a megaphone and soapbox to promote the science of happiness.

His expertise spans the varied fields of philosophy, public policy and economics. He holds a first-class degree from Oxford University and is currently completing his PhD in political economy at Warwick University.

He is the author of the much-publicized book *Happy Mondays: Putting the Pleasure Back into Work*, which calls for revolutionary re-evaluation of modern working life. He has been described by the *Guardian* newspaper as 'Britain's leading expert on workplace trends'. He has also written a pamphlet for the New Economics Foundation on 'The Politics of Happiness'. This important publication argues the case for well-being to be taken seriously by policy-makers.

A former Young Financial Journalist of the Year, Richard regularly writes columns on economics, public policy and work–life issues for the *New Statesman*, *Management Today*, the *Guardian* and the *Observer*. As a business consultant, he tours the world lecturing to the business community on a range of topics, including the future of work, corporate responsibility, motivation and gender.

In the TV series Richard focused on bringing the happiness project to the wider Slough community, and took to the streets to promote the Happiness Manifesto (see page 12). He also ran the *Making Slough Happy* 'Sex Campaign', and got out and about in the town to encourage smiling and positive energy.

Jessica Pryce-Jones

Jessica Pryce-Jones has degrees in both classics and psychology and was with Rothschild's Bank in Paris before working for eight years in the London insurance market. She believes that British culture is afflicted with a population of 'deficit thinkers', who think negatively about new challenges and are subsequently held back from realizing their true potential. As a result of this belief, she set up her own transformational change consultancy, i-Opener. Her aim is to inspire motivation within businesses and organizations by building on individuals' strengths. She thinks that everyone has the power to change and grow: the secret lies in unleashing inner potential.

In *Making Slough Happy* Jessica worked with her business partner Philippa Chapman to bring many of her tried-and-tested techniques to local businesses.

They introduced practical interventions to create an increased sense of trust between colleagues while creating a better work environment.

Jessica and Philippa helped the Slough volunteers address issues concerning their happiness at work.

Philippa Chapman

Philippa Chapman has worked at getting the most out of people all her professional life. With a degree in languages, and postgraduate studies in education, she has made it her aim, both in the UK and abroad, to get people to maximize their talents. Having been a senior bilingual associate with a leading US management consultancy, she is now part of the top team at i-Opener.

Philippa believes that people tend not to value themselves and their uniqueness enough. She says that the most important lesson anyone can learn is that 'it's good to be you', and that this is the key not only to happiness in general terms, but also to greater satisfaction and contribution at work.

Philippa describes her working relationship with Jessica at i-Opener and during the happiness project as 'a beautiful fit', each one complementing and balancing the other.

Andrew Mawson, OBE

Andrew is a social entrepreneur – in other words, a 'practical visionary' – who applies business principles and ideas to social questions. 'We may work on projects to do with homelessness, recycling, health and so on, but it's not the normal charity, voluntary-sector mindset,' he explains. 'We support individuals and their projects, but our aim is for them to become sustainable. It's about empowering people rather than them relying on charity.'

Andrew, whose career in the social sector has spanned over 20 years, is renowned for his pioneering work at the Bromley-by-Bow Centre in east London, which under his direction became the UK's first 'healthy living centre'. In 1998 he co-founded the Community Action Network, with Adele Blakebrough and Helen Taylor Thompson, and CAN is now the UK's leading organization for the development, promotion and support of social entrepreneurs. In 2000, Andrew received an OBE for his role at Bow.

Andrew is a specialist in discovering, fostering and galvanizing the passions of individuals and communities. As one of our team of experts, his brief was to encourage the Slough volunteers to realize their own potential and that of their town, and he used his experience to help organize a big community event that drew the Slough residents together and acted as the series finale.

Happiness Manifesto

Our team of experts came up with a workable 10-point plan, based on the latest research into the science of happiness, that the Slough volunteers could put into practice over the summer. In fact, these ideas work for everyone, and you will be surprised how simple some of them are... Do these things for two months and see the difference they make.

1   **Get physical.** Take half an hour of exercise three times a week.

2   **Count your blessings.** At the end of each day, reflect on at least five things you are grateful for.

3   **Take time to talk.** Have an hour-long, uninterrupted conversation with your partner or closest friend each week.

4   **Plant something** – even if it's just a window box or pot. Keep it alive!

5   **Cut your TV viewing by half.**

6   **Smile** at and/or say hello to a stranger at least once each day.

7   **Phone a friend.** Make contact with at least one friend or relation whom you have not spoken to for a while and arrange to meet up.

8   **Have a good laugh** at least once a day.

9   **Give yourself a treat** every day and take the time to really enjoy it.

10 **Spread some kindness.** Do a good turn for someone every day.

How to Be Happy

'In our quest for increasing our inner happiness we had to look deep into ourselves, our feelings, memories and thoughts – not always an easy thing to do and something that reduced me to the verge of tears more than once. But in doing so, I learnt an enormous amount about myself, so the outcome for me was positive. Overall my life has changed dramatically for the better, and I'm hoping it will continue to do so. My attitudes and thinking are different. Positive things are happening to me that are very fulfilling. But I've realized I need to put in more in order to get more out.'

Slough volunteer

Without exception, the Slough volunteers all had positive experiences as a result of following the manifesto. One observed: 'Since I've taken the Happiness Manifesto to heart, life is so full and interesting that I can hardly remember how I used to spend my time.' Another said: 'I have enjoyed growing things and found great pleasure in taking steps to make the garden a nicer place to be.' Someone else found it a springboard to lots of new ideas, such as 'Happiness breeds happiness' and 'Cultivating curiosity and trying to be surprised by something every day makes life more interesting'. Another remarked: 'Fulfilling the daily Happiness Manifesto goals has become almost automatic now. Life has become very busy – in a good way.'

Regardless of age, nationality or circumstances, people found that the manifesto had only positive results. 'I met an elderly woman in the park and I talked to her in German about the project. She agreed with everything in the manifesto – so it even works in a foreign language!' Even sceptics were won over: 'I began this project believing that it could all end up being a load of "psychobabble". However, I'm quickly learning that it's much more than that. Psychology researchers worldwide are working to uncover the ingredients of happiness. And here in Slough we are fortunate in having some eminent experts and psychologists guiding us on an exciting journey of discovery.'

We hope that the words and experiences of the Slough volunteers will inspire you to take up the manifesto's challenges and change your life for the better too. So come on, join us – what have you got to lose? Only an attitude to life that might be bringing you down and making you feel less than fulfilled. You can be happier, and here's how…

Part 1
The Theory

What Is Happiness?

'Happiness: state of well-being characterized by emotions ranging from contentment to intense joy.'
Dictionary definition

Happiness is an emotional state regarded as central to our well-being. Associated emotions include joy, exultation, delight, bliss and love. The English word 'happy' is derived from the old Norse word *happ*, meaning 'luck' or 'good fortune'. Interestingly, it doesn't have an exact equivalent in some languages.

Finding a precise definition of happiness remains one of the greatest philosophical challenges, and has taxed great thinkers from Aristotle and Plato to the Dalai Lama. Proposed definitions include 'freedom from want and distress', 'consciousness of the good order of things', 'assurance of one's place in the universe or society' and 'inner peace'. More generally, though, it can be defined as the state towards which humans and other animals are behaviourally driven to counter external forces that would otherwise lead to unhappiness (and presumably eventual death).

But there is one point on which almost everyone agrees: happiness is a uniquely desirable commodity. In every culture surveyed the majority of people say that they regard happiness as the ultimate goal in life, more important even than money. The USA even enshrines the right to 'life, liberty and the pursuit of happiness' in its constitution.

20 FACTS ABOUT HAPPINESS

Scientists are beginning to identify the roots of positive emotion. You will be surprised – and encouraged – by the findings of the latest research outlined below.

1. Although genes and upbringing influence about 50 per cent of the variation in our personal happiness, our circumstances (income and environment) affect only about 10 per cent. The remaining 40 per cent is accounted for by our outlook and activities, including our relationships, friendships and jobs, our engagement in the community, and our involvement in sport and hobbies.
2. After basic needs are met, extra material wealth has little or no effect on life satisfaction or happiness. (Broadly speaking you would have to receive a windfall of more than £1 million to transform you from an unhappy person to a happy one – and even then the effect would be only temporary.)
3. Older people are more satisfied with their lives than younger people: a recent survey by the Centre for Disease Control and Prevention found that people aged 20–24 are sad for an average of 3.4 days a month, as opposed to just 2.3 days for people aged 65–74.
4. If you do 20 minutes of exercise three times a week for six months, your general feeling of happiness will improve by 10–20 per cent.
5. People who rate in the upper reaches of happiness on psychological tests develop about 50 per cent more antibodies than average in response to flu vaccines.
6. According to researchers at the World Database of Happiness at Erasmus University in Holland, Denmark is officially the happiest nation in the world, followed by Malta, Switzerland, Iceland, Ireland and Canada.
7. In the USA clinical depression is 3–10 times more common today than two generations ago.
8. Immigrants tend to acquire the happiness characteristics of the nation to which they move, not the nation in which they were born.
9. In nations with high levels of income equality, such as the Scandinavian countries, happiness tends to be higher than in nations with unequal wealth distribution, such as the USA. People tend to prefer more local autonomy and more direct democracy to increased income.

How to Be Happy

10 Richer workers tend to be happier than poorer colleagues, but research suggests that happy people have a greater potential to become rich, so it's a question of well-off chicken and wealthy egg.

11 People who suffer strokes or other debilitating diseases suffer tremendously in the short term, but after a while their happiness is only slightly below the average for the population.

12 When people get married their happiness peaks, but after a while their happiness levels return to where they were before they got married.

13 People in steady relationships are happier than singletons.

14 Women tend to experience their all-time lowest life satisfaction at the age of 37, whereas men experience this at 42.

15 Having 100–200 belly laughs a day would be the equivalent of a high-impact workout, burning off up to 500 calories.

16 Gold doesn't guarantee happiness. Studies of Olympic athletes show that bronze-medal winners are happier than silver-medal winners, and sometimes happier than gold medallists. According to the Australian team's head psychologist, Graham Winters, it feels better to come third when you're not expecting it than to be just pipped for first.

17 The late pioneering social psychologist Professor Michael Argyle, who conducted numerous happiness studies, showed that among the things that make people happy are sport, music and – best of all – dancing. Enticing sports facilities everywhere would dramatically increase the nation's happiness. Group dancing, which combines exercise, music, community, touch and rules, also drastically increases happiness.

18 Several studies have shown that the presence of a pet can reduce blood pressure and stress, promoting health and happiness.

19 According to a new look at a 40-year-old study on child-rearing practices conducted at Harvard, those children who were hugged and cuddled the most grew up to be the happiest.

20 A good mood even has a distinctive smell. Scientists have found that people can judge whether someone is in a positive mood from their body odour alone. In one experiment men and women were shown funny or scary films while their armpit odour was collected on gauze pads. A week later researchers asked strangers to decide which pads had come from people in a good mood and which had come from frightened people. They were able to do this with surprising accuracy.

Can you test for happiness?

Scientists can use techniques such as PET (positron emission tomography) brain scanning to reveal that particular moods or emotions are accompanied by distinctive patterns of electrical and chemical activity in various regions of the brain.

The brain activity patterns associated with happiness and sadness are quite different from each other. Happiness is particularly associated with heightened electrical activity in the left prefrontal cortex of the brain (just behind the left eye). People who register higher levels of activity in this area are found to be better at controlling their feelings and recovering from upsetting experiences.

What is the difference between pleasure and happiness?

The term pleasure is often used to indicate a localized natural high. The chemical messenger substance dopamine is released by the brain in response to food, sex, drugs and other pleasurable stimuli (dopamine is sometimes called the brain's pleasure chemical).

Pleasure is a quick but ephemeral fix of animal sensation, so pleasurable experiences therefore produce only a temporary lift. Pleasure seekers need to increase the dose or move on to a new source.

Happiness, on the other hand, refers specifically to a long-term inner feeling, a sense that life is going well. You want that feeling, rather than the fleeting sensation of pleasure, to be maintained. It is a physical state of the brain, and one that we can induce deliberately. Psychologist and BBC happiness expert Richard Stevens concedes: 'It's not easy to change your feelings at will. But you can decide on what you think about. If you make sure you direct your thoughts along positive lines, good feelings are likely to follow. That's what makes regularly "counting your blessings" such a powerful tool for happiness.'

Pleasure is the high of visiting a nightclub; happiness is reading a great book or acquiring a new skill. There is nothing inherently wrong with pleasure, but a common mistake is to equate happiness with pleasure alone.

WHAT IS HAPPINESS?

For psychologist Richard Stevens, happiness has three primary ingredients:

1 Good feeling and positive mood.
2 Engagement with living and vitality.
3 Meaningfulness – making value choices in your life.

None of the *Making Slough Happy* volunteers had really considered the nature of happiness before the experiment began, and they reached some profound conclusions that touched them deeply. Here is one of their observations.

'Shakespeare's paradoxical idea of "sweet sadness" suggests for me that happiness is often the other side of sadness – it expresses a process of coming to terms with reality. I should not feel unhappy about experiencing sadness because the difficulties and events that bring sadness are often a catalyst for change that leads to something new and rewarding.'

What is happiness for?

Happiness is more than a warm glow. In evolutionary terms, it keeps us alive. Biologists like to talk about natural selection having 'designed' human features for certain tasks. Arguably, two of our greatest joys are food and sex – the first keeps us alive, the second perpetuates the human species. People pursue food and sex because eating and copulating release neurochemicals that make them feel happy. (By contrast, things that are bad for our survival, such as fire, dehydration or prison, are 'designed' to cause us pain.)

The search for good feeling is the mechanism that has preserved the human race. However, happiness is not designed to be a permanent state of mind. If the joy that comes from sex lasted for ever, we would copulate only once in a lifetime – but the euphoria would probably last that lifetime!

'There is no duty we so much underrate as the duty of being happy. By being happy we sow anonymous benefits upon the world.'
Robert Louis Stevenson, nineteenth-century author

MYTHS ABOUT HAPPINESS

Society has a genuine fear of happiness, as we can see in modern film and literature. Many modern novels explore the idea of people being brainwashed into happiness. In Aldous Huxley's futuristic fantasy *Brave New World* (1932), the World Controllers use genetic engineering to create the 'ideal' society in which recreational sex and drugs make everyone happy consumers. More recently Will Ferguson's hilarious satirical novel *Happiness TM* (2001) posits a nightmare scenario where a self-help book actually *works*, transforming people into passive, happy automatons, and bringing down global business because no one needs to drink or smoke or shop ever again.

Myth 1: Happiness is selfish.
The pursuit of happiness can seem selfish, conjuring up images of complacent people lazing around all day. We like to think that suffering ennobles us and gives us distinction. In fact, nothing could be further from the truth. You cannot help others or be truly useful unless you are happy. And you cannot be truly happy unless you are productive, useful and helping others.

Myth 2: Unhappy people are more creative.
Another myth suggests that we have to be unhappy to be creative – that true artists are tortured souls. In fact, research has shown quite the opposite: happy people are more creative.

Myth 3: Happy people are airheads.
Research has shown that even very happy people have appropriate responses to terrible events and do grieve. Like most people, they may experience low moods following failure or setbacks, but they recover faster. And happy people cope with practical problems better because they know when to change tack or give up. They are more resilient but also more realistic about what it is possible to achieve.

What's so great about being happy?

Everything. Happy people believe that they have control over their lives rather than being passive victims of chance. They also assume they have the skills and knowledge to exercise that control. Thinking that you are helpless and at the mercy of others is a form of negative thinking associated with depression.

Everything we desire in life – beauty, fame, wealth – can be seen as a means to a higher end: namely, happiness. But no one ever seeks happiness in the belief that it will bring some higher benefit. Arguably, therefore, it is the purest goal.

'A happy life is not a life full of blissful contentment; it's a life that contains elements of tragedy, challenge, misery, failure and regrets. But it's how we deal with them that makes the difference.'
Richard Reeves, BBC happiness expert

What about genes?

Of course genes (which influence whether we have a sunny, easy-going personality, deal well with stress and feel low levels of anxiety and depression) do play a crucial role in the development of any human characteristic, including happiness.

In 1996 David Lykken of the University of Minnesota published a paper looking at the role of genes in determining people's sense of satisfaction in life. He had gathered information on 4000 sets of twins born between 1936 and 1955 and found that identical ones reared apart were as much as 50 per cent more alike in their happiness levels than fraternal twins reared in the same household. In other words, as much as half of our capacity for happiness may be inherited.

The happiness 'set point'

It seems we all have a happiness 'set point', rather like a thermostat on a central heating system. This is partly genetically inherited, but it also depends on what happens to us in the first five years or so of life. A stable family background, for example, could enhance the set point, while instability could have an adverse effect. Thereafter, no matter what happens in our life – good, bad, fantastic, terrible – we tend to return after a time to our set point. Psychologists call this phenomenon the 'hedonistic treadmill' because happiness may go up and down in the short term, but over the long term we return to equilibrium.

Like a thermostat, this set point will drag our happiness back down even when good fortune happens. A 1978 study of US lottery winners, for example, found that they did not end up significantly happier than a control group of non-winners.

The good news is that after misfortune strikes the thermostat will strive to pull us out of our misery. Even people who suffer terrible injuries tend to return to their set point. A study of paraplegics found that a week after the accident they were angry and anxious, but after eight weeks their strongest emotion was happiness. (This, of course, depended on their level of happiness before the accident.) People are often surprised by how happy paraplegics can be. Nobel-prize-winning psychologist Daniel Kahneman deduced that the reason for this is because being disabled is not the only thing that makes up these people's lives. They enjoy all sorts of things, such as friendships, food and entertainment, and they are involved in and focused on all aspects of their existence, not just the being paraplegic part.

Similarly, kidney dialysis patients recognize that their health is relatively poor, yet in their moment-to-moment experiences they report being just as happy as healthy people. The same is true of those who suffer romantic break-ups: these may seem devastating at the time, but the broken-hearted eventually recover and return to their normal happiness set point. Psychologists call this adjustment to new circumstances 'adaptation'.

Does nurture play a role?

Our capacity for happiness (based on our genetic inheritance and childhood environmental factors) is only up to 50 per cent defined. So the good news is that we all have a chance, and the choice, to increase our happiness.

Unlike other more fixed heritable traits, such as height or eye colour, our capacity for happiness is a very changeable trait – especially during adolescence, but it remains so throughout life. Neuroscientists have found that the brain is highly plastic. This means that it can be 'reprogrammed' for a higher base level of happiness, whether or not we had a bumpy start in life, and even if our parents were themselves depressed.

Adaptation has its limits, of course. There are some bad events we never get used to, or that we adapt to only very slowly, such as child abuse, rape or the terrors of war.

Let's study happiness, not depression

Although many philosophies and religions have studied happiness over the past two centuries, science has ignored it. But now all that is changing. Since 1998, the new field of study called 'positive psychology' has emerged, which focuses on how people flourish rather than how they become ill. In chapter 3 we'll be looking at how this exciting new 'science of happiness' can change your life.

Are You Happy?

Sometimes happiness seems a mysterious, elusive quality that only other people possess. Even to think about it makes us self-conscious.

In a never-ending quest for happiness, we keep changing the external conditions of our life – new car, new job, new lover – in the belief that this will help us to be happier. But what would really make us happy is not getting rich, or slim, or the approval of others, but feeling good about our life. The bottom line is how we feel about ourselves. To improve life, we must improve the quality of our experience.

HAPPINESS QUESTIONNAIRE

The most common way of measuring happiness is to use a questionnaire. For the Slough Project, psychologist Richard Stevens was asked to devise a way of measuring the volunteers' happiness levels throughout the project. Working with psychologists Jane Henry and Linda Corlett, and psychotherapist Nevia Mullan, he selected two established tests of life satisfaction, and constructed three further tests of happiness and mood, specially for the project. Why not take half an hour now and fill in this questionnaire to test your current levels of life satisfaction and happiness? You can then redo the questionnaire in a few months' time, when you have read *How to Be Happy* and tried some of the suggestions and exercises, to see if you have been able to raise your levels of life satisfaction and happiness.

Life satisfaction

1 How satisfied are you with your life?
Please indicate with a number between 1 (not at all satisfied) and 10 (extremely satisfied).

General happiness level

2 In general, how happy or unhappy do you usually feel?
Put a tick against the one statement below that best describes your average happiness.

Extremely happy (feeling ecstatic, joyous, fantastic)
Very happy (feeling really good, elated)
Pretty happy (spirits high, feeling good)
Mildly happy (feeling fairly good and somewhat cheerful)
Neutral (not particularly happy or unhappy)
Slightly unhappy (just a bit below neutral)
Mildly unhappy (just a bit low)
Pretty unhappy (somewhat 'blue', spirits down)
Very unhappy (depressed, spirits very low)
Extremely unhappy (utterly depressed, completely down)

3 What percentage of the time do you feel happy, unhappy and neutral (neither happy nor unhappy)?
For each of the three statements below, give your best estimate between 1 and 100. Make sure the three percentages roughly add up to 100%.

On average, what percentage of the time do you feel **happy**?   %

On average, what percentage of the time do you feel **unhappy**?   %

On average, what percentage of the time do you feel **neutral** (neither happy nor unhappy?)   %

How to Be Happy

Satisfaction with various aspects of your life

4 How happy are you with each of the following areas of your life?
Indicate by placing a tick in one of the boxes on a scale from 1 to 10
(1 = not at all happy and 10 = completely happy).

Area of your life	Not at all happy									Completely happy
	1	**2**	**3**	**4**	**5**	**6**	**7**	**8**	**9**	**10**
Your work (or any unpaid work if not employed)										
Your home										
Your leisure										
Your main relationship										
Your family										
Your local community										
Your local environment										
Your diet										
Your exercise level										
Yourself generally										

'We can't all be happy, we can't all be rich, we can't all be lucky – and it would be so much less fun if we were… Some must cry so that others may be able to laugh the more heartily.'
Jean Rhys, Good Morning, Midnight *(1939)*

Slough questionnaire

5 **Below is a series of statements. Indicate how much you agree or disagree with each statement on a scale from 1 to 10. If you agree completely with the statement, put a tick in box 10. If you strongly disagree, put a tick in box 1. If you only partly agree or disagree, choose one of the other boxes accordingly.**

How far do you agree or disagree with the statements below?	Strongly disagree 1	2	3	4	5	6	7	8	9	Strongly agree 10
1 I can usually deal with the problems in my life.										
2 Nothing seems much fun these days.										
3 I feel valued by other people in my life.										
4 My life seems stuck in a rut.										
5 I'm unclear what I want from life.										
6 I often find myself doing things that fully absorb me.										
7 I can change things in my life for the better.										
8 Most of my daily activities seem trivial and unimportant.										
9 I feel in control of my life.										
10 I feel like a failure.										
11 I have all the energy I need.										
12 To me the world seems a pretty bleak place.										
13 My life is full of interesting possibilities.										
14 Life seems rather empty.										
15 I feel close to people around me.										

How to Be Happy

How far do you agree or disagree with the statements below?	Strongly disagree 1	2	3	4	5	6	7	8	9	Strongly agree 10
16 I have difficulty in arranging my life in a way that is satisfying to me.										
17 My life feels good.										
18 There is not much to look forward to in my life.										
19 Things usually work out for me the way I want.										
20 I'm not doing what I'd like to be doing										
21 I often get overwhelmed by problems.										
22 There is much beauty in the world around me.										
23 I like to get even when others have upset me.										
24 I have many things to be grateful for in my life.										
25 When it comes to it, most people cannot be trusted.										
26 Material possessions are important to me.										
27 Being in nature is important to me.										
28 I find it difficult to find much meaning in life.										
29 I enjoy my social life.										
30 Being happy in myself is more important to me than what others think of me.										

Affectometer (mood scale)

6 Below are some words that describe feelings. For each one, please indicate how often you have experienced this feeling over the last week by putting a tick in one of the boxes, on a scale where 1 means you have never experienced the feeling and 10 means you've felt it a great deal.

Feeling	Never 1	2	3	4	5	6	7	8	9	A great deal 10
1 Optimistic										
2 Bored										
3 Loving										
4 Tense										
5 Irritable										
6 Upset										
7 Enthusiastic										
8 Nervous										
9 Inspired										
10 Lonely										
11 Able to get down to things										
12 Relaxed										
13 Insignificant										
14 Happy										
15 Anxious										
16 Interested										
17 Depressed										
18 Tired										
19 Excited										
20 Withdrawn										
21 Joyful										
22 Peaceful										

How did you do?

Further details about the questionnaire and how to score yourself and interpret the results are given in the Appendix on pages 220–21.

Why do we become unhappy?

By the standards of our grandparents we are healthier and wealthier than ever before, yet an increasing number of us claim to be unhappy. Why else are we flocking to therapists, consulting divorce lawyers or taking Prozac? Many of us reach midlife and feel a tremendous sense of anticlimax. We may have the house, the car, the consumer durables and the partner of our dreams, so why the gnawing sense of dissatisfaction?

The biggest puzzle of all is why, given their wealth, people in the leading Western democracies aren't happier. After all, income levels in Europe and North America have risen steadily since the 1970s, yet satisfaction levels have hardly improved at all, and in the USA they have actually fallen. The number of male suicides in almost all Western nations from the 1970s to the present has risen (despite an overall drop in, for example, the British suicide rate in the last century). In recent years, rich countries seem to have higher suicide rates. Meanwhile, job satisfaction has not increased over the last quarter of a century.

Britain is turning into a nation of petulant tantrum-throwers. In a recent survey 70 per cent of people admitted that they now argue more just for the sake of it, while 67 per cent admitted they are getting angry in public more often. Is it the stress of modern life, or are we simply losing our capacity for joy?

Many of us risk unhappiness by overvaluing the validation and recognition that work brings. Some of us even feel we don't deserve to be successful and therefore happy. We believe that it is better to expect little and avoid the pain of disappointment. If you admit you feel unhappy, you can end up feeling flawed or a failure. (Is it any coincidence that the word 'sad' has come to mean 'inadequate' or 'unfashionable' in modern speech?) The social desirability of being happy – or at least appearing to be happy – is paramount.

But arguably the good thing about the current crisis of unhappiness is that it has encouraged psychologists, social scientists and economists to turn more of their energies to the age-old question: what makes people happy?

So how can you tell if you are happy?

Psychologists explain that happiness is a distinct state in its own right, not merely the absence of sadness and depression. It depends on three elements:

- Pleasure (the emotional sensation of feeling good in the here and now; the savouring of sensory experiences).
- The absence of displeasure (freedom from pain, anxiety; engagement with family, work, romance, hobbies).
- Satisfaction (judging, on reflection, that your life is good; finding meaningfulness in the service of something larger than you).

Of these three components of happiness, sensual pleasure is believed to be the least consequential. Engagement in life and finding meaning in our world are much more important. People who are good at communicating with others, for example, might find long-lasting happiness through becoming involved in politics or voluntary work, while a rock star wanting to save the world might find it in organizing a charity concert. You don't have to be religious to lead a meaningful life.

'I got the results of my Open University exam and I had done well. I was really happy and relieved. In fact I was ecstatic.'
Slough volunteer

Are you an optimist or a pessimist?

A common characteristic of happy people is optimism – a belief that life will go well and future events will be favourable. Optimistic people tend to regard their troubles as transient, controllable and specific to one situation. Pessimistic people, on the other hand, believe that problems will linger, that they are personal and entirely their fault. Small setbacks hurt for days, perhaps months.

The problem with being a pessimist is that if we become afraid of the consequences of failure – criticism, embarrassment or blame – this fear can paralyse us. Our career, our whole life, becomes lacklustre because of such self-defeating anxiety.

Optimists are also healthier. In general, they are less bothered by various illnesses and recover better from cancer and surgery. Scientists at the Mayo Clinic in Minnesota selected 839 consecutive patients who had referred themselves for medical care 40 years ago (and who had submitted themselves to a battery of tests, including one for the trait of optimism). Of these patients, 200 had died by the year 2000, and the optimists had 19 per cent greater longevity than the pessimists.

Of course there are times when it is good to carry out a task in a less then exuberant mood, such as filling in your tax return or sitting an exam. But generally, being happy makes us more creative and more open-minded. We have more to offer.

'When one door of happiness closes, another opens: but we often look so long at the closed door that we do not see the one which has been opened for us.'
Helen Keller, blind and deaf American lecturer, writer and scholar

Do you live in the past, present or future?

According to American positive psychologist Professor Martin Seligman, 'We are better equipped to be happy if we can enjoy the present, plan for the future and not dwell too much on the past.' Do you spend hours lamenting past mistakes, or wish away the present, dreaming of future happiness? Problems occur if we allow ourselves to become too fixated on any one time-perspective. The negative person is sad or bitter about certain aspects of the past, while the past-positive person takes a warm and nostalgic view of things, but is less happy in the other time zones.

The present-hedonist cares only how good things feel at the moment, while the present-fatalist feels swept away by events, and powerless. There's only one future-perspective profile: the ambitious goal-seeker, who creates a lot of stress for himself and those around him. To restore a healthy balance, psychologist Philip Zimbardo advocates that we should actively develop a 'flexible time perspective', where we can learn to savour whichever dimension is going to be most helpful and reflect our true values. 'Too often,' says Zimbardo, 'goals are all about the future. They miss the present moment. As a result, too many of us live in the "not now". Ask yourself, what is important about today? If you could live your best life today, what would you do differently right now?'

Don't sweat the small stuff

Psychologists have found that people think more about the big picture when they are happy, tending to focus obsessively on detail when they are unhappy. According to Seligman, some people can put their troubles aside and go about their life effectively even when a major part of it, such as their job or marriage, is falling apart. Others can't do this at all. When one thing goes wrong, their whole life collapses.

In fact, Seligman says, it is important to make a distinction between universal and specific explanations. If, for example, someone rejects you, it is more helpful and accurate to say, 'He finds me annoying' (a specific explanation) rather than 'I am annoying' (a universal explanation). It's important not to let one painful home truth tip you over into a totally negative cycle of thinking.

What is the difference between self-esteem and satisfaction?

Self-esteem is about liking yourself, which is clearly an important quality for life. Low self-esteem can impair social relationships. If you are not happy with yourself, it is hard to be happy with other people. But satisfaction is about how you evaluate your life in the long term. Do you like the way it is going? In principle, you could have quite high self-esteem yet still be dissatisfied by the progress of your job or relationship.

What makes very happy people?

To find out the secret of being very happy, Martin Seligman and another American psychologist, Ed Diener, investigated individuals who ranked in the top 10 per cent of consistently very happy people. The most interesting factor they discovered is that happy people are well connected to others – they have rich personal relationships, a better social life, spend least time alone, and are rated highest on good relationships by themselves and friends. They did not differ on the amount of sleep they got, their TV watching, exercise, smoking, alcohol intake or religious activity.

Can I change?

We're all different, so what gives joy to one may be insufferably boring to another, but there are certain broad rules you can apply to raise your capacity for joy.

As discussed in chapter 1, it is possible to change the way you think and to optimize your chances of happiness. In fact, that was the purpose of the Slough experiment and is the whole point of this book. To improve your level of happiness you can pick up clues from what you like to think about, read and do with your own free time. You can then set goals that are stretching but not overambitious (unattainable goals are a well-known cause of depression).

If you have built your whole life on doubting your self-worth, learning to value and accept yourself will change everything – how you think, how you get on with people and the choices you make. You deserve to be happy – we all do. Remember that happiness is good for you, so don't be embarrassed about making it a priority. Psychologists have compared the journey to happiness as helping people to open a window and take a look around.

Life is filled with opportunities to feel serene and happy, but it also has moments of fear, irritation and despair. Such feelings are written into our genetic code; they're what it means to be human. To deny the existence of difficult feelings is to live a half-life. But we can be happier.

Remember, life is not a competition. Authentic happiness derives from setting yourself higher goals or standards, not from comparing yourself against others. A joyful life is one that is created by you – a unique creation that cannot be copied from someone else's recipe.

How to Be Happy

'It's like being your own life detective... no one is more expert on bringing happiness into your life than you are.'
Liz Hoggard, author and journalist

ARE YOU A MAXIMIZER OR A SATISFICER?

BBC happiness expert Richard Stevens, drawing on the work of US psychologist Barry Schwartz, argues that a maximizer is a perfectionist who always wants the best. When out shopping, for example, this kind of person looks at all the alternatives before deciding what to buy. The satisficer, on the other hand, says, 'That's good enough – that'll do me.' The maximizer is doomed to misery in the modern world because there is so much choice. Going out for a simple bite to eat and finding a restaurant turns into a trawl for *haute cuisine,* while the satisficer thinks, 'This one looks OK – let's go in here.' For the maximizer it's not only a case of information overload but also of regret afterwards too – for all the choices that weren't made.

Stevens gave the Slough volunteers a questionnaire devised by Schwartz. Those who scored high were encouraged to content themselves with what is good enough rather than always seeking the best, especially where everyday decisions were concerned.

If you are interested in finding out whether you are a maximizer or not, try the test on page 34.

MAXIMIZATION SCALE

Write a number from 1 (completely disagree) to 7 (completely agree) next to each question.

- ☐ Whenever I'm faced with a choice, I try to imagine what all the other possibilities are, even ones that aren't present at the moment.
- ☐ No matter how satisfied I am with my job, it's only right for me to be on the lookout for better opportunities.
- ☐ When I am in the car listening to the radio, I often check other stations to see if something better is playing, even if I am relatively satisfied with what I'm listening to.
- ☐ When I watch TV, I channel surf, often scanning through the available options even while attempting to watch one programme.
- ☐ I treat relationships like clothing: I expect to try a lot on before finding the perfect fit.
- ☐ I often find it difficult to shop for a gift for a friend.
- ☐ Renting videos is really difficult. I'm always struggling to pick the best one.
- ☐ When shopping I have a hard time finding clothing that I really love.
- ☐ I'm a big fan of lists that attempt to rank things (the best films, the best singers, the best athletes, the best novels, etc.).
- ☐ I find letter writing very difficult, even just to a friend, because it's so hard to get it just right. I often do several drafts.
- ☐ No matter what I do, I have the highest standards for myself.
- ☐ I never settle for second best.
- ☐ I often fantasize about living in ways that are quite different from my actual life.

Score
Add up all your numbers.
40 or lower: you are on the satisficing end of the scale.
50: this is average.
65 or above: you are on the maximizing end of the scale.

The Science of Happiness

'Count your blessings and enjoy every minute of life.'
Yoko Ono, American artist

The term 'positive psychology' was invented by the American psychologist Professor Martin Seligman to describe a psychological movement that focuses on people's positive emotions, individual strengths and virtues rather than negative states of mind, such as anxiety, depression and stress. It encourages psychologists to focus on enhancing and extending life's positive aspects.

In the past psychologists believed that the absence of mental illness meant that people were well enough. If help were needed, the goal was to bring patients from a negative, ailing state to a neutral, normal state. Now psychologists believe that they can actually increase our happiness rather than just stop us being depressed.

Positive psychology integrates neurobiology, psychology, medicine, education and social science. It is not intended to replace other forms of therapy but to run alongside them. As BBC expert Brett Kahr remarked: 'I think what's creative and interesting about the Slough Project is that we're taking solid psychological and psychotherapeutic knowledge into the field – namely, Slough. It's been a great adventure, simultaneously exhilarating and terrifying, because none of us has ever done anything like this before.'

The good news is that many of positive psychology's goals and exercises, and the things they helped the Slough volunteers to learn during their experiment with happiness, are extraordinarily effective for use in everyday life.

Positive psychology was born in 1998 when Seligman, who had worked on depression for 30 years, stunned an audience of the American Psychological Association by saying that psychologists had gone off course. Rather than devoting themselves only to lives that had gone desperately wrong, he said, they should focus instead on people for whom everything was going well. By discovering the secrets of a happy life it would be possible to find a recipe for happiness.

The speech was a huge success, and Seligman soon found himself awarded $30 million of research funding, which he has used to set up scientific studies looking into all aspects of positive psychology.

Accentuating the positive

Positive psychologists believe that mental health should be like a form of muscular fitness or athleticism for the mind and spirit. The key is to identify exactly what makes us happy and incorporate more of it into our lives. Easy you might say: just give me more money, sex and fame! But it doesn't work like that.

As pointed out in chapter 2, once our basic material needs have been met, additional money and status don't make us more content. Neither do youth, education or a high IQ. If you trace the trajectory of most people's happiness over time it resembles a U-curve. People typically record high satisfaction levels in their early 20s. These then fall steadily towards middle age, before troughing at around 42. Most of us then grow steadily happier as we get older, with those in their 60s expressing the highest satisfaction levels of all – so long, that is, as they stay healthy.

Although happiness has a large genetic component, none of us are prisoners of evolution. Positive psychology – or the 'science of happiness' as it has been dubbed – is based on the premise that happiness is a state of mind that each of us can cultivate by identifying and using many of the strengths and traits we already possess, such as kindness, originality, humour, optimism and generosity.

'To effect a change you have to change your thinking. Realizing that was a revelation to me and I'm in the process of trying to do it. I'm viewing my situation and my place in the world with different eyes. I hope I keep this change in my train of thought because it is beneficial to me and I actually feel happier. I feel lifted.'
Slough volunteer

Don't obsess about your bad points

Rather than encouraging us to focus on our bad points and try to correct weaknesses, positive psychology advocates concentrating on establishing and building our signature strengths. Ask yourself: when does time stop for me? When do I find myself doing exactly what I want to be doing, and never wanting it to end? By identifying the sources of happiness in our life and making a conscious effort to optimize them, most of us should be able to raise our average satisfaction levels.

But how do we identify our signature strengths? In his book *Authentic Happiness* (and online at www.authentichappiness.org) Seligman describes 24 signature strengths (chosen because they are valued in almost every culture) and provides a questionnaire that helps you to identify your top five. The strengths that he insists

How to Be Happy

are 'measurable and acquirable' include critical thinking, social intelligence, perseverance, leadership, discretion and a love of learning. If, for example, you think your top strength is love of learning, you need to ask if it gives you:

- A sense of authenticity ('this is the real me').
- A feeling of excitement while displaying it.
- A rapid learning curve as the strength is first practised.
- A sense of yearning to find new ways to use it.
- A feeling of inevitability in using the strength ('try and stop me').
- Invigoration rather than exhaustion.
- Joy, zest, enthusiasm, even ecstasy.

Achieving 'flow'

Positive psychology argues that once we know our signature strengths, using them more and more in our daily lives will make us feel happier and more fulfilled. By exploiting our strengths we become completely immersed in what we are doing, whether working, making music or playing sport – a state positive psychologists call 'flow'.

The Hungarian psychologist Mihaly Csikszentmihalyi (pronounced 'cheeks-sent-me-high') has identified that there is a class of flow activities that completely absorb people while they are engaged in them and which they remember afterwards as highly gratifying. These playful or creative activities can range from mastering a three-point turn while driving to executing a perfect salsa step. All of us know the feeling of being so caught up in something that we stop watching the clock. And being able to forget temporarily who we are seems very enjoyable.

'I always describe "flow" as that moment when you're so absorbed in a task that you stick your tongue out. Children do it while they are colouring.'
Richard Reeves, BBC happiness expert

Virtually anything can be a flow activity – reading, working out mathematical equations, telling a story, even socializing – anything you become immersed in. Flow activities have several things in common:

- They set challenges and require skill.
- They involve concentration, stretching the mind or body to its limits.
- They establish clear goals.
- We get immediate feedback.
- We have deep, effortless involvement in them.
- There is a sense of control.
- Our sense of self vanishes.
- Time stops.

Well-being is most authentic, Seligman claims, when it comes from engaging in something we are good at. By contrast, we feel drained when doing something that we struggle with.

Some of Seligman's findings are not new, of course. 'We mustn't forget the decades of effective work by humanistic psychologists, such as Carl Rogers and Abraham Maslow,' advises BBC happiness expert Richard Stevens. 'They devised many techniques for helping people towards personal growth and greater fulfilment in their lives.' Stevens drew on their ideas and methods, as well as on positive psychology, to create the happiness exercises for the *Making Slough Happy* volunteers.

The volunteers understood the concept of flow, even though they weren't familiar with this name for it. And many of them had experienced it too in different contexts. One told us: 'I'd been really stressed out with revision, so my mother suggested we went and played badminton. Five minutes into playing I'd forgotten all about my exam and was simply having fun. I left with a smile on my face.' Another volunteer found singing hugely enjoyable and that it cured his stutter: 'Performing live on stage and connecting with the crowd filled me with so much confidence. Since I've been doing this project, I haven't stuttered one bit. I was really low, but now I've got my energy back. I'm a different person.'

One volunteer even found flow in the unlikely situation of a traffic jam: 'We hit heavy traffic on the motorway, so we decided to take an alternative route home. As my partner was driving, it was up to me to navigate. It's not my strong point, so I felt really pleased with myself when I got us home successfully without getting lost. The feeling was even better because we had turned a potentially unpleasant experience of a traffic jam into a happy adventure.'

WHY IS IT CALLED FLOW?

In his seminal book *Flow: The Classic Work on How to Achieve Happiness*, Mihaly Csikszentmihalyi explains that he (and later Seligman) adopted the term 'flow' because many of the people they interviewed had used it when describing how it felt to be on top form: 'I was carried along by the flow.' Those who attained flow, he claims, 'developed a stronger, more confident self because more of their psychic energy had been successfully invested in goals they themselves had chosen to pursue'.

In addition, he found, the flow experience was enjoyed in similar ways by everyone, regardless of culture, social class, age or gender. The key, he says, is to learn to transform jobs into flow-producing activities, and to think of ways of making relations with parents, partners, children and friends more enjoyable. Even routine experiences, such as mowing the lawn or doing the housework, can become enjoyable provided we restructure the activity by providing goals and rules.

Richard Stevens encouraged volunteers in the Slough Project to use their imagination to find ways of making normally tedious tasks more enjoyable. 'Whether you enjoy something or not,' he says, 'has much to do with your attitude.' So volunteers tried different strategies for livening up their housework, such as washing up at speed, polishing with love, or vacuuming to music.

You could put on an upbeat record, such as Queen's 'I Want to Break Free', and get into the groove as you vacuum away. Or set yourself a time and do it fantastically quickly. It's a question of identifying goals or rules, just as you do when you play a game. Any activity can be made into a game and consume your attention – and give you pleasure – if you set your mind to it.

For the Slough Project, Richard Stevens worked with his colleagues Jane Henry, Linda Corlett and Nevia Mullan to create a set of happiness exercises or tools that the volunteers were encouraged to try out in their own time. These included an exercise to help them experience more flow in their lives.

FINDING YOUR FLOW

Flow, or inner joy, can come from anything that makes you feel excited, exhilarated, high-spirited, invigorated and happy. Everyone finds flow in a different way – perhaps by playing football, going to the gym, singing with a choir, playing with children, going to a party, or watching a good movie.

What are you going to do over the next few weeks to get more flow into your life? Take the time to think about what you enjoy doing and write down a few ideas below. You can then refer to these notes throughout the next few weeks to remind yourself to do more of these things.

I will

_____

_____

_____

_____

_____

_____

_____

_____

_____

_____

_____

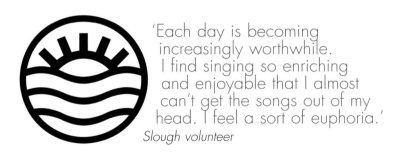

'Each day is becoming increasingly worthwhile. I find singing so enriching and enjoyable that I almost can't get the songs out of my head. I feel a sort of euphoria.'
Slough volunteer

THE POWER OF POSITIVE EXPERIENCE

Over the years information has been systematically gathered from hundreds of surveys measuring happiness across cultures, professions, religions, social strata and economic groups. These surveys use various methods, one of which is 'day reconstruction'. This involves keeping a diary and filling in a long questionnaire detailing everything you did on the previous day, who you were with, and rating a range of feelings experienced during each event.

The method has been used on 900 women in Texas with surprising results. It turned out that the five most positive activities were (in descending order): sex, socializing, relaxing, praying or meditating, and eating. Exercising and watching TV followed. But far down the list was 'taking care of my children', which came below cooking and just above housework!

In national surveys, on the other hand, people frequently cite their children as their biggest source of delight. In a *Time* magazine poll in December 2004 around 35 per cent of readers put their children and grandchildren top. So how do we account for this fluctuation in how people rate positive activities and experiences?

Psychologist Daniel Kahneman of Princeton University attributes it to a disparity between our 'experiencing' self and our 'remembering' self. His studies show that what you remember of an experience is particularly influenced by the emotional high and low points and by how it ends. So if a car driver hoots at you at the beginning of your holiday in Italy when you are trying to navigate in heavy traffic, it could put you in a bad mood and be the thing that sticks in your mind about your trip. But that same experience at the end of the holiday, when you are feeling rested and have happy memories of lovely meals and interesting day trips, will have far less impact.

Dance yourself happy

The British are very uptight about physical intimacy, so Richard Stevens recommends dancing to break down inhibitions and help people to find flow. 'Dancing has key ingredients that can make us happy,' he says. 'It involves the body, our emotional response to music and connecting with others.' As one of the strategies for promoting happiness among the *Making Slough Happy* volunteers, he brought in Patricia Martello (director of the UK School of Biodanza) to run sessions of biodanza, a system devised by South American psychologist Rolando Toro for developing both feelings and the ability to connect with others.

One of the volunteers who tried biodanza described the experience: 'As the music started, my body responded. My energy levels started rising and my feet began tapping. I loved having the opportunity to express myself through movement, no steps to learn, no right or wrong, casting inhibitions aside and allowing my body to respond to the rhythm. I left the workshop feeling full of energy and that feeling lasted for a whole week.'

It doesn't matter what kind of dancer you are: losing yourself in dance gives a fantastic sense of release, both emotional and physical. One participant got extra benefit from it because, as she said, 'I'm good at it and that really gave me a sense of achievement.'

Dreams may come true

Remember your early childhood ambitions? Maybe you can introduce some of them as enjoyable flow activities. In *Making Slough Happy* our psychotherapist Brett Kahr set up a childhood dreams group with the volunteers. As he explains, 'Sigmund Freud once said, "Money never made anybody happy because money was never an infantile wish." I believe that one of the reasons many of us are unhappy, despite having a spouse and 2.4 children and a Jeep and a labrador and a house in the country and a chief executive's job, is that these things were also never childhood wishes. Through psychotherapy I try to help people discover what their early – and often frustrated – childhood passions were, and to see whether we can find some creative way of bringing them to life again now.

'While psychotherapy can't fulfil the wish of a slightly tubby 50-year-old man who's always wanted to be a professional footballer, it can help him find a way of introducing the pleasures of physicality, sportsmanship and male bonding into his life, and this could help him to be happier.'

BBC happiness expert Richard Stevens helped a group of those he was working with to identify what they really wanted to do with their lives and to set up realistic steps towards achieving this goal. One woman devised and performed a stand-up comedy routine, while another wrote the story she had always longed to write, which she read to the rest of the group.

'Thanks to the Slough Project I think I'm experiencing emotions that I haven't had since my carefree childhood. I'm meeting more people, making new friends, doing more. I'm less tired than I used to be and seem to need less sleep, but actually sleep better and wake refreshed and ready to go.'
Slough volunteer

Short cuts to happiness don't work

Although many of us enjoy short cuts to happiness, such as alcohol, sex, shopping or recreational drugs, the high doesn't last. Most of us actually prefer to 'earn' pleasure so that we feel entitled to it. Much of the goodness of life comes from experiencing the journey, not simply arriving.

According to Professor Seligman, gratification activities in which we engage fully – reading a great book, dancing, rock climbing – last longer than bodily pleasures, and build up our psychological capital (happiness in the bank) for the future. Of course, he doesn't want to ban bodily pleasure altogether – he just recommends spacing it out. If we get caught up in a vicious cycle of craving, we need bigger hits more often. And the negative comedown afterwards – hangover, scary credit card bills, a larger waistline – can lead to self-hatred.

Concentrate on what went right

If you want to change the way you think and be happier, start by thinking about what goes right on a daily basis. Whenever you begin feeling negative about things, take a moment out and remind yourself of the stuff that has gone well. It could be anything from a pleasant conversation to a good haircut, or the fact that it didn't rain when you were on your way to work.

If you think about bad things in terms of 'always' and 'never', you have a permanent, pessimistic style, suggests Seligman. But if you think in terms of 'sometimes' and 'lately', blaming bad events on temporary downturns, you have an optimistic style.

'I always try not to take things for granted and to remind myself how lucky I am. Writing down the good things is very helpful. No matter where I am in my life, I've always got that list of positive things to reflect on.'
Slough volunteer

Richard Stevens emphasized to the volunteers the importance of being aware of how they really feel, not how they are supposed to feel. 'Comparing yourself with others is bound at some point to make you feel unhappy. It's crucial to direct your behaviour by what really makes you feel good not what others tell you happiness is.'

Helped by colleagues Jane Henry, Linda Corlett and Nevia Mullan, Richard Stevens ran four all-day workshops on happiness for the Slough Project volunteers. They spent the first morning on strategies to develop a more positive sense of self. One of the exercises they used is on page 44.

POSITIVE THINKING

A key principle in psychology is that what you think affects what you feel. Here are a few ideas to help you to increase the amount of time you spend in a positive mood.

Count your blessings. Make a deliberate attempt at least once a day to reflect on some of the good and maybe wonderful things in your life.

Remember what you like about yourself. At the moments when you are not at your happiest, think about qualities you are glad to have.

Think positive thoughts. When negative thoughts intrude, think about something more positive (you'll get better with practice), or do something you like, even if it's only for a short time.

Think about what you will do over the next weeks to increase your positive feelings and write a reminder list to refer to:

I will

_____

_____

_____

_____

_____

_____

_____

_____

Get away from your pessimistic inner voice

Positive psychology tells us that our reflexive habits – what we say to ourselves when something goes wrong – are usually distortions: mere bad habits of thought produced by unpleasant experiences in the past, such as strict parents, childhood conflicts or a harsh teacher. But because these things now seem to issue from ourselves, we regard them as gospel.

Just because we fear we are unlovable or unemployable doesn't mean it's true. It is important to keep your pessimistic voice at a distance at least for long enough to see if it proves accurate. Very often dark thoughts are over-reactions. For example, if you break your diet once, then think 'I'm a complete pig' and give up on the diet, surely that's the wrong sort of home truth? Ask yourself, 'Is there a less destructive way to look at this?'

Psychotherapist Nevia Mullan, helping with the *Making Slough Happy* Project, advised the volunteers to keep negative feelings in proportion. 'When bad things happen,' she told them, 'it's important you remember all the other positive aspects of your life to stop the one negative event having too much influence on your feelings.'

Of course reframing – learning to recognize and dispute automatic pessimistic thoughts – takes practice. Research shows that it takes 21 days to create a new habit pathway in the brain, and a further 63 days of regular activity to consolidate what you have learnt. You may feel strange at first, but keep on practising and soon it will feel as if you have always behaved in the new way.

Whatever you do, never try to solve things in the middle of the night when you can't sleep. Tell yourself: 'It is the middle of the night and I am in no fit state to solve anything now. Tomorrow will be a better time to worry about this.'

Above all, don't blame yourself for having negative thoughts – that's like punishing yourself twice.

'I think it's good to be positive about life and to believe that tomorrow is going to be a good day.'
Slough volunteer

Ambition and happiness

Before investing great amounts of energy in a goal, ask yourself some important questions.

- Is this something I really want to do?
- Am I likely to enjoy it in the foreseeable future?
- Is the price that I – and others – will have to pay worth it?
- Will I be able to live with myself if I accomplish it?

As Mihaly Csikszentmihalyi observes, a workaholic may come to realize that it 'is more enjoyable to talk with one's two-year-old than to play golf with the company president'.

12 STEPS TO HAPPINESS

Psychologists believe that there are concrete steps we can all take to bring positive psychology, and therefore happiness, into our lives.

1 Do a job that you like.
2 Act happy. Put on a happy face, pretend to be optimistic and outgoing. In experiments people who feign high self-esteem begin feeling better about themselves.
3 Be your own best friend. Stop criticizing yourself and making impossible demands.
4 Be in the present every day by giving yourself a treat or reward – not because you deserve it, but because it's a nice thing to do.
5 Invest time and energy in friends and family. This is far more important for your well-being than where you live or how much you earn.
6 Seize the day. Taking an optimistic approach to life's problems, not exaggerating them and letting them drag you down produces a 'core' on which to build your happiness.
7 Savour life's joys. Focus on the freshness of a green salad or the way the sun dapples the lawn. Psychologists suggest taking 'mental photographs' of pleasurable moments to keep you going in more stressful times.
8 Take control of your time. Set big goals, then break them down into smaller daily aims. As each mini-deadline is met, you will get a delicious feeling of being in control.
9 Develop a strategy for coping with stress and hardship, whether it's your own personal religious faith or positive thoughts, such as: 'The worst has already happened'; 'What doesn't kill me, makes me stronger'; 'This happened before and I survived it'.
10 Listen to music. It's both relaxing and stimulating, and can also boost your brainpower!
11 Take up active hobbies. These tend to make you happier than those carried out slumped in an armchair (gardeners and people who go to the theatre are happier than TV watchers).
12 Channel 'wasted' time constructively. If a friend is late, use the time in a productive way rather than fretting. 'As a society we have very little time to reflect,' says BBC happiness expert Jessica Pryce-Jones. 'We're very busy doing, but we're not that busy thinking or feeling. So to have some time to gather your thoughts is very useful.'

In the happiness workshops done with the Slough volunteers Richard Stevens and his team emphasized the importance of looking after yourself psychologically, particularly when under stress. They encouraged the volunteers to explore their preferred strategies for taking care of themselves.

TAKING GOOD CARE OF YOURSELF

During stressful or challenging times we all need strategies that will help us to regain well-being and happiness, so make a list of what you can do to support yourself. Here are a few ideas:

- Rest/sleep/do nothing for half an hour, or have a leisurely and relaxing aromatic bath.
- Go for a walk, preferably in the country or a park, or do some gardening.
- Listen to music or watch a funny film.
- Arrange to have a haircut, massage, beauty treatment, or healing or counselling session.
- Look around charity shops and buy something for yourself.
- Go to the gym, have a swim or sauna, go fishing or play tennis.
- Write down how you feel, write a letter or a poem, or read an inspiring book.
- Use your imagination to alter or add to this list, taking into account your own personal circumstances and tastes. Ask other people what they do. Make sure you do at least one or two of these activities each week. Concentrate and really enjoy the experience.

Write down a few things you might do to take care of yourself. Keep the list as a reminder to do them.

I will

_____
_____
_____
_____
_____
_____

In keeping with the message of this 'Taking good care of yourself' exercise, Richard Stevens took six of the volunteers to a health spa, where they relaxed in a flotation tank and received massage and aromatherapy.

Boost happiness with kindness

'Helping others is a good way of helping yourself,' says BBC happiness expert Richard Stevens. 'Research shows that happy people help others more. And it also indicates that if you are kind to others, it will lift your mood. So help that stranger pick up the groceries they dropped, slow down and let another car join the flow of traffic, or just open a door for someone. Kindness is a real boost to happiness.'

Some of the *Making Slough Happy* volunteers made a particular effort to be kinder and were delighted with the results. One told us that she simply paid a compliment to an office colleague: 'I saw her face light up. It was cool – I really enjoyed it.'

The gratitude party

Richard Stevens thinks we don't express sufficiently often the appreciation we feel for others. 'When someone does you a good turn or you really value what they do – then tell them how much you appreciate it. This might be in small ways – thanking the bus driver who holds the bus while you run to catch it. Or it can be about expressing appreciation to those who have made a special contribution to your life. This won't only make them feel good but it's virtually guaranteed to make you happy too.'

Following a method used by Seligman, Stevens arranged a 'gratitude party' in which several of the Slough volunteers took part. Each selected someone who had been especially important to them in some way. Two women chose their mothers, two people their close friends, two others their spouses. Each was asked to write a tribute to the person they were grateful to and have it framed or made up in a special way. Without revealing what it was about, the volunteers invited their chosen people to a party and publicly read out the tributes they had written. It proved to be an amazingly moving occasion. Both participants and those watching were several times moved to tears of joy. Stevens concludes: 'We don't have a mechanism for expressing our appreciation in our society, so it's important to set up occasions like this. It is a sure way of making people happy. And judging from our experience with the volunteers, it's a glow that lasts quite a time.'

'Live with love in your heart and always remember to count your blessings.'
Brooke Shields, American actress

Part 2
The Practicalities

4

The Friends Maintenance Programme

'The worst solitude is to be destitute of sincere friendship.'
Sir Frances Bacon (1561–1626), English lawyer and philosopher

FRIENDSHIP FACTS

- Most of us have an average of 30 friends at any one time, six of whom we consider close.
- Over a lifetime we make around 400 friends, but just 10 per cent of these will last. Once a group gets much bigger than 150, everyone finds it hard to keep track.
- Men have on average one fewer close friends than women do. Middle-class men have more friends than working-class men.
- In a recent survey more than 60 per cent of British adults claimed that their friendships were more important than career, money or even family.
- Both men and women find their friendships with women more emotionally satisfying than those with men.
- People with strong social support and intimate friendships visit the doctor less often.
- One in three of us meets most of our friends through work.
- Laughter is 30 times more likely to occur in a group situation than a solitary one.

According to *The Concise Oxford Dictionary*, a friend is 'one joined to another in intimacy and mutual benevolence independently of sexual or family love; a person who acts for one; sympathizer, helper, patron; one who is not an enemy; one who is on the same side'.

Friendship is extremely valuable, and it is also one of the least expensive ways to be happy. People of all ages report the most positive moods overall when they are with friends. Research has shown that personal relationships contribute more to our mental and physical health than money, fame, conventional success or material possessions. As one academic put it, your address book is probably worth more to you than your school or university qualifications.

'Friendliness is an expression of good mental health,' confirms BBC happiness expert Brett Kahr. On average, lonely people have shorter, unhealthier and unhappier lives. Perhaps it's not surprising, then, that happy people make the best friends. We all like being with them. And people with close, fulfilling friendships are happier. This is known as a virtuous circle.

Some people find it tricky to make friends, but it's possible to get better at it by learning how to be more emotionally competent. Changing your mood can really benefit your social network.

'Of all the things that wisdom provides to help one live one's life in happiness, the greatest by far is the possession of friendship. Eating or drinking without a friend is the life of a lion or a wolf.'
Epicurus, Greek philosopher

Freedom in friendship

On one level, friendships are very simple. They are the bonds between people who enjoy each other's company on the basis of common interests and complementary goals. Most of us feel a certain pride about our friends, pleased that they have chosen us and that we have chosen them. We believe that they reflect some important truths about who we are. Long-term friends are the witnesses to our lives: they 'get' us. They reinforce our sense of self rather than trying to change it.

Friendship has been given a special status in our society as a source of pleasure. Unlike the relationships over which we have little control – families, neighbours, colleagues – friends are the joyous, freely chosen part of our lives. They also allow us to practise close attachment without the complications of romance or desire.

The best friendships are unconditional. Friends know what makes us tick and what makes us laugh. Real friends don't disown you if you're going through a broke phase or a fat phase, if you're unwell, if your career is in a less than glittering patch, if you're chronically single or in a wildly unsuitable relationship. If anything, crises are levellers. As one 75-year-old volunteer observed, 'Happiness is to survive, dance, laugh and cry with friends – friends that I still have. They supported me in bringing up my children and helped me cope with my mother, who took seven years to die of cancer.' He and his wife took great pleasure in the longevity of their friendships: 'We visited an old friend at their home and felt the warmth of their embrace. Driving back we felt intense pleasure, and reflected on the path of that friendship over a stretch of 30 years.'

'It is the friends you can call up at 4 a.m. that matter.'
Marlene Dietrich, German-born American actress

Friendship is play

In its broadest sense, friendship is an adult version of children's play. Think of the way we spend our time with friends – sports, jokes and games are all common forms of structured play, along with other communal leisure activities, such as making music, visiting the cinema or going to the pub. A person who finds play easy is open to new experiences and copes better with change. Play, as opposed to serious behaviour, appears to have no immediate benefits, but it actually enables both children and adults to acquire valuable physical, social and mental skills.

The reason play makes us happy is because it promotes a state of optimal experience called 'flow' (see page 37). Flow occurs when you are so absorbed in an activity that you lose all sense of time. You forget about your problems and insecurities, feel at one with yourself and intensely alive.

It is even more gratifying when you experience flow in the company of other people, when you are playing a team game, for example, or are absorbed in a particularly fascinating conversation. Friendship promotes expressive skills – fun, joy, mimicry, telling jokes – so we feel in touch with our real self. One volunteer described such an experience during the Slough Project: 'I went out with the other volunteers and teased one girl by saying that my friend and I had been in a trapeze act. We made the story increasingly ludicrous and she fell for it. Eventually she clicked, but it was fun all the same. It reminded me about being with old friends and unwinding. Teasing each other is fun. Later, I told my wife the story and she couldn't stop laughing.'

How to be a good friend

To have happy friendships, you need the basic social skills to form and then maintain personal relationships. Some of us are good at striking up new friendships, but then, to our bewilderment, they don't last. Of course 'play behaviour' is one of the first things to go when we are feeling bad about ourselves.

Making friends successfully is not just a matter of luck. You need the emotional literacy to deal effectively with both your own feelings and other people's. A socially and emotionally competent person can work out whether someone else is sad, angry, jealous, or simply needs to be left alone. The ability to communicate – to exchange information and feelings with another person – is essential. Sometimes we send out the wrong message without even being aware of it.

Good friendships take motivation and effort. You must want to interact with other people (it is difficult to be lonely and happy at the same time). The more someone is naturally drawn to the company of others, the more friendships they are likely to have, and the greater their chances of forming close bonds. This is one reason why gregarious people tend to be happier than recluses. One of the volunteers experienced this for herself when she made a surprise phone call: 'I decided to ring up the widow of one of my late husband's friends whom I had not seen or heard about for 20 years. We had a really good conversation and it made me feel happy and connected with the world.'

Psychologists have proved that very happy people are more extrovert, more sociable and more agreeable. But they are not especially unique in any other way. They are not richer, or more athletic, or more beautiful, or more successful. They do not appear to experience more good or pleasurable life experiences than the rest of us. It is their capacity for happiness that makes them popular. And the good news is, we can learn to do it too!

'You can make more friends in two months by becoming interested in other people than you can in two years by trying to get other people interested in you.'
Dale Carnegie, American self-help writer

Power of touch

BBC happiness expert Richard Stevens believes that in British culture we don't make enough physical contact with each other. 'Touch is the basic language of love,' he says. 'A child in distress is calmed by being held tight in a parent's arms. Most adults need caresses and cuddles too.' Experimental studies have shown that just touching someone lightly on the arm makes it much more likely that they will respond to you in a more positive way. Stevens also cites some cross-cultural comparisons made by the Canadian psychologist Sidney Jourard, who observed how many times couples touched each other in the course of an hour. Couples in cafés in Puerto Rico scored an average of 120 touches per hour; the people of Paris were not far behind with 110; but in Florida the average was found to be 2, and in London 0!

In an attempt to encourage touch and physical contact, Stevens took two masseuses out on the streets of Slough. He was not surprised to find both passers-by in the High Street and commuters at Slough station quick to queue for a head or hand massage. 'The British may be a bit reserved about touching each other, but most people love it when given the opportunity.'

Friendship prolongs life

In 2005 a study by the University of Adelaide in Australia found that keeping up with friends rather than family is the key to a longer life. Researchers asked 1500 over-70s about levels of contact with children, relatives and friends, and monitored the results over a 10-year period. They found that close contact with children and other relatives had little impact on survival rates, but a strong network of friends and confidants significantly improved longevity. Experts believe this finding could herald a new approach to later life, where friends band together in networks based on similar age and interests.

Another study of 2800 men and women over the age of 65 showed that those with more friends had a lower risk of health problems, and recovered faster if they did fall ill. Meanwhile, a Yale University study of 10,000 senior citizens over a five-year period showed that loners were twice as likely to die from all causes.

Why do we need friends?

Our evolutionary history means that we are 'designed' (by natural selection) to live in relatively small social groups surrounded by individuals who are known to us, and with whom we conduct close relationships. The things that would have helped our ancestors to survive and reproduce – romantic relationships, parent-child love, close friendship – tend to bring us the most happiness. The important thing in any successful relationship is depth of knowledge, which has to be built up over time.

'Almost everybody feels better when they are with other people. It's paradoxical because many of us think we can hardly wait to get home and be alone with nothing to do, but that's a worse-case scenario. If you're alone with nothing to do, the quality of your experience really plummets.'
Mihaly Csikszentmihalyi, Hungarian positive psychologist

The fragmented nature of modern urban society means that many individuals are no longer part of a tightly knit network of family and relatives. Over a quarter of all households in Britain consist of one person living alone. We work the longest hours in Europe, and our increasingly individualistic society means we suffer from impoverished social connections. No wonder we all look for friends with whom we share some common ground as we become more socially, professionally or geographically mobile.

'Friendship has been promoted,' says Philip Hodson, Fellow of the British Association of Counselling and Psychotherapy. And it's a particularly British phenomenon. 'Our traditional families are still important to us, but many of us also set up a sort of second family because we find that the conventional kind doesn't give us all we need.'

A 2002 study conducted at the University of Illinois by psychologists Ed Diener and Martin Seligman found that the most salient characteristics shared by the 10 per cent of students with the highest levels of happiness and the fewest signs of depression were their strong ties to friends and family, and commitment to spending time with them. 'Word needs to be spread,' argues Diener. 'It's important to work on social skills, close interpersonal ties and social support in order to be happy.'

'I stopped to chat with a woman on her narrowboat last night. She was a reflexologist and a Punch-and-Judy puppeteer. We chatted about her boat and my writing. It was great to feel "friendship" with someone I'd never met before and may never meet again.'
Slough volunteer

Case studies

During the filming of *Making Slough Happy*, a very intense and touching friendship blossomed between two volunteers – a gay man in his 50s and a woman in her 40s. They took on the Happiness Manifesto exercise together, and developed a very close bond through the progress of the project. In fact, they discovered that friendship really can make you braver and transform your life. The man, who was self-conscious about scarring on his chest from a series of heart operations, allowed his female friend to persuade him to go swimming at the local baths.

'One's friendships shouldn't just be workplace-based,' advises psychotherapist Brett Kahr. 'You need at least a few good friendships from each decade of your life, and you have to work at them. Friendship is both an art and a skill – a plant that needs constant watering.' Men, he says, are less adept at friendship than women. 'They'll ring to arrange meeting at the pub or a sporting event, but not for the sake of psychological connectedness. And we've got to change that because men are missing out on a big trick here.'

One Slough volunteer, an Asian woman in her late 30s, had given up work and lost contact with most of her friends. Despite having everything that should make her happy – husband, children, house, car – she admitted, 'I'm not happy but I feel embarrassed about saying so.' Brett's task was to help her 'sculpt' the ultimate happiness day, starting with a workout at the gym, going shopping, then visiting girlfriends. 'What about the evening?' he asked. She said, 'I do like dancing, but I never go. I haven't gone in years.' So together they drew up a guest list of friends she hadn't seen for ages and Brett made her phone them, *on the spot*, to book an outing. 'It was a great way to encourage her to foster the connection with friends. The problem was she just didn't tend to them sufficiently regularly.'

Are friends the new family?

For some of us, long friendships have been more important than our romantic relationships or marriages. We stay independent adults for longer as we delay pairing off and having children, or decide not to have them at all. (The average age at which English men marry is now 31, women 29.) The phenomenon of later births means that family takes up a smaller percentage of our lives. We wait years to have children, and we could be 70 before we become grandparents for the first time.

Friends often become our most significant kinship group, a fact exploited in television sitcoms such as *Friends* and *Sex and the City*. These showed groups of friends who were always available for each another, always in each other's lives.

In his book *Urban Tribes* (Bloomsbury, 2003) Ethan Watters applauds unmarried 20- and 30-somethings who make long-lasting friendship groups the centre of their life. Far from seeing them as commitment-phobic, he insists: 'Single life in the city is no longer a phase that needs to be concluded quickly. With little fanfare, we've added a developmental stage to adulthood that comes before marriage – the tribe or friendship years.' The UK website Friends Reunited has proved just how nostalgic we are about our early friendships.

Male and female friendship

Women's friendships are built on disclosure and support, while men's friendships more often revolve around activities. For either gender the best predicator of not being lonely is the frequency of interaction with women. Nonetheless, men still desire the ease of close friendship with someone of their own gender. Bill, a man in his 60s with a wife and children, reports that he is absolutely distraught because his one friend, a man he has known for 40 years, is seriously ill. 'I cannot imagine my life without him,' he says. 'It's been the most important relationship of my life.' David, a salesman in his early 50s, feels that the absence of close male friendship is a huge gap in his life. Career and family have consumed his time for 20 years, and now he feels oddly lonely. John, a musician who is single after the end of a 15-year relationship, wishes that his friends would make more demands on him. He would like to be more involved in their lives.

Being a loner can even be bad for your heart if you're a man. In 2005 a survey by the Harvard School of Public Health in Boston found that men with few social connections have the highest risk of atherosclerosis (hardening of the arteries).

PROGRESSION OF FRIENDSHIP

Relationship expert John Gottman, author of *The Relationship Cure: A 5-step Guide to Strengthening Your Marriage, Family and Friendships*, has identified a typical ladder of needs for a friendship – the steps we take to connect from initial meeting to deeper intimacy:

- Light conversation or small talk
- Humour
- Friendly gossip
- Affection
- Support
- Problem solving
- Connection through discussing deep subjects, such as future goals, worries, values and meanings.

The friendship bank

Friendship is a form of social capital: think of it as a bank account in which you need to invest as well as borrow. The best way to keep your friendships in good working order is to treat them to a regular maintenance programme. Great friendships don't just happen by chance as you get older; you must cultivate them as assiduously as you cultivate a job or family.

Ask yourself the following key questions:

How do you organize your friendships?

Do you distinguish between having deep friendships and casual, transient acquaintances? Are you a flexible person who accepts that you may see certain friends only occasionally? That dates may sometimes be cancelled or that friends may be slow to return calls or emails? Or do you demand committed, totally reliable confidants? Look closely at your friendship group and see if you are making too many 'incompatible' friendships.

Do you believe in having a best friend?

In essence it is better to have a few close, supportive relationships than to be casually acquainted with hundreds of near-strangers. But does everyone, hand on heart, have one true best friend? Keep in mind that no single friend can fulfil all your emotional needs.

Does friendship need a job description?

Friendship is one of those areas full of hidden assumptions and unspoken rules. We only discover the rocky foundations of certain friendships when those assumptions clash. When you make a new friend, ask yourself:

- How much time will you spend together?
- Will one person take the lead in the relationship?
- Would you be happy with a supporting role?
- What is your relationship history?
- Do past injuries interfere with your ability to express affection towards, or accept affection from, your friend?
- Would you like to change this?

Connectedness is the keystone of happiness, yet many of us lack the strong bonds of friendship because we wait for them to occur 'naturally'. If they fail to materialize, we think there's nothing to be done about it but feel sorry for ourselves. This is nonsense because there's a lot you can do to make these friendship bonds happen.

Remember that being happy will make you a better friend. Research shows that when people are happy they are much more likely to spot the similarities between themselves and others, whereas unhappy people are more likely to spot the differences.

'My wife and I visited an old friend. There was a lot of love in the time we shared and I was grateful for our friendship.'
Slough volunteer

Do you work at your friendships?

In the TV series Brett Kahr took six volunteers on a boat trip on the Thames to examine the kind of friendship groups they had – or rather didn't have. 'I was shocked that quite a few people didn't have many well-established friendships at all,' says Brett. 'One man said he spoke to his friend every six months. He was astonished when I said I speak to my two best friends 365 days a year, come hell or high water.

'What became very clear is that we British suffer from a psychological anorexia. Just as anorexics deprive themselves of food, so the British character deprives us of the nourishment of friendship. First, the majority of us are very bad at building friendships, then we're hopeless at maintaining them. I was especially shocked when I asked the group: "Why is it that you don't have more regular contact with your friends?" and they said, "Well, we don't want to bother people," as though the idea of making contact would be an imposition. Far too many of us are privately nursing a fear that we are boring, difficult or overwhelming.'

'A life without a friend is like a death without a witness.'
Spanish proverb

WAYS TO BE A BETTER FRIEND

Good relationships require you to be a good friend, and the key to this is to follow well-defined, realistic goals.

- Be interested in other people. Self-absorption undermines happiness because it stops you from being brilliant at developing and maintaining close personal relationships. By and large happy people do not spend most of their time thinking about themselves and dwelling on their own feelings. They tend to focus on the world around them. People who care about others are happier than those who are more preoccupied with themselves.
- Be more open. Research suggests that to get close friends it is necessary to engage in a high level of self-disclosure. Having lots of friends but talking only about impersonal topics, such as music or sport (a classic male trait), does not prevent loneliness. It is only by sharing personal things about yourself that you win over truly rewarding friendships. So don't feel embarrassed when you're going through a difficult patch in your life and be tempted to retreat from your friendships at the very point when you need them most. Research shows that people relax physically as they confide painful experiences. Like confession, confiding is good for the soul.
- Try out new challenges in friends' company. The richest friendships are based on shared meaning. Are there untapped areas of potential in your relationship? You could take up swimming, travelling or volunteering together, or start a book group. Or simply try learning more about your friend, discovering new facets of his or her unique individuality and disclosing more of your own in the process.
- Act confidently. We often feel envious of people who never seem to feel insecure. However, much of what we think of as genetic is only learnt behaviour. Think of the most confident person you know and ask yourself how they behave, what they say, what they do, what they wear. If you can watch them in action, note everything they do, then practise doing those things yourself. This technique is called 'modelling', and successful people do it without realizing what they are doing. If you find yourself stuck for words, try gesticulating. Psychologists report that moving your hands while you talk helps you to access memory and language.
- Keep active. One of the easiest ways of securing long-term happiness is to take up an activity that involves making friends. Play football, do yoga, learn kick-boxing… it doesn't have to be anything expensive. Research

carried out by psychologist Mihaly Csikszentmihalyi found people were happiest when they were just talking together, when they knitted or gardened.

- Be more trusting. Reciprocity is absolutely central to human behaviour. Results show that the more you trust someone, the more likely they are to trust you. Suspiciousness simply turns people off. Scientists at Zurich University have discovered that the hormone oxytocin, which promotes maternal feelings and fidelity, also makes people trust each other. And, as brain scans have shown, trust makes us feel good.

- Communicate positively. Happy people are good communicators who use every available channel to convey their positive nature. They vary the pitch, rate and volume of their voice to make themselves sound more interesting. They use facial expressions, gestures and body language to show their interest in others. Even touch is part of their armoury because it prompts chemical and physical changes in the brain and body and can have a tremendous impact on people's feelings of well-being.

- Maintain eye contact. 'Eye contact is terribly important,' says BBC happiness expert Richard Stevens, 'because it's part of connecting with and being accepted by others. It can express aggression, affection, interest, enthusiasm… a huge range and depth of emotions. Avoiding eye contact can be powerful in a negative way. It freezes people out.'

- Make an effort. It's so easy at a party to retire into a corner and wait for people to notice you. Instead, spend some time observing the other guests and try to guess who might have matching interests and a compatible temperament to you. Start talking to that person about topics you think they will be interested in. If the feedback is negative, or the conversation turns out to be boring or above your head, don't give up. Try a different topic or a different guest. Remember, you don't have to be the focus of conversation – you can share the floor.

- Learn to be a good listener. Often in a social situation we catch ourselves not listening properly, but instead planning a witty riposte. Concentrate on the here and now, especially if you are being told something personal by a friend. The principle of responsive listening is validation. Your friend wants to feel that he or she has been understood. As they talk, you can punctuate their words with 'Mmm, yes' or 'I understand', or simply nod.

- Use friends as a sounding board. Talking through a dilemma with a friend can help you to clarify the situation and arrive at a solution. Their perspective might encourage you to see things differently, and changing the way you do things is one of the most powerful mechanisms for changing how you think and feel.

- Don't see things in black and white. We've all had evenings with a close friend that simply didn't work out – where you seem to get on each other's nerves, or the friend seems distracted. 'That's it!' you might exclaim. 'The friendship is over. We can never be close again.' That's when you need to think beyond your own feelings and find out what's behind the scratchiness. Don't quit just because your moods don't match.
- Make a friend of solitude. Learn to enjoy being on your own so that your friendships are genuinely chosen rather than endured in preference to being alone.
- Learn to forgive. Write a letter of forgiveness to a friend who has wronged you. Anger and resentment hold you back, so don't indulge in bitterness and thoughts of revenge. You might think it's good to let anger out rather than repress it, but dwelling on things that make you angry actually produces more anger and is associated with a higher risk of cardiac disease.
- Look beyond your obvious social group. If you surround yourself with friends who simply reaffirm your public persona, you will never be encouraged into new ways of being, and will thus miss out on the opportunities that friendship presents. A true friend is someone who makes you think differently, who is willing to share the risks that any increase in complexity brings. Cross-generational friendships are increasingly rewarding. One 38-year-old woman described hers with a friend aged 62. 'It's certainly not a mother–daughter relationship. It's a friendship of equals. I am far more open about things like sex and relationships than I would be with my own mother. My older friend has taught me to be more assertive and not to waste my time on regrets. She spent a lot of her life being a wife and mother, so independence is very important to her. But there is certainly a caring, practical side to her. I go round for supper and we watch wonderful trashy TV – something I never normally allow myself to do.'
- Share advice. Ask friends if they'd like your advice before offering it. If they say yes, share your wisdom. Don't be disappointed when they don't do what you suggest. In turn, ask for advice but don't feel obligated to take it.

Can't Buy Me Happiness

'Gross national happiness is more important than gross national product.'
Jigme Singye Wangchuk,
King of Bhutan

WHERE'S THE MONEY?

- Just 1 per cent of people in Britain share nearly a quarter of the wealth.
- We spend an average of £2050 a year on consumer goods.
- The average Briton will spend £1.5 million in his or her lifetime.
- The average man's cost of living is 21 per cent higher than the average woman's.
- Men spend 40 per cent more than women on nights out, and two and a half times more on electronic gadgets.
- Londoners spend six times more than the rest of the country on home help.
- Parents spend an average of £715 a year per child on toys.
- The average man owes £5000, and the average women owes £3000.
- Merseyside is currently home to 3200 millionaires.

Can money buy happiness? Well, yes and no. Once you can afford to feed, clothe and house yourself, each extra pound makes less and less difference to your sense of well-being. Beyond a certain comfort level, currently covered by about £15,000 per year, more money does little to increase your satisfaction with life.

Let's not be naive though: poverty is a terrible thing, and researchers find that, on average, wealthier people are happier than the less well off. Economist Robert Frank of Cornell University observes, 'There are rich people who are miserable. There are poor people who are happy all the time. But if you're an unhappy rich person, you're going to be happier than if you were poor.'

The connection between money and happiness is more complex than this information suggests. In the past half-century the average income has rocketed in industrialized countries, yet happiness levels have remained static. Britain is approximately twice as rich as it was 1960, and almost three times richer than after the Second World War. Yet clinical depression is more prevalent than it was two generations ago, and about 2 million people are estimated to be taking antidepressants.

If money buys so little well-being, why do we go to such great lengths to get more? By working ever harder, chasing elusive gains, we are on what psychologists call a 'hedonistic treadmill'. Millions of us spend more time and energy pursuing the things that money can buy than engaging in activities that create real fulfilment in life, such as cultivating friendships, helping others and developing a spiritual sense. This seems increasingly misguided, when money isn't even one of the six key factors now scientifically established to affect happiness most: mental health, satisfying and secure work, a secure and loving private life, a safe community, freedom and moral values.

Over the past two decades an increasing body of social-science and psychological research has shown there is no significant relationship between how much money a person earns and whether he or she feels good about life. Indeed, MORI's 2004 survey 'Understanding Life Satisfaction and Trust' found that absolute levels of income are not that important. A *Time* magazine poll reinforced this view by finding that money ranked 14th as a major source of happiness for its readers.

In his happiness workshops, Richard Stevens gave the volunteers a recipe for getting off the materialist treadmill. 'What is most important is to monitor how you feel – what really makes you happy. Try to reduce the impact of advertising (for example, by switching off the TV or doing other things when commercials are on). Try to avoid making comparisons with what other people have. In particular, focus on being rather than having. Think of all the good things you have in your life now rather than what you think you might enjoy if you had the money.'

Wealth is like health: its absence breeds misery, but having it doesn't guarantee happiness. And chasing money rather than meaning in life is a formula for discontent.

'We consistently overrate the importance of money as a happiness producer, and underrate the importance of other attributes. And that means we systematically make choices that undermine our own happiness. We are chasing the wrong lodestar.'
Richard Reeves, BBC happiness expert

The politics of happiness

If money really doesn't make us happy, should governments be pursuing ever-greater financial profits? In a country that is already rich it might be argued that a policy aimed at raising economic growth is of comparatively little value. After all, what makes us truly happy are the emotional ties of family, work, community, friends, health, personal freedom and moral values.

Happiness is a form of social capital because it brings enormous tangible benefits to society. And a society rich in social capital should therefore be better off in many ways, not least because it should need to spend less on hospitals, prisons and antidepressants. Surely, then, we should be subsidizing issues that promote better community life, such as mental health care, education, recycling, green issues and integrated transport. Aren't security and family-friendly policies more important than absolute income?

As economist and Labour peer Richard Layard argues so eloquently in his book *Happiness: Lessons from a New Science*, the American view that work should be in a permanent state of flux with individuals moving jobs, searching for more cash and accepting insecurity as part of an enterprise culture is wrongheaded and actively lowers happiness. Layard, best known for his studies of unemployment, makes an impassioned plea that the pursuit of contentment (rather than narrowly defined 'success') be placed centre stage. He also calls for gentler management, less downsizing and squeezing of labour, and more security of tenure. He has no time for people who want more 'labour mobility', believing it has destroyed secure communities, separated families and contributed greatly to unhappiness.

Layard is at his most passionate on mental health. Depression is largely curable with drugs and therapy, but only a quarter of people suffering from it get treatment. Half the cases of disability in Britain are caused by mental illness, but it claims just 12 per cent of resources. Shifting money within the NHS to alter this state of affairs would, he says, provide a satisfyingly quick improvement.

'I want chancellors of the exchequer and chief finance officers to buy into this research about happiness. I think it is our challenge to demonstrate that there is good science now to help us help people have better lives.'
Richard Reeves, BBC happiness expert

So why is happiness virtually ignored by economists and governments? Shouldn't the quest for personal happiness drive public policy? This, of course, is not a new idea. The eighteenth-century philosopher, social reformer and first major proponent of utilitarianism, Jeremy Bentham, famously asserted that 'the greatest happiness of the greatest number' should be the supreme criterion in terms of legislation and morality. Richard Reeves subscribes to this view and defines the campaign to make Slough happier as 'modern utilitarian philosophy in action'. The challenge within this is to ensure we're making choices that are best for our well-being.

Can you bottle it?

It's all very well being able to define what constitutes a happy life, but how do you take the message into the classroom or the office? As Reeves sees it, this will take a revolution in the way we think about the world – a change of mindset equivalent to that required for the Enlightenment, where people went from believing that their station in life was pre-ordained to challenging those in authority and questioning the received wisdom of the time. If individuals wake up to the true ingredients of well-being, rather than those that are constantly being sold as such, the potential for change is huge.

And Reeves has one more controversial question for us: should we *make* people be happy? If you could add a happiness drug to the water supply and raise people's evaluation of life by 20 per cent, would you do it? After all, we add fluoride to the water for healthy teeth. The answer to this question is important because happiness is a declared goal of politics. If not achieved through the water supply, how exactly will it be done?

KEY QUESTIONS TO ASK POLITICIANS

- Are you happy?
- Do you think MPs are responsible for our happiness?
- Which legislation have you supported that you think will increase happiness?
- Do you think that the UK and Europe, like the USA, should give citizens a constitutional right to the pursuit of happiness?
- Are your constituents happier than the UK average?
- Do MPs set a good example in terms of happiness, for example, do they get enough exercise and sleep, or enjoy family life?
- What is more important than happiness?
- Should there be a Ministry of Well-being?

When money matters

Money does matter in various ways. People earning under around £10,000 are measurably and permanently happier when paid more. People who have been out of work are thrilled when they get a job. People who are sick get much happier when their monetary situation improves. A redundancy cheque can change people's lives, giving them the freedom to travel, to buy their own home, to reinvent their career. For women (who now make up half the workforce) it is still incredibly important to be financially independent.

Sadly, however, money generally makes us unhappy and dissatisfied – especially when we compare our own income with that of others. Yes, richer people are happier – not because of the absolute size of their wealth, but because they have more than other people. And the wealth gap harms the rest of us. Income rivalry makes those left behind more miserable than it makes the winners extra happy.

Part of the problem, Robert Frank argues, is that we spend money on conspicuous consumption – second homes, cars, DVDs, phones and suchlike. But if we used an increase in our income to acquire more inconspicuous 'goods', such as a less stressful job nearer to home, we would be much happier. This was something discovered by one of the Slough volunteers: 'I was working in banking, in a pretty high-powered suit-and-tie job, but then, at the age of 45, I got to the stage where I just didn't want to do that any more. I gave it all up and set myself up as a landscape gardener. What I have now is freedom and flow – pleasure at work – which is so much more important than lots of money. It has completely transformed my perspective on the world.'

'Annual income twenty pounds, annual expenditure nineteen nineteen and six, result happiness. Annual income twenty pounds, annual expenditure twenty pounds ought and six, result misery.'
Charles Dickens, Mr Micawber in David Copperfield (1850)

We get used to the good life

Of course if you hand someone £20, the pleasure centres of their brain lights up as if responding to an offer of food, sex or drugs. But that initial rush does not translate into long-term pleasure for most people. Surveys have found virtually the same level of happiness between the very rich individuals on the *Forbes* 400 list and the Masai herdsmen of East Africa. Lottery winners return to their previous level of happiness after five years. Increases in income just don't seem to make people happier.

The reason for this is that the human brain becomes conditioned to positive experiences. It's what psychologists call 'adaptation'. Getting a chunk of unexpected money registers as a good thing, but as time passes, the response wears off. An expected monthly pay cheque doesn't bring any buzz at all – and doesn't contribute to overall happiness.

The interesting thing is that people judge wealth relatively rather than absolutely: even if you are happy getting a pay rise, finding that a colleague has a bigger one more than wipes out your happiness increment. Competition for money and status is thus a zero-sum game; and the more opportunities there are for comparison – rankings, league tables, advertising – the greater the dissatisfaction will be.

The key seems to be whether you have more than your friends, neighbours and colleagues. In one shocking experiment people were offered the choice between a hypothetical £100,000 salary on the basis that colleagues received £250,000, or a salary of £50,000 while everyone else got £25,000. They all opted for the reduced salary of £50,000 so that they could have more than everyone else.

In lab tests Andrew Oswald, an economist at Warwick University, asked college undergraduates how satisfied they would be with various salary offers for a hypothetical job. He found that the ranking of the offers within a range of possible salaries made a huge difference to the students' satisfaction: they rated a particular salary much more favourably if it was one of the top ones on offer rather than one of the lower ones. Similarly, in a recent survey of more than 16,000 workers in the UK, Oswald found that people reported being more satisfied with a given amount if it ranked higher in the company's salary hierarchy.

'Human beings make the mistake of thinking that another x thousand pounds in an absolute sense will make them better off. It's not that. It's that pounds buy status, and status makes them better off.'
Andrew Oswald, British economist

Keeping up with the Joneses

Many of us suffer from what sociologists call 'reference anxiety'. According to that thinking, most people judge their possessions in comparison with those of others. They tend not to ask themselves, 'Does my house meet my needs?' Instead they ask, 'Is my house nicer than my neighbour's?' If you own a two-bedroom house and everyone else around you owns a two-bedroom house, your reference anxiety will be low. But if you are surrounded by three- and four-bedroom houses, your reference anxiety may rise. Suddenly your two-bedroom house – one that your grandparents might have considered quite luxurious – doesn't seem enough.

Part of the problem, thanks to gossip magazines, TV and the Internet, is that we know so much more about other people's lives. Once upon a time we lived in small towns or urban areas where conditions for everyone were approximately the same. But now we know every detail of how the super-rich live, and that triggers dissatisfaction. As material expectations keep rising, more money may simply increase our desire for more expensive trappings. As we move up the economic ladder, we stop feeling grateful and focus on what we still don't have. So money never satisfies. Over the course of the Slough Project one of the volunteers discovered this for himself: 'I've learnt that experiential things – talking with friends, walking, reading, cooking a great meal – make you far happier than buying things.'

As positive psychologist Martin Seligman observes, too many of us view expensive purchases as 'short cuts to well-being'. In surveys by the Roper polling organization in 1978 and 1994, for example, Americans were asked to list the material items they thought important to the 'good life'. The researchers found that the more of these items people already had, the longer their list was, so the good life remained always just out of reach.

There has often been the assumption that the more people were willing to pay for something, the more utility it had. But it turns out that a £200 item may not generate more happiness than a £20 item, and a Mercedes may not confer much more happiness than a Ford.

Ed Diener, a psychology professor at the University of Illinois and a leader in the science of measuring happiness, interviewed members of the *Forbes* 400, a list of the richest Americans, and found that they were only a tiny bit happier than the public as a whole. The reason, it seems, is that those with wealth often continue to feel jealousy about the possessions or prestige of other wealthy people – so even large sums of money may fail to confer well-being.

'People who value money more than other goals are less satisfied with their income and with their lives as a whole.'
Martin Seligman, American positive psychologist

Think about your attitude to money, what informs it and how you can change it for the better. To help you do so, ask yourself some key questions:

- What does money mean to you?
- How much is enough?
- How important should the pursuit of wealth and material possessions be in your life?
- How was money regarded in your home as you were growing up?
- Do you want money to have the same or a different role in your life?

Hitting the jackpot

You're not alone if you harbour dreams of winning the lottery, but you might be surprised that it doesn't necessarily make for long-term happiness. BBC happiness expert Richard Stevens says 'It's not having lots of money that makes you happy, but knowing that you have enough for what you need. The sense of being in control is central to happiness. Keeping on top of your finances is usually a much more important recipe for happiness than trying to make lots more money.' According to Dr H. Roy Kaplan, author of several books on lottery winners, the initial euphoria is often short-lived, and life doesn't change as much as people imagine. 'You can catapult people from one economic status to another overnight, but a lifetime of beliefs and experiences changes more slowly.'

Kaplan also observes that people who were outgoing and gregarious before winning took the change in their stride, while those who were shy and withdrawn became suspicious and paranoid. (Perhaps that has something to do with being inundated with requests for money from both friends and strangers.)

While many lottery winners keep their jobs, they find their relationship with co-workers changes – and not for the better. Those who quit and move to a palatial estate can quickly find themselves isolated and depressed. They miss the pleasure they used to get from interacting with colleagues and neighbours. It's not surprising, then, that some lottery winners think their lucky day has brought them nothing but bad luck.

Money only reinforces what was already there to begin with, says economist Andrew Oswald. 'People who win the lottery think money is going to change them as a person, but in fact it is their lifestyle that alters. If they were a kind, warm-hearted person before, they will be after.'

'A lot of people who complain about losing money are already rich.'
Patti Smith, American singer song-writer

The happy get rich - eventually!

More productive than hankering after extra money is to look forward to better days. Research has shown that if we think our lot is improving, happiness follows. People living modestly but anticipating better days to come are likely to be happier than people living well but not looking forward to improvements in their living standards.

And there is another compensation to ponder. Psychologist Ed Diener has found that happy people tend to have higher incomes later on in their lives. So while money may not help to make people happy, being happy may help them to make money.

10 HAPPY FACTS ABOUT MONEY

1   We might assume rich people see more of their friends, but they sacrifice relationships for time in the office earning money.

2   Moving to a richer area can cause feelings of disappointment and envy towards neighbours, leaving you unhappier than before you moved – so don't try to keep up with the Joneses.

3   Experiential purchases (holidays, concert tickets) make people happier than material ones (new dress, new car) according to a 2004 survey by Leaf Van Boven and Thomas Gilovitch of Cornell University.

4   Receiving more pocket money does not make children any happier. According to research by Professor Jonathan Bradshaw of York University, 'The key determinates of children's mental well-being are relationships with parents and peers, rather than the level of income they are living on.'

5   Those who value love more than money report much higher satisfaction with life. Studies show that individuals who strive most for wealth tend to live with lower well-being. This is especially so for those seeking money to prove themselves, gain power, or show off rather than support their families.

6   Materialism makes you ill. One study by Tim Kasser at Knox College in Galesburg, Illinois, found that young adults who focus on money, image and fame tend to be more depressed, have less enthusiasm for life and suffer more physical symptoms such as headaches and sore throats.

7   Money buys neither more sexual partners nor more sex, according to a survey carried out by David Blanchflower and Andrew Oswald, using recent data on a sample of 16,000 adult Americans.

8   Shopping is called 'problem recognition' by psychologists. We see something in a shop window and it becomes a problem because we were happy without it five minutes ago.

9   Rich people with a history of mental illness are up to three times more likely to kill themselves than those with less money.

10 Remember, we can choose those with whom we compare ourselves. If we make social comparisons by looking upwards, we are bound to be unhappy. But if we compare downwards, we have every reason to count our blessings. That's why Olympic bronze medallists are happier than silver medallists.

6

Happy at Work?

'Work is much more fun than fun.'
Noël Coward, actor and writer

We spend the majority of our lives at work – more time than with our partners – so it is no surprise that it has a huge bearing on our happiness. What's more, research shows that happy people are more successful at work. A recent study measured the positive emotions of 272 employees, then followed their job performance over the next 18 months. Happy people went on to get better evaluations from their supervisors, and higher pay.

Of course, work offers far more than money. A satisfying job can bring structure and meaning to life, along with mental and emotional stimulation. This is as true for those engaged in unpaid work, such as caring for their children or elderly relatives, as it is for the highest-earning investment banker.

As human beings like to keep busy, we carry our work-shaped traits into the rest of our lives. Even our hobbies – rock climbing, bee-keeping, stamp collecting – are industrious. Most important of all, work offers a regular opportunity to develop the skills of close personal relationships. Nearly one in four of us meets our long-term partner through work.

Psychologist Mihaly Csikszentmihayli argues that work is the place where we are most likely to enter the state of 'flow', where people are so involved in an activity that nothing else seems to matter (see chapter 3).

BUSY BEES

- Nearly 4 million people in the UK work more than 48 hours a week.
- One in 25 men works at least 60 hours a week.
- The average British commuting time is 45 minutes, the highest in Europe.
- Between 60 and 80 per cent of relevant groups are not aware of recent changes in paternity, maternity and parental rights to flexible work or leave.
- People in their 60s are happiest at work, while those in their 30s enjoy it least.
- Workers between the ages of 20 and 49 are most likely to say they lack interesting challenges.
- The average lunch break in British offices is 27 minutes.
- Half of us are too frightened to take our full holiday entitlement.
- The number of people 'downshifting' to less demanding jobs is expected to reach 3.7 million by 2007.
- Some 80 per cent of self-employed people are satisfied or very satisfied with their jobs because they can control their hours and working environment.

Why work can be good for us

At its best, work makes us feel strong, active and motivated (whereas escapist leisure activities, such as watching TV, can sometimes leave us feeling passive and depressed).

In fact, work incorporates many of the conditions of flow. These include clear goals and rules of performance; frequent feedback about how well or poorly we are doing; and an environment that encourages concentration and minimizes distractions. As a result, people often feel more engaged at work than they do at home. Surgeons, for example, say that they find their work exhilarating; the goal is both rational – to set a bone or get some organ functioning properly – and intellectually enjoyable. They know when they have succeeded and get immediate feedback. Indeed, some surgeons say they are at their happiest when performing operations.

But even the most mundane of chores can be turned into a creative, intellectual game. Someone who can create flow experiences in the most barren landscape (a depressing office, a weed-infested urban landscape) is said to have an 'autotelic personality' and signifies someone who is able to make an activity an end in itself.

Of course, there's no denying that work can be a prime cause of unhappiness. When it comes to structuring the working day, our health quickly degenerates if we don't have some control of our own destiny. We need to feel that what we do makes a difference to our situation.

In a world where we are increasingly defined by work, many of us have a very poor understanding of office politics. When an organization is badly managed it can be rife with game-playing and manipulation. In extreme cases, it can take the form of harassment or bullying. Over 15 per cent of the workforce claim to be dissatisfied or very dissatisfied with their jobs. These people tend to work in low-skilled parts of the economy, often with little or no control over when and where they work, and with little say in how.

As work increasingly defines us to ourselves and other people, and largely determines our standard of living, the difference between getting it right and getting it wrong is life changing.

'We spend most of our waking life working. To waste it in bad jobs is a sin.'
Richard Reeves, BBC happiness expert

When work makes us ill

Depression and anxiety are now the most common reasons for claiming long-term sickness benefit, having overtaken back pain as the main reason for time off work. In fact, according to the mental health charity Mind, excessive stress at work is now costing the British economy about £100 billion a year in lost revenue.

Staying late at the office can also push up our weight. Researchers at the University of Helsinki found long working hours (more than 40 per week) and stress at the office increased the risk of obesity. Meanwhile, a 2004 study showed that meeting high-pressure deadlines leaves employees six times more at risk of heart attack in the following 24 hours.

One volunteer who took part in Jessica and Philippa's exercise at Slough engineering company Tunes (see page 79) found that work didn't have to get on top of him if he didn't let it. 'I've learnt to recognize what I am good at, and I tell myself that on a regular basis. I've also changed my attitude. I realize I don't have to be made to feel bad. It's my choice and I'm not going to. If people give me confusing instructions, rather than getting bolshy, I present options back to them and say, "What is it you really want me to focus on?"'

'Without work, all life goes rotten.'
Albert Camus, French novelist and dramatist

Why do we stay in bad jobs?

It's a good question. Why *do* so many perfectly intelligent people end up working in environments that don't suit them? Where the real values don't match their own?

Of course, we would be far happier if we worked in places that respected the qualities we possess. The problem is that we are often slow to recognize that we're in the wrong place. That's partly because we're averse to too much change (and being depressed makes it very hard to institute anyway), but also because there are so many reasons not to change our job. We may tell ourselves we lack money, qualifications or access; that we are especially unlucky and have fewer choices than everyone else. On good days we may even fantasize that if we stay just a little longer our true worth will be recognized. That's a dangerous strategy to adopt.

According to BBC happiness expert Jessica Pryce-Jones, there are three kinds of 'work orientation' – reasons for going to work:

- Job – you're there for the money.
- Career – you're there for the status.
- Calling – you're there because you care; you'd do it even if you weren't paid.

To determine which of these really applies to you, ask yourself these three questions about your work:

- Do you want what you have?
- Do you know what you really want?
- Does your occupation reflect the real you?

The simple advice from experts is that we need to take action to make ourselves happier at work. Here are some proven strategies that apply whether you stay in your present job or decide to look for a new one:

- Match your skills to the job.
- Do something regarded as worthwhile.
- Take control.
- Have interpersonal contact.

At the end of this chapter (see page 86) there are ideas to help you get more happiness from work – because work is really important. 'The mere fact of being in employment raises your happiness level by about the same amount as having an extra £100,000 a year,' says Richard Reeves. Coming home from a job, brimming with stories, enthusiasm and ideas to share with a partner – and being ready to hear theirs – is a hugely positive force in relationships.

We all moan about our jobs from time to time, but research has found that the unhappiest people are the unemployed and the economically inactive who, for various reasons, are unable to go out to work. Their life satisfaction is little more than half of those in work or caring for others. (However, this is not true of unemployed people who do voluntary work or have absorbing hobbies.) According to research by economist Andrew Oswald at the University of Warwick, losing a job damages mental health more than splitting up with a partner. After all, if you're unemployed you never get a day off.

Not just for the money

After basic needs are met, pay has surprisingly little influence on job satisfaction (see chapter 5, page 67). Indeed, a 2004 report published by the Learning Skills Council clearly showed that happiness is more important to workers than money. It also revealed that 93 per cent of teenagers agreed that doing something they enjoy is more important than making money.

Studies suggest that what might actually bring us the deepest and most enduring satisfaction is the respect and appreciation of our workmates. Teaming up to take on life is what humans are designed for, which explains why people who have a best friend at work invariably have better productivity and health.

It's good for the boss, too

Happy employees make for happy employers because research suggests that happiness actually increases productivity and income. They're also less likely to be absent or tempted to leave.

For a modern service company to be successful it needs to score highly in terms of intangibles, such as customer satisfaction, communication skills and flexibility of response. This requires a satisfied workforce willing to give its labour.

Employers therefore need us to be happy. In an employment market where skills are in short supply, companies need to protect the investments they make in recruiting and training people. While poor pay is among the main reasons employees give for wanting to change jobs, it takes more than money to make us happy – or perform well. Rather, staff motivation is rooted in feeling valued, being listened to and having goals clearly communicated.

'All that matters is love and work.'
Sigmund Freud, Austrian founder of psychoanalysis

Workers are human capital

Of course, treating staff well doesn't just mean giving them lots and lots of money: it means creating an environment in which they have a level of autonomy and can actually give their best. If people are treated like robots, they are bound to feel bored and dissatisfied.

'My definition of work is "transforming the world around us". That's why gardening and child-rearing are also work. But if you do a job that doesn't lead you to see the transformations your efforts are leading to, it's not work — it's just a job. And that's bad news.'
Richard Reeves, BBC happiness expert

Good employers communicate with their workers, listen to their concerns and accommodate their needs as much as possible. Employee happiness is not an add-on — it needs to be integrated into an organization's working practices and into what economists call the work contract between capital and labour.

Work can be fun

The idea that the British are a nation of job-haters who long to flee the pressure of endless emails and meetings is out of date. In a 2004 Joy of Work poll more than 2.4 million people confessed to being 'workophiles' — work lovers. A further 42 per cent of those questioned even claimed that their most important relationships were at work. Working with friends, far from being a contradiction in terms or a dangerous confusion, is one of the greatest pleasures life can bring.

For our parents, work was something to be endured. They could only do what they really wanted to outside work hours. But jobs today are more fun than they ever used to be. Creative businesses have 'chill out' areas and meetings in the local coffee shop. Now people do for fun the things they'd do anyway. This approach has fundamentally changed the way we work and interact.

Our working environments have improved, too, with open-plan offices, flexible hours and on-site facilities, such as gyms, dentists and even places of worship. Work is the new home. As Richard Reeves observes, 'We used to learn and then earn. Now we learn as we earn.'

In line with these changes, current figures show that nearly one in two workers is a woman. By 2010 only 20 per cent of the full-time workforce will be white, able-bodied men under 45 years old.

It might not seem possible when the alarm clock goes off on a Monday morning, but a very significant percentage of us look forward to going to work. We welcome the challenges it presents, and are happy to work longer hours because we are passionate about our jobs.

Put simply, the best careers advice is find out what you like doing best and get someone to pay you for doing it. That way your job never feels like work.

'I thought I would show my colleagues how grateful I was for their support, so I bought them all chocolates and a card. I wrote a personal message of thanks for each of them. One lady invited me to her lunch party as a result. Another told me I was very gifted. This was really important to me as I had had a very difficult relationship with both of them. I felt pleasure, satisfaction, contentment. And I'm still feeling great now days later.'
Slough volunteer

HAPPINESS AT WORK – THE 12 COMMANDMENTS

According to our experts Jessica Pryce-Jones and Philippa Chapman, there are 12 key components for finding happiness at work.

1   Getting things done.
2   Having a variety of tasks.
3   Having some control over your job.
4   Being thanked.
5   Using your strengths to do your job well.
6   Knowing what's expected of you.
7   Understanding why what you do is important.
8   Being heard.
9   Having friends at work.
10 Learning new things.
11 Having the right boss for you.
12 Giving and receiving feedback.

As part of *Making Slough Happy*, Jessica and Philippa carried out a work project with an engineering company called Tunes. This small, family-run business, one of the oldest companies on Slough Trading Estate, had a fairly traditional approach to manager–worker relations. There had been no staff meeting in 16 years, and employees had never had an appraisal.

To find out how things could be improved Jessica and Philippa set up a staff exercise around the 12 Work Commandments. They pinned paper cloud-shapes up on the walls with a different commandment written on each one. Participants were then invited to attach their comments to the clouds, explaining why particular commandments were important to them. It proved a revelation, as Philippa explains: 'Three clouds had no comments on them at all: "Being thanked", "Being heard" and "Having some control over your job". So then we knew there was a great gap that needed to be addressed around staff communication.'

Jessica and Philippa worked with employees to request an all-hands meeting. They suggested keeping the agenda to three non-confrontational work issues, such as IT provision in the company, to give everyone a chance to come together in a relaxed environment. Once staff and management had got used to meeting in this way, they could then address more complex issues.

The experts also devised a series of exercises to help the employees learn more about themselves and each other. These were as follows.

Building blocks

Jessica and Philippa gave each employee a pile of interlocking building blocks with different phrases written on them, such as 'salary', 'social relationships at work' and 'optimism', then asked them to assemble the phrases in a tower in order of what they could and couldn't influence.

'This teaches you to be realistic about what you can and can't control at work,' says Philippa. 'People think happiness is totally down to earning more money, but many people can't control how much money they are paid, unless they work on commission, so it's not a constructive area to put your energy into. Far better to concentrate on areas you can control, such as relationships or your own feelings.'

Philippa believes that happiness at work breaks down into three areas. 'These are things you can't control (weather, traffic, the economy, contracts that someone else didn't sign); things you have some influence over (trust, support from others, feedback); and things you actually do control (your feelings, your attitude, optimism, etc.).

'The funny thing is,' says Philippa 'the things that we waste so much time moaning about at work are the things that are outside our control, such as the weather or the traffic.'

 79

Gratitude at work

This exercise reminds people that their performance and job satisfaction are directly linked to other people in the building. For example, you may never meet the person who makes sure your salary is paid at the end of the month, but you'd soon notice if they didn't do it.

Jessica and Philippa put the names of employees at Tunes in a hat and asked each of them to pick one. They then had to thank the named person for their 'role' at work. First up was the accountant, who warmly thanked the man running courier dispatch for bringing a huge delivery of paper into the building after realizing it was going to get rained on. 'I want to thank you,' he said, 'because you saved us a lot of money.'

It was amazing, said Philippa, just how much thanking people individually improved employee morale.

Perception at work

This exercise helps people to understand that not everybody thinks in the same way. Jessica and Philippa showed the employees 3D stereograms very fast (stereograms allow you to see a 3D object, such as a woman's face, hidden inside a picture) then covered them up again, and asked everyone to describe what they had seen. Of course, everyone had seen something different, which pointed up the need to be flexible with colleagues' points of view. Don't shout if they don't understand a task first time. Try to see it from their reality.

By the end of the project, in the areas that had been focused on, staff happiness at Tunes had gone up an astonishing 43 per cent. One of the employees, who was also a Slough volunteer, confessed: 'I've learnt to take time and think about other people's happiness, and not just fly off the handle. What I say and do affects other people, so I need to be more understanding of their jobs and listen to what they say. I now view colleagues as customers rather than people who are expected to do this and that when you want. Respect your fellow workers: we are all part of the same team.'

Another member of staff said: 'People are a lot more responsive and helpful. I feel more in control of events and not so much like I'm being carried along by them. More work gets done in less time. I am also more confident. You get far less problems and hassle, and you are easily approachable, so you get a better response from other workers'.

Making work more fulfilling

In his seminars with the *Making Slough Happy* volunteers, BBC happiness expert Richard Stevens did an informal survey of how much they enjoyed their jobs. Most reported a good level of satisfaction, and in some cases a high level. In addition to using one's particular strengths, Stevens suggests three ways of making work more fulfilling.

1 Try to find some meaning and sense of purpose in what you do.

2 Take control. One way of doing this is through managing your time so that you actually do what is important to you. In doing this try to keep a broader view of what your work is all about and its value.

3 Work on your relationships with your colleagues. Try to make your time together enjoyable. In particular, look for win-win strategies, where you both achieve what you want rather than being in competition with each other.

'Make sure you haven't already got what you want before looking for something else. Always seeking change may undermine your appreciation of what you have and deflect you from exploring how you can make this better.'
Richard Stevens, BBC happiness expert

What sort of person are you at work?

Are you a big picture person or more interested in the detail? Are you an extrovert or an introvert? Are you entirely logical or driven by your feelings? 'Your personality and preferences can affect how you come over to other people at work,' explains Jessica. 'So maybe you rub up against someone the wrong way and bang – you have a row. You need the tools to be able to deal with the person most unlike you at work.' These tools, she explains, include being able to 'mirror' the other person so that you can work with them. 'If, for example, the person says, "Fabulous" 20 times, you can repeat it once to show you are on the same wavelength. You literally pick up the language and thought that other people are using and reflect it back to them – even if it's very unlike you.'

Visual, Hearing, Feeling (VHF)
'People use language in three different ways,' says Jessica. 'From a visual point of view ("I see what you mean"); from a hearing point of view ("I hear what you mean"); and from an emotional point of view ("I feel your unhappiness").' This means that by listening carefully to the register someone uses, you can pick up clues about how to approach them.

'I've actually learnt to say "no". In the past at work I felt like I was being run over by all the tasks I had to do, but now I can assert myself. And I've changed my language. I don't say things like, "Perhaps you could possibly close the door if it's not too inconvenient". If you phrase things more assertively, people will respond in kind.'
Slough volunteer

Body language
The non-verbal messages we all transmit at work are amazingly important. Problem areas, especially for women, are non-assertive eye contact and hand gestures. Assertive gestures are when you move your hand in time with your speech, to mark what you say. 'Male leaders tend to present the back of their hand and knuckles, when they're speaking, which says "I'm in charge",' says Jessica. 'Women tend to show open palms, and tilt their hands up to the ceiling, which is more yielding and inclusive, but doesn't help if you're trying to keep power in a male arena.' One thing she recommends is that women adopt the assertive hand gesture if they want to be listened to. 'It will feel odd at first, but ask yourself how you want to come over. Do you want to play the game or not? I'd also recommend that when you have the floor to speak, stand up. And don't stand on one leg or a back foot when you speak because this tentative posture makes it much easier for someone to challenge you.'

Work-life balance

Workers face a central paradox. We know the importance of getting on and enjoying work in terms of influencing how happy, unstressed and healthy we are. But we also recognize the need to have a satisfying life outside work.

The casualty of our new 24/7 culture is leisure. Britons spend an average of 43.6 hours a week at work – the longest working week in Europe. In fact, more than 4 million of us work over 48 hours a week (the limit set in 1998 by the European Working Time Directive). The TUC has dubbed our long-hours culture a 'national disgrace'.

Some 67 per cent of people believe that there is more to a successful life than making money, and about half that number feel that juggling career and personal life is getting harder. Little wonder, then, that more than a third of the UK workforce admits to be looking for a new job right now, or is planning to do so.

Worryingly, around 400,000 workers are 'wage slaves', earning less than £16,000 a year for working more than 60 hours a week.

When asked why they work long hours, the most common reason people give is to speed up promotion; the next reason is fear of losing their job. Altruistic reasons, such as helping out colleagues, come much further down the list.

However, there are grounds for cautious optimism about the future when we look at recent MORI poll findings about what final-year undergraduates see as the most important aspects of their future job. Some 45 per cent put good salary and training/development opportunities at the top, but the next most important is work–life balance, mentioned by 32 per cent, and well ahead of lots of other traditionally important factors, such as responsibility and travel opportunities.

Meanwhile, industries with a culture of long hours, such as banks and financial institutions, are losing staff. According to a recent survey, one out of every four people training to be a maths teacher has come from the financial services sector. Employers will have to learn to be more flexible if they want to retain staff.

How can you achieve a work-life balance?

Long hours are not good for us: they cause stress; they're bad for our health; they wreck relationships; they make caring for children or dependants more difficult; and tired staff are bad for business. In addition, working long hours doesn't necessarily mean you are more effective.

No one is suggesting that Britain should turn into a nation of clock-watchers, but we need to strike a better work–life balance. After all, who wants their tombstone to state that they were a hard worker?

'I've learnt that work can be seen as something much more than "economic exchange". It's about making connections – making friendships.'
Slough volunteer

As people go through life, their relationship with work changes. In the early days, perhaps when they have young children, they may appreciate the child-care facilities provided. But later they may need time to care for elderly parents. Or they may want to devote more time to education or hobbies.

Work–life balance is about people having a measure of control over when, where and how they work. To facilitate this the government set up the Work–Life Balance Team in 2000 to promote workplace practices that benefit both employees and employers. Employees with a happy work–life balance, the team point out, tend to be more motivated and productive, while flexible working arrangements mean that employers can reduce absenteeism and maximize their available labour. These practices also help more people to reach retirement in a good state to enjoy it — and that is where happiness can really kick in.

WORK QUESTIONNAIRE

Of course we all want promotion, but make sure you want it for the right reasons. As discussed in chapter 5, we seriously overestimate the amount of happiness that earning more money will bring. Surveys that track job satisfaction by levels of income over time show that job satisfaction is not very strongly related to levels of wages at all. As we get more, we want more, so our satisfaction level remains fairly constant. Worse still, the new expensive lifestyle that often comes with more money becomes a classic form of addiction.

The best reasons for wanting promotion or changing your job are to make the most of your abilities, to stretch yourself mentally and to enjoy the challenge. As Richard Reeves observes, 'There is absolutely nothing wrong with wanting nice stuff, but it cannot compensate for spending most of our waking hours in an activity that we hate.'

Before you make any major decisions about your job, take time to think through the positive – and negative – aspects of your situation. Are you, for example, a 'people person' or are you more interested in process? Do you need the support of working with a team, or are you best going solo?

Think about all aspects of your working life whether you're at home caring for an elderly relative or a child, working in an office or out on the road selling. Think particularly carefully about the following areas.

Environment
Think about your commute to work, your physical working environment and even the view from your desk. Do you find these elements of your working life acceptable or do they get you down? Is there anything you could do to improve your working conditions?

Colleagues
Do you regard any of your work colleagues as friends? Are you treated with respect by them and your manager? If you are under pressure or need help, are your colleagues supportive? Do you feel part of a team?

The work
Do you feel challenged in your job? Are you confident in your abilities? How involved in decision-making processes are you? Does your job provide enough variety and stimulation? Are you ever bored at work? Are you committed to the work you do?

Future prospects

Can you see a future for yourself with your company? Are there opportunities for promotion and are you encouraged to apply for them? Can you see yourself doing a higher-status job currently done by one of your colleagues? Do you feel optimistic about your future career prospects?

Pay

Compared with other similar organizations, does your company pay you enough? Is your pay in line with that of other members of your company who do a similar job? Is earning more a constant career goal?

Work–life balance

Do you feel that you spend enough time with your family and friends? Do you find it easy to switch off after work? How long does it take you to unwind after a hard day? Do you regularly feel stressed? Do you find yourself thinking about work at weekends, and do you feel apprehensive on Sunday evenings?

Your typical day

Think back over your most recent day at work: how typical was it? Which parts of your day did you enjoy most and why? Are there any parts you dreaded or did not enjoy? Do you talk regularly to someone – a friend, partner, colleague – about your day at work?

General approach to work

When someone asks how work is going, what is your immediate response? How did you choose your career path and if you could go back, would you make a different choice? Are you happy at work?

'Blessed is he who has found his work: let him ask no other blessedness.'
Thomas Carlyle, nineteenth-century historian and critic

10 DYNAMIC WAYS TO BE HAPPIER AT WORK

If you feel like a square peg in a round hole, don't worry – you're not alone. In fact, in a 2003 government survey almost 60 per cent of people said that they regretted the career choice they had made and would choose a different career if they could start over again.

The good news is that there's plenty you can do to change your situation, whether it's training in the workplace or moving to another career altogether. Some people build up a portfolio career, where they might, for example, be a solicitor during the day and a yoga teacher at night. Remember, you are not trapped – there's always another way.

Use your answers to the exercise on pages 84–85 to think about the changes that you could make to improve your general happiness at work. Below are some ideas for improving your working life.

1 **Live close to work.** People who commute long distances to and from work are measurably unhappier than those who work closer to home. However, the average journey is only 8.5 miles, so get out of that car, bus or train and try cycling. Tell your employer that it would be good for business to provide bicycles, clothes lockers and power showers.

2 **Work for a small company.** Research has shown that people who work in small, cohesive groups tend to be the most satisfied with their job. A survey published by *Personnel Today* found that staff in organizations employing fewer than 500 staff tend to feel more involved, enjoy being recognized by their co-workers and feel that their contribution makes an impact.

3 **Choose a 'happy' profession.** It doesn't really matter what kind of work you choose so long as you feel that it's important in some way. Hairdressing topped a recent survey as having the happiest workers. Next came the clergy, chefs, beauticians, plumbers and mechanics. By contrast, social workers, architects, civil servants and estate agents came at the bottom of the table.

It is well known that the most important elements in what makes for a happy job are personal control and social relationships – clearly hairdressers get lots of both these factors. Lawyers, on the other hand, suffer from the adversarial and aggressive nature of their job. Although highly paid, they are more likely to divorce, retire early or leave the profession altogether. Pessimists do better at law, but that mindset doesn't always make you happy as a human being.

4   **Work to your strengths.** What are the five qualities or signature strengths that matter to you most? Here are some possibilities:

Patience, Confidence, Empathy, Humour, Creativity, Optimism, Energy, Practicality, Daring, Honesty, Openness, Generosity.

Choose work that lets you use the qualities you value, every day. If honesty is top of the list, for example, there's no point in working for an unscrupulous loan shark. You'll feel you're betraying your integrity and lose respect for yourself.

- Are you patient, and good at conveying information? Perhaps a career in teaching, science or journalism would suit you.
- Are you practical with a technical bent? You could try engineering, construction or manufacturing.
- Are you ethical and socially aware? Perhaps the law, policing, fire-fighting, politics or charitable work would appeal.

According to BBC happiness expert Jessica Pryce-Jones, the important thing is to have a 'big idea' about yourself and make sure it fits with whatever you're doing. Look at Sarah Tremellen who set up the Bravissimo bra company. In a recent interview she said she wasn't just selling bras – she was 'celebrating women's curves'. That's the big idea that motivates her. Identify your own big idea and you're on your way to a happier working life.

5   **Avoid falling into a negative spiral.** When work is frustrating it's easy to become resentful and fall into a mindset where you think, 'I hate these people. I don't want to be here.' A more constructive approach is to think of yourself as a dispassionate observer: 'What's going on here? How

interesting…' This allows you to sidestep the emotions of the situation. Tell yourself you're on your way to a better job and that you're working hard to find what will suit you.

Positive self-talk is also an effective strategy with workplace bullies. 'The minute you start reinforcing a negative, your mind actually works with it,' Jessica explains. 'You think, "Oh, he's watching me, he thinks I'm bound to drop all these papers. Oh no, I've dropped them." Don't create a negative self-image you can't shift.' Instead, she suggests, you can train yourself to create your own personal happiness 'triggers' to enable you to move away from those negative self-images and focus on, and trigger, more positive feelings.

'Look at your own hand,' she suggests, 'and choose a place that nobody else touches in normal work contact – maybe your third knuckle on the left hand. Now think of a truly lovely moment you have experienced in your life. Start going into that memory, evoke what you were seeing, hearing and feeling. If there was any taste, make it extra delicious. If anyone was there, keep them smiling at you. As you're growing the memory, touch the spot on your hand that you've chosen. Now you have a 'trigger', and you can simply press your knuckle to recall that feeling whenever you need to. You can use your happy memories to lighten the load at work when things get tough.'

6 **Turn a stalled career into a calling.** Use your signature strengths at work to 'recraft' what you do, advises psychologist Mihaly Csikszentmihalyi. Enjoying the state of flow on the job transforms it from a chore into a pleasure. For example, a kitchen worker can decide to be a food artist and make each dish as beautiful as possible. Or a nurse, worn down by changing beds, can take an interest in patients' families, involving them in the process of recovery and using this to boost the morale of the patients. With the right attitude, any job can become a calling; without it, any calling can become a job.

7 **Persuade your employer to be flexible.** Flexitime allows people to vary the start and finish times of their day, provided they work certain core hours. Encourage your employer to consider allowing this option. You could also ask him or her to think about allowing job sharing, part-time working, staggered hours (which allow

employees to have different start, finish and break times to facilitate extended opening hours), and compressed working hours (where people work an agreed number of hours over a shorter period of days).

Put your request for any of these options in writing, outlining the effect you think it will have on the business and how this could be dealt with. Emphasize the value of what you do, and if you are using the extra time to study or learn new skills, make it clear how your employer will benefit.

8   **Ask for a career break.** If you feel burnt out, ask for a career break – a period of unpaid leave from work that usually lasts between one and five years. Make an agreement with your employer that you will return to your old job or a similar one in the future. Although often taken by people raising young children, career breaks are increasingly requested by employees who want to have a 'gap year' travelling or doing charitable work. The advantage is that you have a guaranteed job to return to and the company will retain your skills.

9   **Try downshifting.** Taking a job that involves a drop in pay and more modest living conditions in return for freedom from the drudgery that was getting you down is known as 'downshifting'. It can mean working from home, or it can mean becoming a smaller fish in a smaller pond, but the outcome – less stress and a happier life – could be well worth it. The number of people downshifting is expected to reach 3.7 million by 2007.

10 **Work for yourself.** To uncover your real potential, make a list of your five best qualities (see page 87). Then ask yourself how you could use them in providing a valuable service that others would gladly pay for.

There is plenty of advice for people who want to start up in business. The government's Small Business Service website, for example, has information on a variety of issues. Your local Business Link office should also be able to help you draw up a business plan, advise you on all areas of small business and put you in contact with relevant organizations in your area.

Leaving your job and going it alone can be scary and expensive. But if you are unhappy or have a great idea or skill for going it alone, it might be the best risk you ever took.

Love Makes the World Go Round

OUR LOVE LIFE

- The average British marriage lasts 11 years.
- The number of couples who get married in England and Wales is set to fall by 10 per cent in the next 25 years.
- Getting married is the equivalent to a financial boost of £72,000 (i.e. you would have to pay a single person that sum every year to make them as happy).
- The average age at which British men tie the knot is 31; for women it's 29.
- We spend an average of two hours and 30 minutes a day with our partner.
- According to US therapist Shirley Glass, 56 per cent of men who have affairs say they are in happy relationships; only 34 per cent of women say the same.
- Around 58 per cent of young men aged 20–24 still live at home; the figure for young women of that age is 39 per cent.
- Homosexuality has no statistically significant effect on happiness.

We are biologically programmed to find other human beings the most important objects in the world. Only in their company do we feel complete. We need other people and we need to be needed. In fact, there are few stronger predicators of happiness than a close, nurturing, equitable companionship with one's best friend. People who are in loving relationships with another adult have better hormonal balance and better health.

People are also more satisfied with their lives if their partner is happy. A 2005 survey by Nick Powdthavee at Warwick University found that if your lover is happy, it can even outweigh negative experiences in your own life, such as ill health and redundancy.

Love is a dynamic, ongoing process that provides social connectedness, which is very important to human beings. It is the emotion that makes another person irreplaceable to us. We idealize their strengths and virtues, and downplay their shortcomings – and they do the same for us. A crucial measure of love is the discrepancy between what your partner believes about your strengths and what your friends believe. The bigger the discrepancy in a positive direction, the bigger the romantic 'illusion' your partner has of you. The rather wonderful thing is that the bigger the illusion, the happier and more stable the relationship. We're lucky love is blind! We may even try to live up to our partner's idealized vision of us, so it becomes a self-fulfilling prophecy.

MADLY IN LOVE

Neuroscientists who have taken brain scans of people in the early stages of love say that we become quite unhinged by it: activity patterns show a mixture of dementia, obsession and mania. These prompt compulsive acts, such as the need to constantly phone your partner, which may even resemble psychosis.

Planets apart

Why do men and women understand emotions differently? The simple answer is that there are physical differences in the brain. Women have more grey matter in parts of the limbic system, which is involved in emotion processing, and they also have a larger orbital frontal lobe, which inhibits aggressive behaviour. A 2005 study by psychologists at St Andrews University found that a man's brain cannot pick up the facial expressions showing how his partner feels – supporting the long-held belief that men are emotionally clueless.

But all is not lost. Men can improve on their recognition of emotions reflected in the face by learning to 'mirror' what they see in others. A study at the University of California found that when people copied the facial expression they see in a partner, they were able to experience what the other person is feeling. It enabled them to understand what expressions denoted disgust, fear and especially sadness and surprise, which they often failed to recognise previously.

How do we choose a happy partner?

Research suggests that a relationship is more likely to be successful if the people involved share similar values and interests and are broadly similar in attractiveness. We therefore need to develop realistic attitudes to choosing a partner, and find a way to balance immediate sexual attraction and the other ingredients needed to sustain a long-term relationship. We also need to encourage our children to develop this attitude.

Of course there is a difference between the capacity to love and allowing yourself to be loved. Drawing on the ground-breaking research of Dr John Bowlby, the eminent British child psychoanalyst, and the American psychologist and researcher Professor Mary Ainsworth, positive psychologist Martin Seligman has identified three emotional types in adults, which have their origins in early childhood. These are:

1 **Secure type** – 'I find it relatively easy to get close to people and am comfortable depending on them, or with them depending on me. I don't often worry about being abandoned, or about someone getting close to me.'

2 **Avoidant type** – 'I am uncomfortable being too close to others. I find it difficult to trust them completely or allow myself to depend on them. Partners often want me to be more intimate than I am comfortable with.'

3 **Anxious type** – 'I find others are reluctant to get as close as I would like. I often worry that my partner doesn't really love me or won't want to stay with me. I want to merge completely with another person and this sometimes scares people away.'

Secure lovers remember their parents as available, warm and affectionate. They have high self-esteem and other people like them. They strive for intimate relations with those they love, and try to find a good balance of dependence and independence. They admit when they are distressed and try to use it for constructive ends. They are sensitive to care-giving, understanding when it is and isn't wanted. They avoid one-night stands and don't think sex without love is enjoyable. When a relationship is in trouble, secure people seek support from others.

Avoidant lovers remember their mothers as cold and rejecting. They regard other people as dishonest and untrustworthy (guilty until proved innocent). They lack confidence, especially in social situations. They are distant and don't disclose feelings. They are more approving of casual sex and enjoy sex without love more than with it. When a relationship is in trouble, they don't seek support from others: they try to forget it. Anxious lovers remember their fathers as unfair. They feel that they have little control over their lives, finding others hard to understand and predict. They cling, constantly fear rejection and discourage independence in people they love. They flaunt their distress and anger, but when the other person becomes angry or impatient they become too solicitous. Sexually, women (but not men) are more likely to get involved in exhibitionism, voyeurism and bondage. When a relationship is in trouble, anxious lovers focus obsessively on their own state.

The bottom line is that securely attached people do better in both life and love. At the end of this chapter (see page 99) we offer tips that can help you feel happier and more secure in your relationship or marriage.

'Passion and jealousy are especially powerful emotions because they are generated at the deepest level. They stem from our evolution where unconsciously we want to ensure the propagation of our genes, and from unconscious childhood memories of love and fear of desertion.'
Richard Stevens, BBC happiness expert

Marriage

If you want to be happy, get married – all the statistics prove it. When the National Opinion Research Centre surveyed over 35,000 Americans over the last 30 years, 40 per cent of married people called themselves 'very happy', while only 23 per cent of never-married adults made the same claim. This was true of every ethnic group studied.

Although living together is now very common, it has not so far proved as stable a form of relationship as marriage (unmarried parents are, on average, twice as likely to split up). So-called 'smug marrieds' tend to live longer, enjoy better mental and physical health (they smoke and drink less) and are less likely to commit suicide. Curiously, they also tend to have better-paid jobs. Indeed, a British survey of 20,000 men found that married men live three years longer and earn £3000 a year more on average than single men.

Although marriage has a good track record for making people happy, it must be said that happy people tend to be more likely to get married in the first place. This makes sense when you remember that they are usually more out-going and sociable than depressed people.

During the first year of marriage a couple's happiness level shoots up. However, a study released in 2003 by Dr Richard Lucas of Michigan State University found people adapt to married life and return to their personal 'set point' of happiness (see page 21). The researchers, who studied 24,000 people over a 15-year period, focusing on the relationship between their marital status and their state of happiness, claim the results highlight the role of adaptation in determining life satisfaction: in other words, we can get used to a good thing.

Of course, marriage is not a universal panacea. Today one in three British marriages will end in divorce or separation. You are statistically more likely to divorce if you married young, if you gave birth before you were married, or if you have been divorced previously.

And let's not forget that an unhappy marriage undermines well-being and even makes us physically ill. Research has found that for people in 'not very happy marriages', their level of happiness is lower than the unmarried or the divorced.

> 'I have realized since doing the happiness experiment how much pleasure and happiness I get from seeing people I love enjoy themselves.'
> Slough volunteer

Does being single make you unhappy?

A 2003 survey revealed that 30 per cent of households in the UK contained just one person, which translates as nearly 25 million adult singletons. And many people do find happiness living solo. A person who is very satisfied with life probably has a rich social network – in effect a 'para-family' of friends, ex-lovers and colleagues – and has less to gain from the companionship of marriage. On the other hand, a person who is lonely and therefore somewhat dissatisfied can gain much by marrying.

In a 2005 poll for market research group Mintel, more than half of single British women said they were happy to stay unattached. In fact, the biggest gripe among single women was that people always assumed they wanted to be in a relationship.

> 'A woman needs a man like a fish needs a bicycle.'
> Gloria Steinem, American feminist

While the Mintel poll found that 56 per cent of single women were 'very happy' with their lives as they were and had no desire to be married, it found that some 46 per cent of single men felt the same, but almost half said the biggest downside of living alone was 'not having enough sex', and one in four said they missed the 'comfort and closeness of a hug'. Some 39 per cent of men and 35 per cent of women said they considered themselves 'apathetic about love'.

While the term 'singleton' may conjure up images of fast-living, high-spending *Sex and the City* types, the reality is rarely so glamorous or affluent. In fact, single people can be among the poorest members of society, particularly if they have dependents or are elderly. And even for young professionals, any break in income – be it through redundancy or illness – can be stressful if there is no other breadwinner to fall back on.

When a marriage ends

International survey data shows that the greatest dampeners on happiness are being separated, closely followed by being widowed and being unemployed.

Getting separated is the equivalent of suffering a £132,000 drop in an average lifetime's pay, but the year of divorce is the worst in terms of depression. After that, men return usually to their 'set point' of happiness (see page 21), but women continue to suffer.

The death of a spouse is the unhappiness equivalent of a £168,000 drop in pay. It takes a widow 5–8 years to regain her previous sense of well-being.

Do children make you happy?

The relationship between children and happiness is complex. Having a child can bring joy and bind a couple together, but it can also cause anxiety and strain. Women are more likely than men to state that their children make them happy than men, despite the fact that the most acute trade-offs between employment and childbirth tend to be made by women. Fathers are more likely to attribute happiness to a wider definition of 'family and friends'. However, all the parents surveyed were quick to affirm that they have no regrets – and many insisted that having children had made them a nicer person.

While there is great rejoicing when children are born, within two years parents revert to their original level of happiness.

Those without children can see them as a threat to their lifestyle, finances and relationships. But at the same time they often consider children a natural progression, and an unfulfilled desire for a child can be all-consuming and lead to high levels of unhappiness.

You can be happy with or without children, though the happiness you experience may be derived from different sources. In a 2001 World Values Survey, only 12 per cent of British women and 20 per cent of men thought that a woman had to have children to be fulfilled.

HOW TO BE HAPPIER WITH YOUR PARTNER

Build up a relationship 'bank'

In the normal course of events happy couples exchange emotional information hundreds of times a day. It doesn't have to involve deep intimacy: it might be a question, a look, a gesture, a touch, a phone call or text message. John Gottman, a professor at the University of Washington in Seattle (and author of *The Relationship Cure: Five Steps to Strengthening Your Marriage, Family and Friendships*) calls this 'making a bid' because you are literally bidding for your partner's attention and letting them know that you want to feel connected to them. It tells the recipient:

- I hear you.
- I'm interested in you.
- I understand you (or would like to).
- I'm on your side.
- I'd like to help you (whether I can or not).
- I'd like to be with you (whether I can or not).
- I accept you (even if I don't accept all your behaviour).

Of course when two or more people get together to accomplish anything, sooner or later there's bound to be a conflict, however loving the relationship. But, says Gottman, building better emotional connections can help you to maintain a happy, stable relationship as you discover how to live with your differences.

Couples who react positively to one another display greater humour, affection and interest during arguments. Rather than shutting down, they stay present and therefore have a much better chance of resolving issues and repairing hurt feelings. Remember, you can express your feelings without having to act on them. For example, you could say, 'I'm so angry I want to scream' or 'I feel so upset I want to leave'. This tactic allows you to stay and talk rather than screaming or leaving.

Gottman's research has found that 69 per cent of marital conflicts never go away. If a couple clash over a particular issue – money, housework, sex – they're likely to have the same conflict for ever. But the good news is that if you keep talking to each other and explaining your position, you may reach a point where compromise is possible and you can say, 'I know we don't agree on this issue, but I understand that you are as committed to your point of view as I am to mine, and I respect you for it.'

People don't get married and have children with the intention of allowing their relationship to fail. But often that happens because we don't pay enough attention to the emotional needs of others. We're not acting mindlessly, but we get too caught up in our own concerns to focus on the people around us. For example, a husband and wife may be putting so much time into raising their children and doing up the house that they have no energy left for their own primary relationship.

Repeating the past?

You'll be surprised how much of your own family's emotional philosophy you have absorbed. 'Half of marital angst is directed towards your own mother or father, but gets projected on to your partner instead,' observes BBC happiness expert Brett Kahr. 'When you're screaming at your wife, you're also screaming at your mother for past psychological injuries.'

Inevitably, this colours the way we see and interpret events. This can be a problem if you react to new people in your life as if they were 'just like my mother' or 'just like my step-dad'.

Some emotional injuries still feel hugely sensitive today. That's why the goal of so many forms of therapy is to help the patient revisit painful events from the past to gain new insights. You don't have to keep reacting to new events and relationships with the same automatic painful response.

John Gottman recommends that you ask yourself some key questions in order to determine your attitude and feelings towards your past.

- Can you describe the philosophy of emotion in your home when you were growing up?
- Did your family believe it was important for people to understand their own feelings and express them to others? Or did they believe it was better to keep them bottled up?
- Was it OK to express anger or joy?
- Could you be sad sometimes without being told off for being gloomy?
- How does that philosphy affect you now? Do you sometimes feel guilty for having difficult emotions such as anger and fear?

Handling conflict

Some couples are so good at handling conflict that they make it look like fun. It's not that they don't get cross, but when they disagree they're able to stay connected and engaged with one another. It's almost as if all the good feelings they've accumulated form emotional capital in the bank. When an argument arises, they can draw on this reservoir. For example, a husband might think, 'God, she's really driving me mad at the moment, but she always listens when I complain about my job, so I should give her a break.'

No one should interpret abusive expressions of rage or frustration as bids for connection. However, research shows that a little understanding can go a long way towards recognizing why the bids that often lie beneath a partner's mask of anger, sadness or fear have failed. For example:

- An ambiguous bid to connect may be made to avoid vulnerability or emotional risk.
- Poor communication may be unintentional.
- A bid may be phrased in a negative way that makes it hard for others to hear or accept it.
- The person making the bid has failed to acknowledge their needs in the first place.

MOST HATED HABITS

Scientists at Louisville University, Kentucky, have identified a list of the most annoying habits that can cause a rift between couples. They include:

- Making up or exaggerating anecdotes at dinner parties
- Keeping your partner waiting in shops
- Leaving wet towels around
- Laughing at your own jokes
- Flatulence
- Taking too much luggage on holiday
- Failing to replace the toilet roll
- Using babyish terms of endearment in public
- Men being scared of horror films
- Complaining about your partner's clothes
- Changing settings on the car radio.

According to Michael Cunningham who led the research, 'The first experience of any of these things is likely to be a negative one, but repeated exposure may produce a social allergy – a reaction of hypersensitive annoyance or disgust.'

TIPS TO MAKE YOUR MARRIAGE WORK

Relationship expert John Gottman says that devoting just an extra five hours per week to a marriage makes all the difference. Here is what you should do:

- Touch affectionately – a kiss, a pat, a squeeze (5 minutes × 7 days).
- Find out one thing that you are each going to do that day (2 minutes × 5 days).
- Have a low-stress conversation when you reunite at the end of each workday (20 minutes × 5 days).
- Go on one weekly date, just the two of you, in a relaxed atmosphere (2 hours); it's a good idea to pre-book the restaurant or hotel to you make sure you do it.
- Give genuine admiration and appreciation at least once every day (5 minutes × 7 days).

By watching hundreds of couples interact for 12 hours a day for an entire weekend in his 'love lab', Gottman can predict divorce with 90 per cent accuracy. The clues are:

- Immediate harsh words of disagreement
- Criticism of partner rather than complaints
- Displays of contempt
- Hair-trigger defensiveness
- Refusing to listen to a partner's point of view
- Negative body language.

10 STEPS TO A HAPPIER MARRIAGE

1 **Stop thinking of your partner as perfect.** People with the highest expectations of wedded bliss often set themselves up for the steepest decline in happiness, according to a 2004 study published by psychology professors James McNulty of Ohio State University and Benjamin Karney of the University of Florida. Their four-year study found that high goals for happiness – when they're not backed up by equally robust communication and relationship skills – eventually lead to disappointment during the difficult points of a relationship.

2 **Delegate.** 'Let your partner do more to help out with chores, such as cooking and cleaning,' advises BBC happiness expert Jessica Pryce-Jones, 'otherwise you end up with what Martin Seligman calls "learned helplessness". It's very easy for a man not to know how to use the washing machine because you're the one who always does so.'

3 **Turn negatives into positives.** Instead of complaining about your partner's obstinacy, choose words that are less provocative: 'I respect him for his strong beliefs, and it makes me have confidence in our relationship.' Similarly, you might say of a volatile or passionate partner: 'At first I thought she was crazy, but now I think our relationship would suffer if this attribute were to disappear.'

4 **Be true to your strengths.** Seligman argues that marriage goes better when we use our signature strengths – from steadfastness and loyalty to integrity and kindness.

5 **Practise responsive listening.** Good listening validates the person who is talking, so concentrate and offer positive encouragement, such as 'I understand' or 'I see what you mean' or even the non-committal 'I can't blame you for that'. Save disagreeing with your partner until it's your turn to speak. If there is a genuine distraction – children, phones ringing – be upfront: 'I'd like to talk this over with you but let's wait till we won't be disturbed. Can we put it off for a little bit?' When you start talking, begin by paraphrasing what your partner has just said to show you have listened: 'I understand that you're having a bad time at work. Is there anything I can do to help?'

Richard Stevens adds: 'It's important not simply to blame your partner for behaviour you don't like. You need to own your feelings here. Different people see the world differently. Good communication is about sharing your experiences and becoming aware of your partner's, not about defining what's right and wrong.'

How to Be Happy

6   **Adopt the speaker–listener ritual.** For couples in troubled marriages almost every discussion can escalate into an argument. Seligman advocates labelling these 'hot-button issues' so that you both have a chance to take the floor. Say upfront, 'This is one of my hot-button issues, so let's use the speaker–listener ritual.' You can take turns to stand on a symbolic piece of carpet or paper. If you don't have the carpet, you are the listener and can't interrupt. When you are the speaker, talk about your thoughts and feelings, not your interpretation of what your partner is thinking and feeling. Use 'I' as much as possible rather than 'you'.

7   **Ask open-ended questions.** Don't ask the kind of questions that can be answered with simple one-word responses. Instead, ask your partner questions that allow them to explore their point of view and elaborate. Open-ended questions get to the heart of your partner's values and dreams. And if he or she does express an unrealistic dream – leaving their job, buying a new sports car – don't turn against them with sarcasm or ridicule. Try to enter into the language of the 'dream' ('I can see how that would make you happy') and let them work out whether it is really achievable.

8   **Be optimistic.** When your partner does something that displeases you, try to find a temporary and local explanation for it, such as 'She was tired' or 'He had a hangover' rather than 'She goes out too much' or 'He's an alcoholic'. Similarly, if they do something fantastic, advises Seligman, build it up with permanent and pervasive character traits, such as 'She's a great leader' rather than 'What a lucky day she had'. Interestingly, when an optimist and a pessimist marry, a happy marriage is possible. But when two pessimists marry and something dreadful happens in their lives, a downward spiral can ensue.

9   **Discuss your need for independence.** If you feel your partner is turning away, it might be that they need to gain more autonomy in the relationship. Be upfront: talk about your relative needs for independence. How much freedom and autonomy do you each need? Will you allow others to become as close to you as you are to each other? Yes, it can be scary to discuss this topic, but to avoid having this discussion simply leads to hurt feelings and maybe even the dissolution of the relationship.

10 **Create a relationship 'map' together.** To become more familiar with the details of each other's lives, make a list of 50 questions from 'favourite meal' to 'best recent day'. Answer the questions about your partner, and see where the gaps are.

Richard Stevens gave the volunteers an exercise in intimacy to use with close friends and partners. This requires finding at least an hour where you can both be undisturbed. Each partner is given 10–15 minutes to express his or her feelings without interruption. At the end the person listening can express what they have been feeling while listening but should not criticize. Then the partners swap roles so that the talker now becomes the listener and subsequently expresses what he or she was feeling while listening. 'This simple technique can be a remarkably effective way of finding out what each person feels,' says Richard, 'and in so doing, strengthens the bond between you.'

One of the Slough volunteers spoke about the experience of talking undisturbed to her partner for an hour: 'We've been together for 12 years now, and last night we went out for a few drinks and dinner (I'm an old-fashioned girl at heart). We had a great time being away from home and family. It gave us a chance to talk and be open with each other, which is something we don't often do. It was helpful to listen to what my partner had to say – and boy did that man have lots to say! I was blown away by his openness. I now think that talking and listening to each other will make us stronger in every way. It's just a question of finding the time. But I will!'

During the TV series one married couple, who are very much in love, worked with Richard on their different personality styles. The wife is very much a take-charge type, while the husband is quiet and gentle. He finds decision-making – even something as simple as choosing a restaurant – very difficult. His wife would like him to be more assertive. So Richard set the husband the task of creating a 'very special day' for his wife. Part of his role was to make all the decisions about it, from deciding the destination to organizing the transport and including an extra treat, without her knowing anything about it. This is a great exercise to help a partner practise being more assertive in a relationship.

'Our wedding anniversary today. It was a lovely day, full of laughter and quite a bit of emotion underneath. Thirty-three years to mull over, and a lot of gratitude for all they have brought us. Inevitably it brought up memories of our first meeting, first outing, first holiday together, work we have shared and troubles we have survived. The question that now challenges us is "What next?"'
Slough volunteer

How to Be Happy

Sexual Happiness

STRANGE BUT TRUE...

- Married people have better sex lives than single people.
- France is the sexiest country, with couples having sex 137 times a year (British couples clock in at 119).
- The British spend 22.5 minutes on foreplay.
- People around the world have had an average number of 10.5 sexual partners.
- We spend two minutes 42 seconds per day having sex.
- The average global age for first sex is now 17.7.
- The typical British man lasts seven minutes 37 seconds in bed (six seconds more than American men).
- People who were 16 when their parents divorced have more sex than average.
- Almost half the British population have been unfaithful to their partner at some point.
- A higher income does not buy more sex or more sexual partners.
- People aged 35–44 are having the most sex.
- Highly educated females tend to have fewer sexual partners.

'Marriage is a wonderful invention, but then again, so is the bicycle repair kit.'
Billy Connolly, comedian

Most people will be delighted to know that you should have as much sex as humanly possible to be happy! In a 2004 study of 1000 employed women, sex was rated retrospectively as the activity that produces the single largest amount of happiness.

The statistics throw up some surprising facts, including that married people have more sex than their single counterparts, and that those hanging from chandeliers with multiple sexual partners are far from being the happiest. Psychologists have calculated that the number of sexual partners that would make us happiest in a year is… one. Their research shows that you will have happier and better sex with the same partner.

All in the head?

Sex makes us feel wanted and attractive, needed and admired. We feel emotionally connected to the person we're having sex with, and touching and orgasm release endorphins (feel-good chemicals), which create a feeling of well-being. In fact, endorphin production can increase 200 per cent from the beginning to the end of sexual activity.

Although there is a link between intimacy with a loving partner and happiness, there are definitely benefits from the physical act itself, whether it's 'going solo' or with a partner. Satisfying sex boosts our immune system and makes our blood pump furiously. It's also good for the heart, both physically and emotionally.

Ongoing physical contact, and not just sex alone, also helps produce endorphins, including oxytocin. Together these substances act like natural opiates and help stabilize a relationship by inducing a drug-like dependency. Although there are many reasons why two people choose to maintain a close and loving relationship, endorphins could well be a factor.

Research also suggests that semen acts as an antidepressant because it contains a range of hormones, including testosterone and oestrogen, both of which have been shown to improve mood.

Successful human reproduction is not a matter of quick fertilization followed by both parents going their separate ways. For immature, dependent offspring to thrive they need parents who stick around to mentor and protect them. Women in stable relationships ovulate more regularly, and continue ovulating into middle age, reaching menopause later than women in unstable relationships.

Famous sexologists William Masters and Virginia Johnson discovered in the 1970s that sexual pleasure involved the brain as much as the body. They proclaimed that sex is 'psychophysiological', which basically means that if you get your attitude right, the impact on your body will be enormous. The brain is the biggest erogenous zone, so you need to spend more time on 'brain sex', such as fantasies, role play, variety, surprise and anticipation.

Typically, a new couple will have a high sex drive in the first 18 months of their relationship (this is an evolutionary pattern designed to lead to pregnancy and pair bonding). Later the frequency of sex will naturally diminish, so don't feel guilty or worried that you're going off each other. Having said that, relationship expert Tracey Cox is convinced our sex lives can 'age' well: 'As you get older together as a couple, you're more likely to move from genital/orgasm-based performance to more holistic sex.'

'A relationship I think is like a shark... it has to constantly move forward or it dies.'
Woody Allen, Annie Hall *(1977)*

Mars and Venus

As you've probably noticed, male and female desire is not always in sync. On average, men take two and a half minutes to reach orgasm, while women take 12. In addition, men tend to be on a five-day cycle when it comes to wanting sex, and women are on a 10-day cycle.

According to Dr David Goldmeier, a consultant physician at St Mary's Hospital in London, 'Men are "penile-centric". If we have erections, we feel sexy in our penises.' Sex for women, however, tends to start in the brain – perhaps after a nice gesture, such as being given a bunch of flowers or cooked a nice meal.

Studies suggest that one in three marriages in Britain and the USA struggle with problems associated with mismatched desire. And, says Tracey Cox, one of the greatest sources of unhappiness for couples is the myth that women always have an orgasm from penetrative sex. 'Fewer than 30 per cent of women orgasm through intercourse – and half of those are probably faking. Which begs an obvious question: if women not climaxing through intercourse alone is such a common problem, why are we all lying about it?' Accepting that the female orgasm is nearly always clitoral would make us all a lot happier, she argues. 'Couples who are happiest in bed are the ones who get past that and don't get hung up about it.'

'Husbands are like fires. They go out when unattended.'
Zsa Zsa Gabor, Hungarian actress and socialite

Mismatched desire

Why do we insist on matching up with people who don't feel the same way about sex as we do? Well, one good reason is that relationships and love aren't based entirely on sex. We fall in love and decide to settle down for lots of reasons, not just sexual compatibility. The other reason, says Cox, is that it's really hard to tell in the beginning what sort of sex drive your partner has.

'Our libido is strongly influenced by hormones and other substances, which tend to go bonkers during that heady phase at the beginning. During infatuation, the body releases high levels of phenylethylamine and dopamine, and even people who usually couldn't care less experience a sensational surge in desire.'

This means someone with quite a low sex drive acts and feels like a person with a high libido. But, of course, hormone boosts don't last, and within 18 months they return to their true levels. Happily, there's lots that can be done to redress the balance and keep both partners in a relationship sexually and emotionally satisfied. 'But,' says Cox, 'there's one crucial piece of advice that makes all the difference here: you must stop blaming each other. Our natural testosterone level (high = high desire, low = low desire) is beyond our control.'

GOOD SEX CAN KEEP US YOUNG

Men and women who have sex four or five times a week look more than 10 years younger than their contemporaries who have sex twice a week. So says Dr David Weeks, a neuropsychologist at the Royal Edinburgh Hospital and author of *Secrets of the Super Young*. Dr Weeks, who carried out a 10-year study involving 3500 people, believes that the pleasure derived from sex is a crucial factor in preserving youth. 'It makes us happy and produces chemicals telling us so.'

However, he found that indulging in promiscuous sex did not have the same benefits as enjoying loving sex in a long-term relationship, and that it was more likely to promote the ageing process rather than reduce it.

How
to Be
Happy

'I had the best sex ever in my whole life with my wife last night. I've been following the Happiness Manifesto, talking uninterrupted to my partner, hugging, smiling, recognizing the blessings in my life – and it works! I've never felt so close and intimate with anyone.'
Slough volunteer

Role confusion

'The agony of romantic love is that there are such enormous transferences that cloud the love relationship,' observes BBC happiness expert Brett Kahr. Someone who starts out as a romantic partner loves and cares for you, and so tips over into a mother/father role. 'We turn to our partners for sexual intimacy, for companionship, for procreative purposes… but the parent–child relationship also gets activated. So if your partner says, "Shall I rub your back/make you dinner/iron your shirt?" you suddenly find at a deep unconscious level that you don't know whether you're with an adult-genital partner or with your mother.

'The birth of a child can also cause strain. When your wife has a child, you don't know if she is abandoning you and having a new love affair with this baby at her breast, you don't know whether you're still allowed to have sex with her when she's clearly enjoying this very intimate physical relationship with the baby. One of the design faults of the human unconscious is that we become confused about intimate relationships – not knowing if they're horizontal [peer] relationships, where you're on the same plateau, or vertical relationships, where it's parent–child.

'And then, once those different roles have become muddled, there is tremendous scope for confusion and anguish. Unless the roles are sorted out in one's mind, in my experience that is when marital problems begin to rear their ugly head.'

'There's this perception that you don't have to work at sex, which is odd when you think that everyone accepts you have to work on other aspects of your life, such as career, body and diet. People think if you have to work at your love life, there's something wrong. In casual or short-term relationships it's perfectly possible to have great sex without love. But long term it is almost impossible to have great sex without a good relationship supporting it.'
Tracey Cox, sex therapist

15 WAYS TO HAVE A BETTER SEX LIFE

1   **Try to vary the routines** of eating, sleeping or shopping together because sex starts long before you reach the bedroom. Sexual play can lose its first excitement in a long relationship, so it's worth making an effort to talk together about new topics of conversation, visit new places or make new friends.

2   **Be upfront** about your different sexual needs and rhythms. Problems often arise when one partner is more interested in sex or sensual pleasure than the other. Knowing that such differences can be based on an individual's brain circuitry could help. With this understanding, says Professor Gottman, one partner is less likely to feel personally rejected when the other acts uninterested. Rather than judging each other as 'cold' or 'too horny', partners can see their differences in a more objective light.

3   **Value sleep.** What could be more symbolic of the trust and intimacy in a relationship than the act of taking off your clothes, lying down and falling asleep in the same bed with another person? Try to let go of the tension of the day, and regard sleeping as a temporary ceasefire from arguments.

4   **Plan to have sex.** Some people believe love-making should be totally spontaneous, but family life can get so busy that it may never happen. Is there a specific, regular time during the day that you can plan to be together – maybe at the weekend when the kids are off at music lessons, or during a lunch hour?

5   **Share fantasies.** Many couples have an interval in their love-making that's considered 'uncensored', when it's OK to reveal secret desires and fantasies. You're not required to tell all, but sharing can be fulfilling. And fantasies are by definition the free play of the creative imagination.

6   **Go to a fancy dress party.** 'People have the best sex ever after fancy dress,' claims Tracey Cox. 'Masks also work for the same reason.'

7   **Have a private code for initiating or refusing sex.** The older generation used the sweet euphemism of 'leaving the heating on overnight'. Psychologist Lonnie Barbach suggests that you talk about desire on a scale of one to nine, where nine is 'extremely lusty' and one is 'not in the mood at all'. That way you can communicate how you are feeling without your partner feeling rejected.

How to Be Happy

8   **Be generous.** In a long-term relationship our bodies inevitably age. A good lover has the ability to see a partner's faults but focus on the good bits of the body.

9   **Write a love letter.** Spell out each word using your tongue as a pen on your partner's most intimate body areas. This ensures that you're varying your movements and won't overstimulate one particular part of their body, says Cox.

10 **Experiment with role play.** This allows you to act out a safe but erotic scenario. It's often best to this away from home (perhaps on a 'dirty' weekend) because it's much easier to pretend that you're someone else when you're in unfamiliar surroundings. 'Divide the plot into four parts,' advises Cox. '1. Where/how you meet. 2. What happens when you do. 3. How it all starts happening. 4. What happens when it does (most detail here). Make it real by thinking about it.'

11 **Affair-proof your relationship.** The couple who play together tend not to play apart. 'Variety is what most of us want, but we tend to want it with the same person,' says Cox. 'Yes, we're very up for doing naughty things, but if most of us h we'd rather do it with our long-term partner than a We think it's all about the lure of new flesh, but most o not. People have affairs not just for newness but b crave variety.'

12 **Obviously practice makes perfect** – knowing w to press to make your partner happy. But the most imp is to be flexible and open to change. 'You can desensit – you've done the same thing for so long that your bo kick to push it over the edge,' Cox says. 'Avoid knee-jerk reactions or judging partners who want to try "kinky stuff".'

13 **Reject sex, not the person.** Say, 'I don't feel like sex, but I do feel like holding you because I love you so much.' It's infinitely preferable to pushing the person away and rolling over.

14 **Have sex even if you don't really fancy it.** Lots of people enjoy it once they get started, and there's evidence that making love regularly boosts the body's production of testosterone – which will make you want to have sex more often in the future.

15 **Make sure you have a good time before and after sex** – not just during. Cuddling and affection are very important.

Our man on the ground

Research shows that more and better sex with one partner is a key to happiness. 'For plenty of people, more sex rather than more money will bring happiness,' comments BBC evangelist Richard Reeves. During filming he bravely took on the *Making Slough Happy* 'Sex Campaign'. As part of his research, he visited a hair salon, a barbershop, a sex shop and a rugby club – all of which are staffed by what he calls society's 'confessors': i.e. the people to whom we confide intimate details of our lives.

To his surprise, he found that it was women, *not* men, who wanted to have more sexual partners. 'They were much more up for it and more honest. Their attitude was, "Well, you only live once, you should experiment before you settle down." Men, on the other hand, claimed to want only one woman and that they never slept around. Maybe they felt they had to be more PC on camera when their wives and girlfriends would be watching. I didn't quite believe the men had reached such a stage of sexual maturity, which was why I went to the rugby club to get some more realistic locker-room talk.'

Richard thinks it is this dissembling that causes men so many problems. 'I think men are driven, perhaps biologically, but, even more importantly, socially, towards forms of sexual behaviour that turn out not to be in their best interest or for their happiness. And the sex paradox might be that men behave in ways that are not in their best interest for reasons of cultural history. Women, however, are the 'new men', saying, "Yeah, party time!", which is kind of interesting and refreshing.'

What he found particularly encouraging was that people were quite happy to talk about sex openly. 'People did recognize that a healthy sex life reflects the health of society generally. If you haven't got the time or energy for good, strong intimate relations, then maybe we've got something wrong. The most worrying thing was when I asked the blokes whether they'd rather have twice as much money or twice as much sex… To a man, they said money. When young blokes say that, all hope for future relationships is lost.'

'A happy marriage is a long conversation that always seems too short.'
André Maurois, French writer and biographer

How to Be Happy

Erotic dancing

'I think some people live very unintimate lives,' says BBC expert Richard Stevens, 'which is a pity because intimacy is a wonderful base for happiness. It provides a kind of emotional security and depth, and validation of one's self.'

To encourage the *Making Slough Happy* volunteers to connect with each other and learn about the importance of touch, Richard introduced biodanza into the workshop sessions. This uses different types of music to arouse feeling and sensitivity to others. No one speaks in biodanza: communication is through look, gesture and touch. This reduces the opportunity for people to hide behind an assumed mask or role. Biodanza requires freedom, trust and spontaneity in the participants. People connect with each other as experiencing individuals. Eye contact is central to this, which can make biodanza an emotionally charged experience. Far from being terrified, the group took it on with gusto.

As one of the participants recounts: 'The biodanza workshop was great fun. To begin with I found myself uncomfortable and had to leave because it was very erotic in places, but it was also very therapeutic. Strange things came out of it, like the experience of looking into someone's eyes, which was very intimate and intimidating at the same time. Doing this with a man I knew made me laugh as I felt so awkward, but with other people it seemed that a very deep and emotional message was being communicated.'

'If you would be loved, love
and be lovable.'
Benjamin Franklin, American statesman

Happier Families

'Where does the family start? It starts with a young man falling in love with a girl – no superior alternative has yet been found.'

Winston Churchill, statesman

FACTS ABOUT FAMILY LIFE

- More than two-thirds of the 24.7 million households in the UK are families.
- Around seven in 10 households are headed by a married couple.
- Households with two adults and two children spend an average of £611 a week.
- The size of the average British household fell from 2.91 people in 1971 to 2.31 people in 2002.
- In 2001, 10 per cent of all families with dependent children in the UK were stepfamilies.
- Britain is the single-parent capital of Europe, with nine out of 10 lone parents being lone mothers.
- Around half of all divorces involve couples with children.

Some of our most intense and meaningful experiences are the result of family relationships. While individuality is very important to the developing adult, there are great opportunities for joy and growth that can only be experienced within family life. Occasionally setting aside your own needs and goals for the pleasure of belonging to a mutually supportive group can be tremendously satisfying. In the overall aim of increasing happiness, the family is exceptionally important, and this chapter will help you to improve that area of your life.

A common mistake people make is to assume that family life takes care of itself. Like all relationships, those within the family need the investment of time and care. While these relationships can be difficult, even volatile, achieving closeness is not impossible – far from it. It's a skill and it can be learnt. If all parties are willing to try to change direction when they make mistakes, the relationship can be rescued.

The integrated family

In an integrated family each person's goals must be considered equally important. But there also need to be shared goals in order to unite the family emotionally and physically. Start small, such as playing Scrabble together, and build up to bigger projects, such as buying a new sofa or planning a holiday.

Whatever the goal, you all need to respect each other's individual preferences. If your son wants to go ice-skating and your daughter wants to go to a concert, it should be possible for everyone to do skating one weekend and the concert the weekend after. As with any flow activity (see page 37), good lines of communication and feedback are essential.

Does your extended family work?

Now that people travel so widely for work, the nuclear family – parents and children – has become the norm, often living far away from other relatives. The extended family of grandparents, siblings, aunts, uncles and cousins still exists, but tends to meet up only on high days and holidays. Ask yourself: What was the role of the extended family in the home where you grew up? Do you want it to be different or similar in your own life? Is your extended family a reasonably happy and cohesive unit, or are people constantly at loggerheads?

'Happy' is a subjective term; it means different things to different people – and to different families. For some raised voices could be traumatic; for others this could be the usual form of communication. We all have a vision of how we'd like family life to be, and it is possible to improve relationships with extended-family members if you are all open about how much time you want or expect to spend with each other.

'I went to a family wedding and met cousins that I hadn't seen for years. They were all my age and we reminisced about what we did as children together. I came away feeling very happy.'
Slough volunteer

Don't fight!

As BBC happiness expert Brett Kahr observes, 'We often treat our loved ones with emotional cruelty, partly because we know that we can – we know that they are unlikely to abandon us, so we use and abuse them as a means of venting our most aggressive impulses.'

Christmas, birthdays and family holidays can turn into a minefield because many of us are simply not used to spending 24 hours a day with our loved ones. Old grievances and arguments are activated, someone storms out, and before you know it a major family feud has occurred where people don't speak to one another for months.

The best strategy with family arguments and feuds is to avoid having them in the first place, and the best way to do this is to learn the art of compromise. Relationships are all about compromise from the very start. During childhood we are taught to share and to resolve difficulties peaceably, so we should continue that practice into adulthood. Treat each other with the courtesy and respect that you would extend to friends and colleagues. Family connections do not deserve lesser treatment.

But how can you resolve arguments once they've occurred? 'There are two ways of going about it,' Brett advises. 'For severe cases of family or marital dysfunction, professional psychotherapeutic help is crucial to get to the roots of it, and to create a safe professional context in which very difficult emotions can be aired and examined.' (For help in choosing the right professional help, see pages 206–9.)

If you're dealing with a silly spat that can be resolved informally, Brett suggests you take the plunge and phone the relative. 'Better to sort out a problem before it becomes a major haemorrhage. Stimulate conversation and try to arrange a pleasant outing – perhaps a picnic or trip to a sports event.

'In either case the mature approach is to acknowledge the argument straight away, "Listen, I'm really hurt and I'm feeling very sad that we had such a strained conversation when we spoke last time. Can we talk about it?" It's not that difficult, but so many of us are flooded with intense feelings of shame that we find it hard to say something as simple as, "I'm sorry if I hurt your feelings," and we end up spoiling potentially rewarding relationships as a result. As my wise, late Jewish grandmother said, "It's better to be the bigger person".'

HOW TO STRENGTHEN FAMILY TIES

- Use family rituals to create shared meaning. A ritual involves two or more people coming together around a common activity. It might be based around a religious festival, such as Christmas or Ramadan, or a family event, such as a birthday, holiday or shopping trip. Marking life's major transitions – weddings, moving house, loss of a loved one – in the company of friends and family is a way to feel connected to a larger community of support.

  Don't be too rigid in your expectations of the ritual, and don't let one family member bear all the responsibility for organizing it. If you prefer to keep things on a small scale, you could create an informal ritual out of activities you already do, such as watching TV, cooking, supervising homework, after-dinner coffee.

- Get rid of your television. As part of the Slough experiment, the volunteers had their televisions taken away. They all found this difficult at first, but later remarked on the benefits: 'When the film crew took the TV away, I was devastated, but in fact we have used the time talking and laughing together as a family. I've joined the pub quiz and even written some poetry.' Someone else said: 'The children are still a bit wistful about the TV being taken away, but I love the fact it's made us all communicate more. Even though returning it would make life easier with the kids, I'm tempted not to have it back!'

- Create a family archive. Every family has its own unique history, so why not pool your resources to create a shared archive of memories? Gather together your photos and home videos. Interview elderly relatives about their life. Research the family tree or commission a new series of portraits. Some artists also create bespoke pieces that celebrate a family relationship or event. For example, textile artist Natasha Kerr works with old family photographs and stories to build up layers of text, paint and embroidery, thus creating an 'heirloom' for the future.

- Plan a reunion. Ideally, this should be held on neutral ground – a country park, a hotel, village hall or restaurant. Keep activities light-hearted and optional; no one should feel obliged to go hiking or play games. Spread the work around and involve everyone in the planning.

  One Slough volunteer told us how he and his family organize their get-together: 'My wife and I have six children from our first marriages, so it has always been a mission of mine to build ties between the two streams of the family. My son has hired a scout campsite to gather the two families together for a weekend celebration. This will be a joint experience to help everyone bond as long-term friends. It gives me enormous joy that we all do this. We meet for a joint family get-together every second year.'

Siblings

Brothers and sisters are a big part of the happiness equation. Despite having the same parents and growing up in the same family environment, they are often remarkably different from each other in terms of personality and behaviour. In fact, scientists have found that shared early experiences might make them more different from each other, as each unconsciously tries to find their own, individual niche in the family. Birth order, age difference and gender may also give them different perceptions of the same childhood experiences – differences that can be hard to reconcile.

While a shared past can be a bond, it can also lead to problems because siblings know so much about each other. At the very least it means we know how to push each other's buttons. At worst it may serve as a constant reminder of their imperfections.

Parents do treat siblings differently, and children are highly sensitive to this. The practical implication is that parents should try to treat their children fairly, but this doesn't mean trying to treat them equally: that is virtually impossible.

Rivalry tends to flourish in families where affection and attention are rationed, or redistributed with the arrival of a new baby. This can lead to feelings of loss, envy and even hatred. Interestingly, sibling rivalry is less of a problem in families where affection is not in short supply.

Despite the potential for rivalry, having brothers and sisters can be a great source of happiness. They provide mental and social stimulation, and provide us with important skills, such as learning to fight and reconcile, to cooperate and manipulate, to share and care. Later they may help us understand our shared past.

'The times we share with loved ones may be short... so tell them you love them at every opportunity. You might not have a chance tomorrow.'
Slough volunteer, following a bereavement

HOW TO BE HAPPIER WITH SIBLINGS

- Listen to your siblings' memories of childhood – even when they're hard to hear or conflict with your own. Reconnecting through a shared history can draw you together, especially as you approach middle age and want to find deeper meanings in your life stories. And remember, siblings are the support team who will help you care for your parents as they age and help you cope with their death.
- Don't let the past dominate. Try to 'stay present' with your siblings, seeing them as they are now rather than as the bossy older brother or meddling younger sister. Ask questions such as, 'How are you now?' or 'What's happening in your life at the moment?'
- Treat each other as you would your friends – with the same respect, courtesy and interest.
- Watch your tone. An apparently simple question, such as 'Have you called Mum yet?' can have different meanings depending on the intonation. It could be an excited request because you know she has some good news to pass on, or it could be a veiled rebuke.
- Try to have more fun together. Many sibling relationships end up being about duty, so make spontaneous arrangements, such as going out for a meal or to the cinema, to break the pattern.
- Plan a sibling getaway without partners or children. Just plenty of time to talk and walk, away from the distractions of everyday life.

'Happiness is having a large, loving, caring, close-knit family in another city.'
George Burns, American actor and comedian

How to Make Happy Children

FASCINATING FACTS ABOUT CHILDREN

- The average number of children per family in the UK is now 1.8.
- The British birth rate is the lowest since 1924.
- Children who take part in community action are happier, less prone to depression and physically healthier.
- Talking about your own ideals and dreams (even frustrated ones) in front of your children will help them to develop the ambition to succeed.
- A mother's ability to 'read' her child's mind and accurately judge his or her emotions is more important to the child's development than her social status or income.
- Children need time to digest information and think about things, so don't expect immediate answers.
- Parents who voice low expectations lead children to expect less of themselves.
- If you want your children to be happy, love them for who they are, not for what you would like them to be or to achieve.

Wanting your child to be happy is not selfish. Happy children develop into better students and better employees. They are more popular and more persistent in the classroom. They are also faster at learning and performing mental tasks when they are in a happy mood. Raising happy children who develop into fully rounded adults benefits society as a whole.

A good parent can do a great deal to help children flourish and become happier. And almost any adult has the capacity to be a good parent, even if some lack confidence in their own ability.

Of course, many factors go into making a happy child: education, genes, health and environment all contribute. But parenting is, in fact, one of the most crucial influences. From infancy onwards, a child's very survival depends on adults noticing them and taking action. If children can't connect with parents through positive behaviour, they will do it by acting up.

Good family relationships in childhood have a bigger influence on individuals' later career success and earnings than how well they did in school. Securely attached children begin exploring and mastering their environment sooner than those who are not. And to become securely attached infants must be wholly confident that their primary care-giver (usually but not always the mother) is consistently responsive to their needs and available to give help whenever it is needed. Children who feel unconditionally loved and secure are better able to cope with uncertainty, and can therefore afford to explore, play and take risks. They are also better at understanding and dealing with negative emotions, such as sadness and anger.

By contrast, children who lack emotional literacy find it hard to manage their own feelings or understand other people's, have more problems coping with anger and aggression, and are more likely to smoke, take illicit drugs or abuse alcohol. And if children don't learn how to connect emotionally with a parent (or another care-giver), they will encounter difficulty in connecting in all sorts of relationships for the rest of their life.

In one study mothers of two-year-olds were asked to teach them a difficult task: the same group was then assessed a year later. The study found that children who had been encouraged with praise, guidance and constructive criticism, when being taught something, were more persistent. Other children who had received only negative criticism were ashamed and reluctant to risk exposing themselves to further mockery.

'... the trouble with children is that they are not returnable.'
Quentin Crisp, writer and performer

What do children need to be happy?

In a year 2000 study of children's attitudes towards parents conducted by the National Family & Parenting Institute, eight out of 10 children said that if parents want to raise happy children, they should make them feel loved and cared for, while seven out of 10 said that parents should make children feel listened to and understood. Being clear about what is right and wrong was also considered important in raising happy children. Less important were parents not being married, not giving children all the material things they wanted, and living apart if they really don't get on with each other.

'I'm very fond of children, but I couldn't eat a whole one.'
W.C. Fields, American actor, comedian and vaudeville performer

Play is important

Children and young animals spend a lot of time engaged in play. It might look pointless, but it is actually an important biological mechanism. It helps children to develop physical, social and mental skills, and teaches them how to cope with the world. In fact, play is the prototype gratification. It almost always involves mastery and engenders 'flow' (when time seems to stop) in a child of any age. Play also builds muscular and cardiovascular fitness.

And children need recreational time. 'Hothousing' them – overscheduling their lives with such things as piano lessons and ballet classes – leaves little time for them simply to enjoy themselves. Watching TV, which consumes three hours a day of the average child's time, is another major enemy of active play. 'Play is an essential building block of life, essential nourishment for healthy development,' advises Doug Cole, chairman of the International Play Association. Research has also found that children who go to less academic nurseries, where they spend more time playing, tend to have better social skills and job success as adults.

Overprotective parents often ration play, says Paul Martin, author of *Making Happy People*. 'Play, especially of the outdoor or rough-and-tumble variety, is viewed as potentially nasty, or even dangerous: the child might be upset, bullied, hit or worse. The problem here is that attempting to insulate children from risks will also deprive them of opportunities for play and social interaction, which can be crucial for their development.'

Loving boundaries

The key element in raising happy children is to love them unconditionally, but also offer boundaries. 'Children need boundaries, but boundaries are very different from discipline,' says BBC happiness expert Brett Kahr. He believes that the word 'discipline' has an inherently punitive quality to it, and overtones of a master–slave relationship. Truly loving parents will always want to set boundaries rather than discipline their child. In practice, this means granting them considerable autonomy while setting clear rules about what is and isn't permissible, then stepping back and letting them get on with it. All children find it easier to develop their potential if they know that, no matter what happens, they have a safe emotional base in the family.

Of course, you must keep a close eye on what your children are up to, but do not interfere unnecessarily. It is also worth being reasonably honest with them: love them unconditionally and praise their achievements, but don't try to convince them everything they do and say is perfect.

If children do misbehave, the golden rule is not to criticize them or their character, only the specific action. Spanking, grounding (barring them from going out) and blanking or ignoring them are rarely effective in the long term. Brett Kahr says: 'I wouldn't even criticize the behaviour. Instead, try to understand the meaning of the behaviour. We have such a punitive attitude towards our children in this country. Rather than saying, "I love you but what you did is hateful", which is also going to make a child deeply ashamed, the parents should sit the child down and say, "When you stole £2 from my purse, I think it was a cry for help. I think you feel you're missing something. Let's talk about what's making you unhappy." If you treat children as human beings, they will respond in kind.'

The myth of quality time

Are you spending enough time with your children? The time you spend together can make a huge difference to their happiness. Busy professionals might be tempted to think that spending only an hour a day together is fine so long as it's 'quality time', but that is unlikely to maintain a rich, consistent and nurturing relationship. According to the survey conducted by the National Family & Parenting Institute, the groups who are least likely to say they can talk to their parents about problems are boys, 15–17-year-olds, non-white children, and those from single-parent households.

'Parents learn a lot from their children about coping with life.'
Nancy Spain, journalist

Help your child to be more resilient

Why are some children able to overcome extreme circumstances – poverty, parental absence, a violent neighbourhood – and find happiness, while others are defeated by minor setbacks? Scientists are increasingly studying the psychology of resilience – the ability to bounce back from disaster – but some feel that whether or not we have this ability to not let life's problems defeat us is sheer luck. Often we carry the scars, but we do eventually adapt.

Werner, who lived through the saturation bombing of Germany during the Second World War, has studied resilience in youngsters since the 1950s. Some characteristics appear to be fundamental, but the strength of the parental bond established in the first three years of life seems to set the tone for the rest of our days. Studies that follow children to adulthood show that these bonds influence future success almost more than any other factor. So does being born with an easygoing temperament or a certain amount of intelligence.

But can children born in 'challenged' families learn skills to help them overcome adversity? The answer is a qualified yes. You can't teach resilience, but certain skills – such as developing a sense of autonomy or being a good reader – increase the chances that a child will be a productive member of society. Belief systems, whether something as straightforward as believing you have a future, or a specific religious faith – also play a critical role.

Resilience, researchers agree, is a complex process. 'It's not a one-dimensional thing,' explains Arthur Reynolds, a professor of social work at the University of Wisconsin. 'There is a sort of chain reaction that leads to resilience later, and the chain reaction begins when children are very young.'

In fact, resilient children are good at drawing people to help them because they are usually open and engaging rather than reserved and sullen. They may also use humour to make you want to help them, and they have become good enough judges of character to know who to call on in an emergency. If one person lets them down, they find another. And those who rebound from adversity in childhood, when they were often required to help others, tend to be more altruistic as adults.

Factors that weaken resilience include violence, physical or sexual abuse, direct exposure to alcoholism and removal from the home. If resilience is strength under adversity, then multiple-risk exposure (to four or more of the weakening factors) will limit emotional endurance.

BBC happiness expert Richard Stevens observes: 'We don't question the fact that we need to pass a test and get a licence to drive a car. Bringing up children probably has as much if not more potential for hurting others. So why shouldn't parents be expected to take courses and pass a test in parenting?'

WAYS TO FOSTER RESILIENCE IN CHILDREN

Encourage a talent. Children who are resilient have often found something to be better at than someone else. Kelly Holmes trained to be an athlete and won Olympic gold despite the fact that her father walked out when she was a child. Actress Samatha Morton survived being shuttled between foster families to be Oscar nominated, while Barnado boy Bruce Oldfield became a major fashion designer.

Be a mentor. Teachers make excellent 'champions', as do grandparents and police officers.

Teach the skills and tools for staying safe. Staff who work with the children of alcoholics at the Betty Ford Centres in California and Texas use a game called 'wheel of fortune', where kids brainstorm ways to handle being yelled at by a drunken father or mother, or stop their parents driving home when drunk.

The role of education

Education helps to make happy people. During their years at school and college, young people acquire the skills, knowledge and experience that underpin long-term happiness.

We tend to assume that attending a good school is a passport to satisfying and well-paid work. But there is far more to education than acquiring qualifications. A good education is one that fosters social and emotional competence, resilience and a lifelong love of learning. The last of these is desirable for all sorts of reasons besides earning money and avoiding unemployment. It equips children for life. Indeed, an inherent desire to learn in old age is strongly linked with mental and physical well-being, and helps to counteract the slowing down of mental processes.

In his book *Happiness: Lessons from a New Science* economist Richard Layard advocates that alongside teaching core subjects, such as maths and English, schools should run well-designed courses in emotional intelligence. Topics would include understanding and managing feelings (including anger and rivalry), work and money, love, family and parenting.

As Paul Martin observes, making happy people is rarely an explicit aim of education. Schools are geared up to deliver measurable academic achievement, not something fuzzy and liberal like happiness. He believes that the repeated assessment and comparison of factual knowledge and academic skills more resembles an obstacle course than a preparation for life. Governments do not set performance targets for schools to produce happier children – but they should.

'I think we educate for unhappiness rather than happiness. Business studies A-level strikes me as a crime against humanity. If anything should be compulsory in the national curriculum, it should probably be philosophy.'
Richard Reeves, BBC happiness expert

What kind of parent are you?

Research shows that some styles of parenting tend to promote the development of happiness, while others do the opposite. Ask yourself some key questions:

- What does it mean to you to be a good parent?
- How does your understanding of good parenting differ from your own parents' view?
- How do you want your child's environment to be similar to, or different from, the home you grew up in?

You can do a great deal to change your children's happiness for better or worse. Building on the pioneering research of British child psychiatrist Dr John Bowlby (who identified the importance of the 'securely attached' child), Paul Martin has come up with four categories of parenting. Read about each one, then decide which category you fall into. This is not an exact science, so perhaps you straddle more than one.

1 **Authoritative parents** love their children unconditionally and accept them for who they are. They keep a close eye on them, provide plenty of support, set firm boundaries, and grant considerable freedom within those boundaries. Authoritative parents monitor their children and intervene when necessary, but let them get on with things when there is no need to interfere. Authoritative parents are loving but not overindulgent or neglectful.

2 **Authoritarian parents** have a colder parenting style, which is more demanding but less responsive to their children's real needs. They intervene frequently, issuing commands, criticisms and occasional praise, but in an inconsistent way. They may use emotional tactics, such as making their children feel guilty, ashamed or unloved. At the extreme, some highly authoritarian parents resort to physical or emotional abuse in their attempts to

control their children, which can cause lasting psychological damage. Children who are beaten or denied affection are at significantly greater risk of becoming abusive parents themselves.

3   **Indulgent parents** are responsive but undemanding and permissive. They are warm and loving but lax, setting few clear boundaries. Punishments are seldom threatened, let alone carried through, and the children often appear to have the upper hand in the relationship. Indulgent parents try to be kind, but shy away from conflict or difficulty.

4   **Uninvolved parents** are unresponsive, undemanding, permissive and set few clear boundaries, largely because they don't really care very much. They are neither warm nor firm, and they do not monitor their children. Instead they are unresponsive to an extent that can sometimes seem reckless. In extreme cases, uninvolved parenting can stray into outright neglect.

'I had a meal for Father's Day with my children. We had a great time together. I wish I saw them more often. I felt real pride and joy in my children.'
Slough volunteer

Large amounts of psychological research shows that authoritative parenting tends to be associated with better outcomes. On average, children of authoritative parents are happier, academically more successful, emotionally better adjusted and have better relationships with their peers. Martin believes that authoritative parenting promotes many of the personal characteristics that typify happy people. These include good social and emotional skills, freedom from excessive anxiety, a sense of control, resilience, self-esteem, optimism, playfulness and freedom from excessive materialism.

By contrast, the children of highly authoritarian parents interpret other people's intentions as hostile, even when they are not, which makes them more likely to behave aggressively.

'Human beings are the only creatures on earth that allow their children to come back home.'
Bill Cosby, American entertainer

15 WAYS TO BE HAPPIER WITH YOUR CHILDREN

1   **Build three 'portions' of play into their day.** Make one 'free physical play', such as cycling, horse riding, skateboarding or hide and seek. Another should be 'imaginative play', such as dressing up or play-acting. The third is 'free creative play', which includes painting, model-making, cooking and singing without the structure of lessons and parental supervision. Don't stop your children when they are absorbed in play. If time is limited, interrupt briefly to say, 'Ten minutes before we have to stop'.

2   **Discourage excessive materialism.** A 2003 study by psychologists at the Queen Elizabeth Medical Centre in Western Australia found a high incidence of depression among young children who believe happiness is something achieved by money, fame and beauty. The children of authoritarian parents often develop a strong desire for money as they grow up, maybe as a response to feelings of insecurity caused by cold, controlling parents.

3   **Be relaxed.** A parent who consistently overcontrols a child is sending a message that the world is a hostile place, which can cause the child to become shy and clingy. Sociologist Frank Furedi calls this 'paranoid parenting'. Of course you want to keep them safe, but driving children everywhere rather than letting them walk or cycle with friends, deprives them of valuable opportunities for social interaction. Better to teach them how to become a 'safe' pedestrian.

4   **Don't scold every mistake.** Children who are constantly scolded tend to become less confident and more inclined to avoid difficult tasks. Instead offer good support, which includes telling them when they have got something wrong and advising them how to do it better. Set goals that are challenging but realistic.

5   **Allow children to fail.** We need to fail in order to feel sad, anxious and angry, and therefore learn how to deal with those feelings. Offer children a good role model by admitting when *you* make mistakes.

6   **Don't give in to sulking.** Giving in to bad behaviour simply reinforces its effectiveness in the child's mind. It also teaches children to get what they want by being unhappy. Parents should teach children exactly the opposite – namely, that they are more likely to get what they want by being happy.

7   **Encourage children's signature strengths.** You can do this by giving them simple chores to which they are suited. For example, a kind and nurturing child could groom the pets, while a more energetic one could have fun washing up. You can chat while you work alongside each other. Having chores as a child is an early predicator of positive mental health later in life.

How to Be Happy

8   **Use 'yes' more than 'no'.** Psychologist Martin Seligman believes that 'no' is a very important word in the life of a child because it signifies limits and dangers. However, parents should not confuse what is dangerous with what is inconvenient. Used too frequently, 'no' can damage a child and make him or her freeze when approaching a new situation, while 'yes makes the heart sing'.

9   **Don't allow sibling rivalry to flourish.** After the birth of a new baby, make a point of entrusting the older child(ren) with a new position of responsibility. It could be helping with changing the baby, running its bath and so on. That way older siblings are 'promoted' in rank, which reinforces their sense of security and specialness.

10   **Create a 'love map' together.** To become more familiar with the intricate details of your child's life, make a list of 50 aspects of his or her life, from 'favourite meal' to 'best friend'. Fill in the answers together and see what you get right. It's not a competition but a chance to connect.

11   **Encourage children to practise making choices.** This will help them to explore their own independent vision later on. Start with simple things, such as choosing one of three different cereals that you select at the supermarket, or give them a clothing allowance to spend. It shows you take them seriously.

12   **Don't let mealtimes be a battleground.** If family meals always involve a power struggle, make a simple rule: *you* are in charge of what's served, but your child decides how much to eat of it. If the child doesn't like the dish, allow him or her to have a sandwich and a piece of fruit, but they must make it themselves and not complain.

13   **Limit TV watching.** It takes up far too many of children's waking hours and can adversely affect family communication. Choose programmes you can enjoy watching together, then talk about them afterwards. How did the show make everyone feel? Did it connect to situations the child's life? Use it as a way to connect.

14   **Make sure children get plenty of sleep and exercise.** Happiness may be a cerebral concept, but it is rooted in the physical.

15   **Have a relaxing chat at bedtime.** Encourage children to describe their best moments of the day and to preview what will happen tomorrow (to promote future-mindedness). In an exercise called Dreamland, Seligman suggests you also help children to visualize a 'happy' picture because their last thought before drifting into sleep becomes the basis of their dreams. As Freud taught us, dreams filled with losing, defeat and rejection are tied up with depression, so it helps to equip children with a happy counter-image.

11

Eat Yourself Happy

HOW DO WE FEEL ABOUT FOOD?

- Britain is a nation of comfort eaters – 43 per cent of adults admit they eat to stifle boredom, loneliness and stress, or after arguing with their partner.
- Around 40 per cent of British adults believe that they are overweight.
- We spend 84 minutes a day eating and drinking (21 minutes goes on breakfast).
- A 2001 MORI survey found that women think what they eat is more important to their personal well-being than their sex life.
- The brain is over 60 per cent fat.
- We each spend an average £229 a year on food consumed 'on the move', mostly when commuting.
- In a 2004 National Diet and Nutrition Survey, no young man interviewed had consumed the recommended five portions of fruit and veg a day, and only 4 per cent of young women had done so.
- One in 10 six-year-olds and 17 per cent of 15-year-olds are now classed as obese.
- A recent survey of 200 people found that 88 per cent reported a significant improvement in their mental health after changing their diet.
- Only 38 per cent of British families take their evening meal together every day.
- Some 33 per cent of women have felt guilty after eating.
- Three times more men than women prefer to stay in and create a meal for family and friends than go out.

You are what you eat

While no one is suggesting that you stick to a diet of lettuce leaves (surely the fastest route to unhappiness), healthy eating and lots of fruit and veg can improve how you feel and you can do a great deal to boost your level of well-being by eating mood-enhancing foods.

Like sex, eating is one of the basic pleasures built into our nervous system. Even in our hi-tech urban society people still feel most happy at mealtimes, and what we eat and drink has a large part to play in how we feel. Alongside sleep and exercise, diet has been shown to have not only a significant effect on overall health, but also to contribute directly to happiness.

Research into the effects of food on happiness can be explained as 'brain chemistry'. Chemicals that connect the neurons in the brain can influence the way we feel, and these chemicals are affected by the food we eat.

This chapter is not about counting calories or grams of fat, nor is it about following a restrictive diet from which you're almost certain to stray. It is designed to show you that making some simple food changes will get your body chemistry and brain chemistry back into balance.

If you feel bloated, suffer mood swings or depression, or simply feel exhausted, it may be that you are eating foods that trigger these responses. We need to understand how our moods – and physiology – are inextricably linked to what and how we eat. To be happy, our bodies need a healthy and consistent fuel to draw from.

Remember, your brain is the greediest organ in your body, with some quite specific dietary requirements.

Food and the brain

Research has shown that certain food-dependent chemicals in the brain regulate our moods. To maintain mental and physical health, serotonin, beta-endorphins and blood sugar need to be kept in balance; if not, depression may result. Although balance can be achieved by taking antidepressants, it can also be done by eating the correct foods – which most people would agree is a preferable way of making yourself feel happier.

Let's look at some of the nutrients you need to keep the body functioning well, and that contribute to feelings of well-being.

Glucose
The body uses a very simple form of sugar called glucose as its basic fuel. During digestion all the carbohydrates you eat are broken down into glucose, which is carried by the blood throughout your body to be used as energy by the

cells as needed. All our cells, particularly in the brain, need a steady supply of sugar at all times. The level of sugar in the blood fluctuates with eating, sleeping and other activities. When you eat, your blood sugar level goes up. When you use energy, your blood sugar level goes down. When your body has the optimal level of sugar in the blood, you feel good. When your blood sugar is too low, the cells don't get what they need, so you feel tired or irritable.

Carbohydrates

Most of the sugar in your blood comes from the foods you eat. The rest comes from the extra sugar stored in your liver, to be used when you run out of food for energy. The most efficient source of sugar for the average person is carbohydrates because they require the least amount of work for the body to convert them. Carbohydrates can be 'simple', like those found in beer, table sugar and white flour, or they can be 'complex', like those found in potatoes, oatmeal and whole grains. The simpler a carbohydrate is, the more quickly it can be broken down into glucose (the simplest sugar) and released into the bloodstream. The more complex a carbohydrate is, the longer it takes to be broken down and released into the blood. This means that in health terms the complex carbs are preferable because they release energy in a more sustained fashion.

LOW-CARBOHYDRATE DIETS

Some people on low-carb diets, such as the Atkins and South Beach diets, report unusually high feelings of anger, tension and depression. Judith Wurtman, director of the Women's Health Program at the Massachusetts Institute of Technology, advocates a diet high in complex carbohydrates for weight loss and stress relief. She says that her studies on rats have shown a connection between a diet low in carbohydrates and low levels of serotonin – a neurotransmitter that promotes feelings of happiness and satisfaction. The same rats binged once starch was reintroduced into their diets.

Wurtman believes that the same effect occurs in humans on low-carb diets and leads to pronounced feelings of depression and sadness, even rage. 'People feel very angry, and their antidepressants don't work well either,' she says.

Granted, dieting isn't easy no matter how you do it, but many think low-carbohydrate approaches are particularly hard on your happiness. Wurtman goes so far as to call them dangerous for those who already struggle with depression or bipolar disorder.

Protein

Found in meat, fish, beans, eggs, cheese, nuts and seeds, protein provides the raw materials to help the brain and body grow and heal. Most important of all, protein provides the tryptophan needed to make serotonin, the chemical responsible for mood, sleep and appetite control.

Serotonin

Among the many chemicals in the brain that affect how we feel and act, serotonin is particularly important because it makes us feel relaxed. It also influences self-control and the ability to plan ahead. Low serotonin levels make us depressed and anxious.

Eating foods that contain tryptophan is one way of boosting serotonin levels, and they are best eaten with carbohydrates to improve absorption. A baked potato, which combines both tryptophan and carbohydrate, is a simple way of getting both these ingredients. This correlation may be why we feel cravings for sugary or starchy foods when mood levels are low. Depressed people tend to consume more carbohydrates in their diets than non-depressed individuals, and they show a heightened preference for sweet carbohydrate or fat-rich foods during depressive episodes.

Tryptophan

Foods containing tryptophan increase the body's level of endomorphins – substances that produce a natural high. They are found in chicken, turkey, tuna, salmon, kidney beans, rolled oats, lentils, chickpeas, seeds, avocados, bananas and quinoa. The absorption of tryptophan into the brain is thought to be greatly enhanced by eating carbohydrate-rich foods; in fact, carbohydrate cravings have been explained as a subconscious drive to increase serotonin levels. Complex (slow-release) carbohydrates can help tryptophan to be absorbed across the blood–brain barrier without creating a corresponding dip in blood sugar. Eating 500 mg of tryptophan a day is considered a good way to keep the blues at bay (see the box on page 132 for ideas of how to achieve this).

Dopamine and noradrenalin

These two brain chemicals are responsible for making you feel alert, and low levels can lead to depression, apathy and lack of motivation. You can enhance the levels of these chemicals by eating protein-rich foods (see above).

Other good mood foods

Fat

When you realize that the brain is more than 60 per cent fat, it make sense to include some fat in the diet. Fats are essential for the proper structure and functioning of the brain, and a certain amount in the diet is essential to emotional and mental health. Low levels are associated with symptoms that range from anxiety and depression to hyperactivity and schizophrenia.

Research is also showing the importance of fat in brain development. Scientists at Oxford University's department of physiology have found that children with behavioural problems and learning disorders such as dyslexia benefited from fish oil supplements high in the omega-3 series of essential fatty acids. In some cases children improved their reading ages by up to four years.

So not all fat is to be avoided, and some fats are even to be encouraged.

GOOD MOOD VITAMINS AND MINERALS

Vitamin/mineral	Function	Sources
Antioxidants	Counteract reactions to alcohol and pollution and stresses to the brain; also contain vitamins A, C and E and various trace minerals	Fruit and vegetables
B-vitamins	Unlock energy from food, fuel the body and improve energy, mood and mental functioning	Avocados, bananas, beans, carrots, eggs, fish, lentils, meat, milk, nuts, seeds, whole grains
Folic acid	Brain function and foetal brain development; improves mood, cognitive and social functioning	Avocados, lettuce, walnuts, spinach, greens, beans, nuts, seeds
Magnesium	Helps balance neurotransmitters and process essential fatty acids; low levels are associated with nervous tension, anxiety, irritability and insomnia	Beans, nuts, seeds, greens
Manganese	May guard against schizophrenia and epilepsy	Beetroot, berries, grapes, lettuce, watercress, oats
Potassium	Helps maintain healthy nervous system and correct acid–alkali balance in the body	Apricots, avocados, bananas, cauliflower, mushrooms, nuts, seeds
Zinc	Good mental and emotional health; metabolism of essential fatty acids and production of serotonin	Nuts, seeds, corn, pasta, whole grains, lettuce, meat and certain fish

Herbs to make you happy

In many cultures, herbs have long been used for their medicinal properties. Those relating specifically to happiness are:

Coriander: reputed to have a refreshing, stimulating and uplifting effect on the mind; may help with tiredness and tension.
Ginger: a warm and stimulating herb that can lift the spirits.
Kava kava: a member of the pepper family, particularly effective for symptoms of anxiety; also helpful for insomnia, stress and depression.
Marjoram: calms the nervous system and reduces anxiety and feelings of stress.
Peppermint: a cooling herb that can reduce angry feelings and nervousness; can also help with mental fatigue.

KEEP A FOOD DIARY

An easy way to find out the connection between food and mood is to keep a diary, charting everything you eat and drink and your corresponding moods and physical symptoms. Be honest with yourself. Learn to read your body and hear what it's telling you. This should highlight any sensitivity you have to specific foods and enable you to cut them out of your diet. Common problem items are: caffeine, chocolate, dairy products (milk, butter, etc), eggs, oranges, soya, sugar, tomatoes, wheat (bread, pasta, cakes, etc) and yeast. Note that alcohol can also cause problems because it contains both sugar and yeast.

A food diary might look something like this:

Day/date	Breakfast	Lunch	Dinner	Snacks/drinks	Reaction

How to Be Happy

'Eating together is a social event. It's as much about the rhythm and pattern of conversation as eating, and our binge-drinking culture ignores this at its peril. We need a more European attitude – one that encourages the idea that eating together is to be savoured and lingered over. Tapas is ideal for ensuring you eat alongside drinking.'
Richard Reeves, BBC happiness expert

Eating as an art form

Affordable travel has introduced us to exotic cuisines, and cooking has become a spectator sport rather than a chore, transforming the business of eating into an art form. As we become familiar with unusual ingredients and learn new methods of preparation – even new methods of eating – fuelling the body takes on a new dimension. In the best-case scenario it can become a flow activity, transporting us from the mundane to the extraordinary and making time seem to stand still.

However, psychologist Mihaly Csikszentmihalyi points out that the pleasure will be less authentic if we simply jump on the bandwagon of fine food because it's the fashionable thing to do. He suggests that 'a cultivated palate provides many opportunities for flow if one approaches eating – and cooking – in a spirit of curiosity, exploring the potentials of food for the sake of the experience rather than as a showcase for one's expertise.'

TREAT CAFFEINE CAUTIOUSLY

Caffeine, which is found in tea, coffee, cola drinks and chocolate, is probably the most widely used behaviour-modifying drug in the world. We often choose it when we are feeling tired and irritable because it gives us a boost. Having a cup of coffee or tea has positive psychological associations because it often accompanies a break in work or a chat with a friend.

Too much caffeine, however, can cause anxiety, panic attacks and depression. It also lowers your brain's melatonin level, which is what gives you a good night's sleep, so it's best avoided in the evening.

---

15 FOOD TIPS TO INCREASE HAPPINESS

There are a number of easy and delicious ways that you can maximize the positive effects of food on mood.

1   Eat carbohydrates to increase levels of serotonin and improve your mood (see page 130).
2   Eat protein at every meal. This will help keep up your levels of tryptophan, one of the body's feel-good chemicals (see page 131).
3   Enhance your beta-endorphin level. You can do this by reducing or eliminating sugars and white foods, and eating a range of different-coloured vegetables
4   Eat out. Those who eat out with friends are less stressed or depressed because dining out acts as closure to the day's stressful events.
5   Allow yourself a few scoops of ice cream. Scientists have found that a spoonful lights up the same pleasure centre in the brain as winning money or listening to your favourite music.
6   Have favourite foods only occasionally. This maximizes the pleasure they provide and prevents feelings of guilt.
7   Keep to regular mealtimes. It's a mistake to go longer than six hours without a meal (two or more nutritious foods at any one sitting) because your energy level plummets and you can become depressed. Eat foods that release energy slowly, such as oats and unrefined whole grains.
8   Don't skip breakfast. The brain needs a steady supply of glucose, ideally from slow-release complex carbohydrates to function efficiently and happily.
9   If you can't face solids in the morning have a smoothie made from low-fat yoghurt, fruit and nuts. Research published in 2003 showed that children breakfasting on fizzy drinks and sugary snacks performed at the level of an average 70-year-old in tests of memory and attention.
10 Fish really is the best brain food. It contains omega-3 fatty acids, and is an excellent source of the good mood nutrient, which keeps the brain in great working order.
11 Carry a snack to maintain your glucose levels on stressful days. Nuts, seeds, rice cakes, bananas and avocados provide some of the feel-good chemical serotonin.
12 Avoid junk food, especially highly processed goodies, such as cakes, pastries and biscuits, which contain trans fats. These not only pile on the pounds, but are implicated in a slew of mental disorders, from dyslexia and ADHD (attention deficit hyperactivity disorder) to autism.

13 Eat at least five portions of fresh fruit and vegetables daily. The natural sugars in fruit have a gentler effect on blood sugar levels than added refined sugar.
14 Eating garlic regularly reduces the risk of a range of diseases, from bowel cancer to heart disease. Best of all, it can boost performance in the bedroom! Researchers at the University of Berlin discovered that it could combat male impotence by improving blood circulation in the groin.
15 Eat oysters. The long-held belief that they act as an aphrodisiac may be true, partly because of their high levels of zinc.

IMPROVE WHAT YOU EAT AND DRINK

Remember, you are what you eat. In the next two weeks commit yourself to changing at least one thing about your diet. Richard Stevens gave the Slough volunteers the following exercise:

- Eat less red meat, animal fat, salt and sugar (don't forget the sugar content in soft drinks).
- Eat more fresh fruit and vegetables (at least five portions a day).
- Eat more nuts and seeds.
- Drink less caffeine, alcohol and sugary drinks.
- Drink more water (at least 6–8 glasses a day), herbal teas and freshly made fruit juice.
- Eat organic whenever you can. It's a bit more expensive, but free of chemicals and pesticides.
- Think about taking a vitamin supplement – especially one containing vitamins C (at least 1000 mg), B, D and E.

Decide on the changes in your diet that you think you can achieve, and write down your commitment below.

I will

_____

_____

_____

_____

The following recipes are from the *Optimum Nutrition Cookbook* co-authored by Patrick Holford and Judy Ridgway. Holford is founder of the Institute for Optimum Nutrition, director of the Brain Bio Centre and a leading expert on nutrition and mental health.

Lemon and dill turkey escalopes

with carrot and tarragon potato mash and beetroot relish

As well as being high in mood-boosting tryptophan (from the turkey), this delicious dish is packed with antioxidants from the carrots and beetroot, which help keep your brain and body young.

Serves 2

zest and juice of ½ a lemon
1 tablespoon freshly chopped dill
1 teaspoon extra virgin olive oil
2 turkey escalopes, well flattened

Carrot and tarragon potato mash
300 g (10½ oz) potatoes, scrubbed
300 g (10½ oz) carrots, peeled and sliced
freshly chopped tarragon (to taste)
1 tablespoon skimmed, soya or rice milk
1 teaspoon extra virgin olive oil

Beetroot relish
1 medium to large beetroot
zest and juice of ½ a lemon
2 spring onions, trimmed and finely chopped
5 mm (¼ in) thick slice fresh ginger, grated

1 Mix the lemon zest and juice with the chopped dill and olive oil, then spread over each side of the escalopes. Leave to stand until required to cook.

2 To make the mash, steam the potatoes in their skins. Add the carrots to the steamer after about 10 minutes, depending on the size of the potatoes. Cook for another 15–20 minutes until both vegetables are tender.

3 Peel the potatoes and mash with the carrots, tarragon, milk and oil. Beat until smooth.

4 To make the relish, peel the beetroot and shred on the finest part of the grater. Place in a bowl with the remaining ingredients and mix well.

5 Put the escalopes under a hot grill and cook for 2–4 minutes on each side. Check to see that the meat is cooked through. There should be no pinkness in the centre. Serve the escalopes on a bed of the carrot and potato mash with the beetroot relish on the side.

How to Be Happy

Salmon and monkfish kebabs

with coriander and sunflower seed pesto

Fish, particularly salmon, is the best brain food, being high in tryptophan, as are the sunflower seeds and quinoa (pronounced 'keen-wah'), a gluten-free grain that looks like millet. Eat this dish to beat the blues.

Serves 2

250 g (9 oz) piece monkfish
250 g (9 oz) salmon steak
juice of ½ a lime
1 teaspoon extra virgin olive oil
freshly ground black pepper
150 g (5½ oz) rice or quinoa

**Coriander and sunflower
seed pesto**
a bunch of fresh coriander,
   approximately 25 g (1 oz)
25 g (1 oz) sunflower seeds
1 garlic clove, peeled
1 tablespoon cold-pressed
   mixed seed oil

1 Remove the skin and bones from the two pieces of fish and cut each one into six large chunks. Thread on to skewers.

2 Mix the lime juice and oil, season with black pepper and pour evenly over the kebabs. Leave to stand until required for cooking.

3 Cook the rice or quinoa according to the packet instructions.

4 To make the pesto, place the coriander, sunflower seeds and garlic in a food processor and process briefly. Do not allow the mixture to become too fine. Moisten with the cold-pressed seed oil and keep to one side.

5 Place the kebabs under a hot grill for 2½–3 minutes on each side until just cooked through. Do not allow the fish to overcook or it will be hard and unpleasant. Serve with the rice or quinoa and the pesto.

Spicy mackerel with couscous

Mackerel is pretty much the best source of omega-3 fats, which keep your mind sharp. Here the fish is combined with spices to stimulate the senses.

Serves 2

a little extra virgin olive oil
1 small onion, peeled and chopped
1 garlic clove, peeled and crushed
1 teaspoon ground cumin
½–1 teaspoon harissa or chilli
  powder
1 small red pepper, seeded and
  chopped
125 g (4½ oz) courgettes, diced
1 x 200 g (7 oz) can tomatoes
150g (5½ oz) couscous
1 mackerel, approximately
  300–350 g (10½–12 oz), cut into
  2 fillets

1 Preheat the oven to 180°C/350°F/Gas 4.

2 Heat the oil in a small, heavy-based saucepan and stir-fry the onion and garlic with the cumin and harissa or chilli powder for 1–2 minutes. Add the red pepper and courgettes and cook for another 2 minutes, stirring all the time.

3 Pour on the tomatoes and bring to the boil. Simmer for 10 minutes, stirring from time to time.

4 Cook the couscous as directed on the packet.

5 Place the mackerel fillets on a non-stick baking tray, cover with foil and bake in the oven for 10 minutes or until the fish is cooked through.

6 Arrange the fish on a mound of couscous and top with the sauce.

Vegetarian chilli

with taco shells and green salad

Whether you're vegetarian or not, beans are the brain's best friend because they're high in protein, which is needed to make neurotransmitters, and carbohydrate, the best source of energy. This recipe provides the perfect balance for energy and mood, plus vitamin-packed vegetables.

Serves 2

1 small onion, peeled and finely
 chopped
1 garlic clove, peeled and crushed
1 teaspoon extra virgin olive oil
125 g (4½ oz) mushrooms, finely
 chopped
1 small aubergine, finely diced
1 tablespoon tomato purée
100 ml (3½ fl oz) vegetable stock
1–2 teaspoons chilli powder
 (to taste)
½ teaspoon ground cumin
a pinch of dried mixed herbs
150 g (5½ oz) red kidney beans,
 canned or home-cooked, drained
6–8 taco shells

1 Gently cook the onion and garlic in the olive oil until soft. Add the mushrooms, aubergines, tomato purée, stock, spices and herbs and bring to the boil.

2 Reduce the heat and simmer for 30 minutes, stirring from time to time. Stir in the kidney beans and cook for a further 10 minutes.

3 Heat the taco shells as directed on the packet, stuff with the chilli mixture and serve.

Baked aubergines

with peppers, quinoa and broccoli salsa

Aubergines are a good source of potassium, antioxidants and mood-boosting folates, and a whole one provides three of the recommended five daily portions of fruit and veg. The quinoa is high in protein, while the peppers and broccoli are full of vitamin C, so altogether you have a delicious and healthy meal.

Serves 2

2 medium aubergines, cut in half lengthways
a little cold-pressed mixed seed oil
4 small whole red or orange sweet peppers
100 g (3½ oz) hummus
10–12 black olives, stoned and chopped
2–3 spring onions, trimmed and chopped
1 tablespoon freshly chopped tarragon or 1 teaspoon dried tarragon
150 g (5½ oz) quinoa

Broccoli salsa
100 g (3½ oz) broccoli, broken into small florets
1 small red or orange pepper, seeded and finely chopped
1 spring onion, trimmed and chopped
1 cm (½ in) fresh root ginger, peeled and grated
juice of 1 lime
1 teaspoon cold-pressed mixed seed oil

1 Set the oven to 200°C/400°F/Gas 6.

2 Cut a criss-cross pattern on the cut surface of the aubergines and brush all over with a little mixed seed oil. Place on a baking tray cut side down. Brush the peppers with oil and place on the same tray. Bake for about 25–30 minutes, or until the vegetables are almost cooked through.

3 Mix the hummus with the olives, spring onions and tarragon and keep to one side.

4 Remove the aubergines from the oven, turn them over and spread with the hummus mixture. Return to the oven for another 5–10 minutes until fully cooked.

5 Meanwhile, cook the quinoa according to the packet instructions.

6 Mix all the broccoli salsa ingredients together just before serving and hand round with the baked vegetables and quinoa.

Being Happy Makes You Healthy

'Happiness is good health and a bad memory.'
Ingrid Bergman, Swedish actress

HOW HEALTHY IS THE UK?

- One in six of us suffers depression or anxiety and we spend £395 million a year on drugs to treat it.
- Absenteeism for stress-related illness has increased by 500 per cent since the 1950s partly because 70 per cent of adults claim to feel under pressure in everyday life.
- 1.4 million people have angina.
- There are 300,000 heart attacks each year.
- Heart disease is still the biggest killer of women.
- According to an ICM poll, 25 per cent of Brits ruin their Sundays by working, worrying or feeling depressed about the week ahead.
- A recent study suggests that pessimists are 30 per cent more likely to develop Alzheimer's.
- Suicide is the most common cause of death for young men aged 15–24.
- Mental health problems account for a third of all days lost from work for ill health.
- Smokers are much less likely to be happy than non-smokers.

Happiness is seriously good for your health. Happy people tend to have lower levels of the stress hormone cortisol (high levels are linked to conditions such as type 2 diabetes and hypertension). And they are more likely to recover from major surgery.

When we have a happy experience, the body chemistry improves and our blood pressure and heart rate tend to fall. In fact, especially good experiences can have long-lasting positive effects on our health.

As if that weren't enough, happy people also tend to have a more robust immune system. Those who rate in the upper reaches of happiness on psychological tests develop about 50 per cent more antibodies than average in response to flu vaccines.

Of course, happiness in its various forms – optimism, wisdom and humour – is a great foundation for personal relationships and helps to provide a buffer against stress.

A 2005 study led by Professor Andrew Steptoe of London University (part of a major government health initiative) tested middle-aged Londoners – 116 men and 100 women – in a number of different situations, including at work, during leisure time and in a laboratory. The subjects, who ranged from those who never felt happy to those who felt occasional happiness and those who felt happy most of the time, were asked whether or not they were happy in the various situations, and an average of happy moments was taken over the course of a day.

Those who were happiest overall experienced lower levels of stress hormone during a working day than those who rated themselves as less happy. However, the main chemical difference was that the unhappier subjects had a higher amount of plasma fibrinogen in the bloodstream – a major predictor of cardiovascular disease risk.

'Recently I pioneered a well-being day in the office for my work colleagues. The purpose was to encourage them to reflect on their work routines and focus on how keeping healthy is vital to their working practice. I organized a masseur to come in and work with staff, as well as "therapeutic drummers", who kept everyone relaxed as they worked. There was also a free healthy lunch for everyone.'
Slough volunteer

CHAPTER 12

Health is our most important priority

According to a MORI survey carried out in 1981, and repeated in 1991 and 1997, the prime consideration of subjective happiness for most people is their state of health. When asked to judge which several factors among a list of 10 or so things were 'most important for you personally in determining how happy or unhappy you are in general these days', most people said 'health' (59 per cent), followed by 'family life' (41 per cent), 'marriage/partner' (35 per cent), and 'job/employment of you/your family' (31 per cent). These factors stood well above 'education received' (7 per cent), 'housing conditions' (9 per cent) or even 'financial condition/money' (25 per cent).

Optimism is the best medicine

It pays to be positive. Tests have revealed that happiness or related mental states, such as hopefulness, optimism and contentment, appear to reduce the risk of cardiovascular disease, pulmonary disease, diabetes, hypertension, colds and upper respiratory tract infections.

Harvard health psychologist Laura Kubzansky studies optimism. She has tracked 1300 men for 10 years and found that heart diseases among those who called themselves optimistic are half the rate of those who didn't. The outcome of her study was extraordinary as it showed that the difference in the levels of heart disease for optimists compared with non-optimists was as big as the difference between smokers and non-smokers. Optimists also did better on pulmonary (lung) function (poor pulmonary function can be fatal).

Nun so cheerful

Arguably, nuns have the most blameless lifestyle of us all: they don't drink or smoke, they eat a bland diet, and they have no sexual history. Yet there are still big differences in their life expectancies based on whether they have optimistic or pessimistic tendencies. A famous 2001 study of happiness and longevity in 180 elderly Catholic nuns found that 90 per cent of the most cheerful quarter were alive at 85, as opposed to only 34 per cent of the least cheerful quarter. Similarly, 54 per cent of the most cheerful quarter were alive at 94, while only 11 per cent of the least cheerful quarter survived to that age.

When scientists analysed 'autobiographies' written by the nuns many years earlier they found that those who had expressed the most positive emotions in their early 20s were significantly more likely to be alive 60 years later.

Unhappiness can make you ill

For years scientists and doctors have understood that clinical depression can aggravate heart disease, diabetes and a range of other illnesses. (Significantly, the neurochemistry of depression is much better known than that of happiness.) The World Health Organization has estimated that by the year 2020 depression will be the second biggest cause of disability in the world, after cardiovascular disease.

Just as the workings of the body can affect our mental state, so our emotions can affect the body. Chemical imbalances can cause depression, and depression can lead to comfort eating and obesity. But in fact all chronic diseases have a psychological dimension; diabetes, for example, is often accompanied by serious psychological distress. Yet handling the psychological dimension properly can improve blood-glucose control as effectively as certain medications. Researchers found that patients who received stress-management training, which included breathing exercises and visualization techniques, improved their blood-glucose control by about the same amount as those treated with drugs.

'I thought I wasn't feeling well enough to go to my singing group, but I pushed myself. To my surprise, the session made me feel physically and psychologically better. I woke up feeling great in the morning, thinking today's a joy.'
Slough volunteer

Happy people look after themselves

It comes as no surprise that happiness promotes physical health. Happy people generally have a well-developed capacity to control their immediate urges and to take the long-term view. They are less likely to smoke, drink too much, eat badly or avoid exercise, partly because they are confident and future-minded, and partly because they don't want to spoil a good thing.

Happy people seek out and absorb more health-risk information and are better at health maintenance. Psychologist Robert Emmons of the University of California at Davis randomly assigned 1000 adults to one of three groups. All three groups kept daily journals, but the people in the first also rated their moods on a scale of 1–6; those in the second listed the things that had annoyed them throughout the day; and the members of the third had to write down every day all the things for which they were grateful. The last group not only had a predicted jump in their overall happiness, but spent more time exercising and were more likely to have medical check-ups and wear sunscreen.

How to Be Happy

'I've had a series of heart attacks and two heart-bypass operations. Recently I experienced a few sudden chest pains that made me seek medical advice. In the past I used to worry myself into a "downward spiral", which led to hospital admission and drugs. I'm determined to avoid that again at any cost. I won't be irresponsible or negligent, but I am more relaxed since starting this happiness project. I feel I've taken control by seeking medical advice.'
Slough volunteer

Finding happiness after despair

Even people with serious illnesses and disabilities often regain near-normal levels of happiness once they have had time to adjust to their condition. One American study found that more than 80 per cent of people who were paralysed in all four limbs considered their life to be average or above average in terms of happiness, and 90 per cent were glad to be alive.

Positive psychologist Martin Seligman says that objective good health is barely related to happiness. More important, it seems, is our subjective perception of how healthy we are. 'It is a tribute to our ability to adapt to adversity that we are able to find ways to appraise our health positively even when we are quite sick.' However, people who are ill shouldn't feel pressured into positive thinking or feel obliged to smile through their suffering.

'I don't do stress.'
Ricky Gervais, writer and actor

Is there such a thing as 'good' stress?

Stress, which has become one of the most talked-about afflictions of the twenty-first century, can lead to an imbalance of the feel-good chemical serotonin in the brain, and also lower the immune system. (Just getting someone to recall a painful event can produce this latter effect.)

We are in fact programmed to manage stress because two aspects of our nervous system are designed to handle it. The sympathetic nervous system works as an accelerator, releasing hormones necessary for 'fight or flight', and the parasympathetic nervous system acts as a brake, releasing hormones that promote relaxation.

The body's ability to manage this chemical fluctuation is key to both mental and physical health. Richard Davidson, professor of psychology at Harvard University, has found that mild to moderate doses of bad experience may be beneficial in teaching us to bounce back. In animal studies he compared groups that had been moderately stressed when young to those that never were, and found the former were better able to recover from stress as adults. Just as a vaccination gives you a tiny bit of a disease to build up your resistance to it, a little stress can strengthen and build up our ability to deal with bad experiences.

Meanwhile, research by the British Longevity Society has found that short-lived nerve-racking situations, such as dashing to the airport, can help you stay healthy and live longer. The right kind of stress, researchers found, increases the production of proteins that help repair body cells, including those in the brain, and enables them to work at peak capacity. 'Exercising' this self-repair mechanism can therefore help people look and feel younger.

HOW TO PUT UNWELCOME THOUGHTS OUT OF MIND

BBC happiness expert Richard Stevens taught the *Making Slough Happy* volunteers some neurolinguistic programming techniques to deal with stressful situations. Among these was 'fast-forward thinking', which can be used to get rid of a distressing thought that keeps coming into mind. 'Visualize the situation – perhaps a bad encounter with the boss or a colleague at work – replaying it in your mind, rather as you would a video of the incident. Then try it again speeded up. Keep speeding it up each time you play it over until the characters in the scene start moving like cartoon characters in fast, jerky and comical ways. When you have the scene running really fast, finish by swishing it all out of your mind. It's a great way to get rid of things you would rather forget.'

'I found fast-forward thinking incredibly helpful in combating my anxiety. I thought about images of things that worried me and literally put them into fast-forward in my mind. This meant I got them out of my head more quickly and found calmness again.'
Slough volunteer

Sleep is essential for health

If you want to be happy, make sure you get enough sleep – that means eight hours a night. Tired people are less emotionally resilient and often feel 'out of touch' with what's going on in their lives. In extreme cases, sleep deprivation can lead to feelings of persecution and paranoia, depression, weight gain, impaired performance and damaged social relationships. After just one night of sleep loss, your level of cortisol (the stress hormone) will typically be raised by about 45 per cent the next evening.

Sleepiness is a major cause of accidents and injuries, and persistent poor sleep may even damage the immune system and make us more susceptible to infection. Lack of sleep can also affect our physical appearance (it's not called 'beauty sleep' for nothing).

The fact is, we can survive for longer without food than sleep. There is even some tentative evidence that people who habitually go to bed early live longer.

What does sleep do for us?

We spend a third of our lives – around 25 years – sleeping. It is a uniquely private experience, even if we share a bed. And sleep is not just a biological necessity, it is a neglected source of pleasure. It offers us refuge from pleasant – and unpleasant – life events.

Sleeping also makes us brainier. We spend two hours a night dreaming, a form of creative play, and during this time the brain processes new memories, practices and skills: it even solves problems. Think of it like mastering a new computer game. Instead of grinding away into the small hours, you would be better off playing for a couple of hours, then going to bed. While you are asleep, your brain will reactivate the circuits it was using as you learnt the game, rehearse them, then shunt the new memories into long-term storage. When you wake up, hey presto! You will be a better player.

Unlike early human beings, who tended to sleep when it was dark, we have the technology to prolong light, and as a result we are marginalizing sleep. In fact, many high-fliers regard it as a waste of time and have accumulated a chronic sleep debt. It's like a bank account from which we keep borrowing but pay nothing in.

Humans are not built to work at night and sleep by day, but many do. In industrialized societies shift work turns the normal sleep pattern on its head and makes people weary. We are ignoring our biological clocks and battling against our own physiology. No wonder we feel awful.

What is sleep?

There are several stages to sleep. The 10-minute period of light sleep when we're drifting off is called Stage One. Stage Two is deeper and lasts about 20 minutes. Stages Three and Four are types of deep sleep.

Deep sleep is what our body and brain most need to recover from the day. It's sometimes called 'delta sleep', after the delta waves generated by the brain at this stage. We don't dream during this time. After about 90 minutes of deep sleep comes a period that includes rapid eye movement (REM). You appear to be completely out of it, but your brain is intensely active: you are being bombarded with stimuli, not from the outside world, but from within the brain.

During a normal night, people usually pass through the various stages of sleep several times. Problems arise when the pattern is broken. You will feel exhausted the next day, and over time your body's healing potential will be affected. Your levels of growth hormone will be reduced. And young men take note – testosterone may fall during the day.

Power-napping

Richard Stevens showed the Slough volunteers how to 'power-nap', which he says is a great method for staying fresh when you are under pressure or getting tired. 'You can do it pretty much anywhere. Preferably find somewhere comfortable where you won't be disturbed. Relax your body, breathe slowly and easily, and try to switch off all thoughts. Do this for about 10–15 minutes. Make sure you don't nap for more than 15 minutes (set an alarm if necessary), otherwise you will enter a deep-sleep cycle and could wake up feeling worse than before.'

15 STEPS TO HAPPIER SLEEP

1   Pay off your accumulated sleep debt by going to bed half an hour earlier for a few weeks. This could make all the difference to your alertness.

2   Keep a sleep diary, noting such things as the time you went to bed, the time you awoke, and how much sleep you are actually getting. Be honest.

3   Remember that staying awake for more than 21 hours makes the mind behave as if its owner is drunk.

4   A good night's sleep is normally preceded by a drop in core body temperature, so don't do vigorous physical exercise, eat spicy food or have the electric blanket on just before you go to sleep.

5   If you take a hot bath, do so an hour or two before sleep as it will raise your body temperature, which can keep you awake.

6   Eating a meal three hours before bedtime can help you sleep.

7   A 15-minute 'power nap' during the day makes you sharper and more energetic. Practise dozing after lunch. As Paul Martin observes in his book *Counting Sheep*, 'the siesta is an expression of human biology'.

8   Dairy products are rich in trytophan, an amino acid that also acts as a hypnotic, hence the popularity of milky drinks to aid slumber.

9   Your bed is arguably your most important item of furniture. Spend more on it than anything else, and spend plenty of time there.

10 Keep the bedroom as peaceful, airy and dark as possible – it should be for sleep and sex, nothing else.

11 Turn off any computers or TVs in children's rooms well before bedtime.

12 Beware of caffeine. Superficially it masks the symptoms of inadequate sleep and makes us feel more alive, but it is a stimulant that sabotages our natural brake, which is designed make us feel sleepy.

13 Avoid alcohol as a sleep-inducing nightcap. Progressively more is required to achieve the same sedative effect, and it disrupts the amount of REM sleep during the second half of the night. (The next day's hangover is no fun either.)

14 Find a decent work–life balance. You might be better off getting more sleep than working for a pay rise.

15 If you really can't sleep, relax and apply the principles of REST (Restricted Environmental Stimulation Therapy). Research has shown that this can work wonders. After a day of quiet on a comfortable bed in a dark, soundproofed room, people often emerge refreshed and with new self-control.

FACTS ABOUT ALCOHOL AND DRUGS

- 12 per cent of men and 3 per cent of women are dependent on alcohol.
- In 2003–4, 75 per cent of men and 60 per cent of women in Britain had an alcoholic drink on at least one day during the previous week.
- 48 per cent of the population drink more than twice per week.
- 2 per cent of the population drink six or more alcoholic drinks daily or almost daily, and 17 per cent drink six or more drinks weekly.
- Among those aged 16–59, 35.6 per cent have used one or more illicit drugs during their lifetime.
- Men are about twice as likely as women to have used any illicit drug and/or Class A drugs in the last year.
- 10.8 per cent of 16–59-year-olds have used cannabis in the past year; 2.4 per cent used cocaine and 2 per cent ecstasy.
- Men are more likely than women to be heavy smokers (11 per cent compared to 7 per cent) or ex-smokers (27 per cent against 19 per cent).
- Smoking is most prevalent among the 20–24 age group (44 per cent smoke).
- Smokers are more likely to take other drugs too: 24 per cent used them in the past year compared with 5 per cent of non-smokers.
- Smokers are more likely to be divorced or cohabiting than married, and have fewer qualifications than non-smokers.
- 70 per cent of current smokers say they would like to give up.

Alcohol

In moderation alcohol can reduce feelings of anxiety, lower inhibitions and make you feel more sociable. It produces an artificial high, but it is in fact a depressant, which means it slows down brain activity.

Official guidelines recommend no more than 3–4 units a day for men, and no more than 2–3 for women. This might not sound a lot, but it takes the body an hour to process one unit of alcohol, so it doesn't take a genius to work out that if you're downing lots of units your body won't be able to cope.

Nonetheless, population studies do associate light or moderate drinking with better emotional well-being and social adjustment. Of course, it could be that the socializing associated with it provides the emotional benefits rather than the alcohol itself, just as going to the pub often improves mood.

In the TV series one of the Slough volunteers began to realize he had a problem with alcohol and that it didn't make him happy. 'I was trying to be happy, but everything I tried was out of control as soon as alcohol came into the picture. It was only because of the Happiness Manifesto saying "talk to someone" that I actually did. I learnt from that and talked to my wife about it. I now tell anyone who'll listen that happiness to me is my wife – she loves me!'

Drugs don't work

No one wants to be a spoilsport, but taking 'recreational' drugs can't bring us long-term joy. The pleasure is temporary, and after the initial 'hit' it may be necessary to take larger and larger doses to achieve the same effect. Molecular changes in the brain make these chemical highs increasingly difficult to control.

Indulging in drugs is intrinsically selfish because it takes us into our own little world and stops us connecting with other people. In addition, the high it provides doesn't last long enough to make us happy. For sustained mood enhancement, we should look to our relationships, work, family and community.

CANNABIS

Although many people extol the pleasures of cannabis as a relaxant, and some say that it eases the pain, nausea and vomiting in advanced stages of cancer, AIDS and other serious illnesses, its carcinogenic activity is greater than that of tobacco and its effects on the cardiovascular system and heart rhythm are potentially lethal. Research also increasingly suggests that psychotic breakdown is much greater among those who are cannabis smokers.

Frequent cannabis use increases the risk of developing depression and schizophrenia in later life. In one study of 1600 students from Australian secondary schools, frequent cannabis use appeared to result later on in a rise in depression and anxiety among girls. Another long-term study, in New Zealand, found that people who had used cannabis by the age of 15 were four times more likely to show an increase in 'schizophrenia symptoms' by the age of 26.

Smoking

Dependency on tobacco can be an indicator of unhappiness. Around 12 per cent of heavy smokers perceive a severe lack of social support compared with 7 per cent of non-smokers. In fact, 10 per cent of smokers have a primary support group of less than four people compared with 4 per cent of non-smokers. They are also less likely to have seen more than two friends in the past week.

HOW TO BE HEALTHIER WITHOUT GOING TO THE GYM

1   **Forgive people.** You can't hurt someone by holding a grudge, but you can set yourself free by forgiving. Physical health, especially in cardiovascular terms, is likely to be better in people who forgive.

2   **Calm down.** People who are always stressed and angry or hostile have higher blood pressure, heart rates and cholesterol.

3   **Put on a happy face.** Psychologist Martin Seligman advises trying to think of pessimism as a sort of behaviour rather than a way of thinking. This allows us to choose to behave differently.

4   **Keep a log of what makes you angry.** When the situation next arises take deep breaths before reacting, and ask yourself if this is a familiar trigger that has upset you before. Do you know why?

5   **Believe in what you do.** We become unhappy when we take on something that is alien to us, or behave in a way that is not really true to our nature. This can result in anger, frustration and anxiety, which are the emotional equivalents of disease or illness.

6   **Look forward to things.** This can open up dopamine pathways that help us to feel good about life.

7   **Be grateful.** People who are grateful view their bodies and themselves generally in a better way. When you are grateful you tend to view life and health as precious gifts to be cherished – and you make sure you look after yourself.

8   **Incorporate mildly stressful but enjoyable activities into your free time.** These might include redecorating a room at the weekend, or shopping for a dinner party in your lunch hour. The pleasure you gain will boost your natural defences against illness.

9   **Talk to people face to face.** Communicating effectively in person helps manage stress. Psychologists have found that reliance on text messages/email can inhibit the development of good verbal skills.

10 **Practise altruism.** A selfless act will give you a glow that won't swiftly be followed by a credit card bill or a hangover.

Exercise: Why a Pedometer Beats a Vibrator

HOW FIT ARE BRITS?

- Six out of 10 men and seven out of 10 women are not active enough to benefit their health.
- The average person spends 18 hours a week in front of the TV.
- Two-thirds of us are overweight, and within this group 22 per cent of men and 23 per cent of women are obese.
- People who are more active exhibit lower levels of anxiety and depression.
- Exercise stimulates brain-cell regeneration and gives us a sense of purpose.
- Exercising 3–5 times a week for half an hour releases feel-good endorphins.
- Seven out of 10 gym members think their general mental well-being would suffer if they stop exercising. One in three report that exercise improves their performance at work.
- Around the age of 30 DNA starts deteriorating in our muscles' energy centre. This means we get weaker and the body becomes less flexible, so exercise is even more important.
- Children should be doing 60 minutes a day of moderate to vigorous exercise.
- Men spend more time on sporting activities at almost all ages than women.
- Cycling 4 miles a day reduces your chance of a heart attack by 50 per cent.

The Latin saying *Mens sana in corpore sano* (a sound mind in a sound body) is quite true. While everyone knows that exercise can improve overall physical health, there is also significant evidence to show that it can improve your mental health (and with none of the side-effects of many pharmaceutical remedies). It does this by triggering the release of endorphins, anti-stress hormones that block pain signals from the brain and produce a natural high, and serotonin, the chemical compound that affects mood, emotion, sleep and appetite.

Exercise on prescription

The *Making Slough Happy* volunteers were given pedometers by Richard Stevens and his team, and encouraged to increase the amount and quality of exercise they took. In fact, doctors increasingly prescribe exercise as part of wider treatment for mental illnesses, such as depression and seasonal affective disorder (SAD). Physical activity plays a role in establishing and maintaining a positive mood and self-esteem. It also improves social integration and decreases anger (try swimming 20 lengths and see if you're still angry). It's less passive than popping a pill, and makes us feel that we are regaining control of our life. Research among young offenders, people recovering from drug and alcohol abuse, and those diagnosed with schizophrenia suggests that they benefit too.

In addition to all these things, exercise can relieve symptoms of pre-menstrual syndrome and promote restful sleep. Best of all, perhaps, is that it improves our sex life. People who exercise regularly reportedly have more frequent and better orgasms!

> 'Richard taught us to do *t'ai chi* in the park. At first I worried it would be a bit intense, but it's a very gentle way of exercising mind and body, using slow, meditative movements. It's far less intimidating than going to the gym. But you're soon hooked.'
> *Slough volunteer*

Our best insurance against ageing

Exercise is extremely beneficial to older people, both in terms of keeping mobile and in getting out and about. Scientists have also found that cognitive functioning (mental ability) in the elderly improves with exercise. They believe this could be linked to the fact that exercise improves the body's ability to pump blood and increases the blood's oxygen-carrying capacity. (A good supply of oxygen is essential for healthy brain function.)

A 2001 study led by James Blumenthal, a psychologist at the Duke University Medical Center in Durham, North Carolina, found that exercise had beneficial effects on functions controlled by specific areas of the brain. These included memory, planning, organization and the ability to juggle different tasks. The elderly – especially those with coronary artery disease or hypertension – are thought to suffer some degree of cognitive decline in part due to a reduction in blood flow to the brain, but just as muscle tone and function are improved by good blood flow during exercise, brain function can be improved by exercise too.

Senior citizens who walk regularly perform better on memory tests than their sedentary peers. What's more, over several years their scores on a variety of cognitive tests show far less decline than those of non-walkers. Every extra mile a week has measurable benefits.

'I successfully finished the London to Brighton bike ride. I did it to celebrate my 50th birthday and raise funds for the British Heart Foundation's Help-a-Heart week. It made me happy and joyful. It gave me a real sense of achievement.'
Slough volunteer

How does exercise combat pain?

Prolonged, continuous exercise, such as running, long-distance swimming, aerobics, cycling or cross-country skiing, appears to increase the production and release of beta-endorphin. This chemical has a molecular structure very similar to morphine and produces a feeling of euphoria that has been popularly labelled the 'runner's high'.

Beta-endorphin may also contribute to what some athletes call a 'second wind'. It blocks the pain and exhaustion experienced while running, and may help them to feel limber and energized towards the end of a race.

Exercise boosts brain as well as brawn

Simply walking sedately for half an hour three times a week can improve abilities such as learning, concentration and abstract reasoning by 15 per cent. Researcher Angela Balding from the University of Exeter has found that schoolchildren who exercise three or four times a week get higher than average exam grades at ages 10 or 11. The effect is strongest in boys, and Balding suggests that aerobic exercise may boost mental powers by getting extra oxygen to the brain.

Another reason why the brain loves physical exercise is that it promotes the growth of new brain cells. Until recently, received wisdom had it that we are born with a full complement of neurons and produce no new ones during our lifetime. Fred Gage from the Salk Institute in La Jolla, California, disproved this myth in 2000, when he showed that even adults can grow new brain cells. He also found that exercise is one of the best ways to achieve this.

In mice, at least, the brain-building effects of exercise are strongest in the hippocampus, which is involved with learning and memory. This also happens to be the brain region that is damaged by elevated levels of the stress hormone cortisol. So if you are feeling frazzled, do your brain a favour and go for a run.

'I'm usually completely manic and find it very hard to switch off,' but by the end of a *t'ai chi* session I felt completely relaxed and chilled.'
Slough volunteer

GENTLY DOES IT

Yoga can do wonders for your brain. In 2004 researchers at the University of California reported results from a pilot study in which they considered the mood-altering ability of different yoga poses. Comparing back bends, forward bends and standing poses, they concluded that the best way to get a mental lift is to bend over backwards.

Exercise is the best antidepressant

A survey by the charity Mind found that 83 per cent of people with mental health problems looked to exercise to help lift their mood or to reduce stress. Two-thirds said that exercise helped to relieve the symptoms of depression, and more than half said it helped to reduce stress and anxiety. Some people even thought it had a beneficial effect on manic depression and schizophrenia.

Six out of 10 said that physical exercise helped to improve their motivation, 50 per cent said it boosted their self-esteem and 24 per cent said it improved their social skills. Mind found that people with mental health problems were more likely to get their exercise from everyday activities, such as walking, housework and gardening.

Start off with moderate exercise

The biggest barriers that prevent us from taking physical exercise are motivation problems, the cost of sport and lack of confidence. Only 20 per cent of people in the UK get enough exercise to maintain a healthy lifestyle and satisfactory fitness level. The main excuse is lack of time, but exercise can be fitted into even the busiest of lives. For example, half an hour of active gardening, such as weeding, raking or mowing the lawn, is enough to raise the heart rate and improve circulation.

For exercise-phobes the good news is that moderate exercise fitted into daily life is much more likely to benefit your overall health than vigorous and irregular bursts of activity. A study conducted by Maastricht University found that regular moderate exercisers expended more energy overall than those who did short bursts of high-intensity exercise and were then relatively inactive. It's also the case that moderate-intensity activities are better tolerated by the middle-aged or obese.

Walk your way to health

When we're out of shape the last thing we want to do is bare our flab in an open-plan changing room. But the fact is we don't have to. The ideal way to start exercising is by walking – so discreet that nobody need know you're trying to get fitter. Buy yourself a pedometer and set yourself an achievable goal. The aim is to build up to 10,000 steps a day – which works out at about 5 miles – but that includes day-to-day movement, such as going to the shops or walking around at work. Start by getting off the bus or train a stop earlier than usual, or park the car further away. It can be a genuine thrill to see how many steps you average without thinking. Make sure you congratulate yourself when you reach each milestone.

THE BENEFITS OF WALKING

- Walking 1 mile in 15 minutes burns the same number of calories as running the same distance in 8.3 minutes.
- Walking 2 miles a day, three days a week can reduce your weight by 1 lb every three weeks.
- Every minute you walk adds between 1.3 and 2 minutes to your life.

Walking is particularly good for people suffering from depression or anxiety, who may feel it's too much to go to the gym or learn a new sport or skill.

---

10 TIPS FOR HAPPIER EXERCISE

1 Do the exercise you most enjoy. There's no point doing 20 sit-ups if you hate it. Much better to do something that makes you feel good. It doesn't even have to be exercise in the usual sense of the word. Activities that keep you on the go, such as amateur dramatics, shopping, dancing, gardening or playing with the grandchildren, all make your heart work harder and are good for your health.

2 Get a dog. Pet owners who walk every day enjoy better physical health, and dog owners always say their animals make them friends.

3 Fitness is not just for the young or agile. Even elderly muscles can be trained. Studies in the USA and UK have shown improved muscle strength among over-70s who trained three times a week for three months.

4 Try reducing periods of inactivity during waking hours. If you want to increase your metabolic rate, exchange low-intensity activities, such as sitting in front of a screen, for moderate-intensity ones, such as walking or cycling (fun, affordable and environmentally friendly).

5 Find a walking group in your area. The Ramblers Association organizes walks to suit all abilities, while the Walking Is the Way to Health Initiative website (www.whi.org.uk) gives details of 'calorie-burning' maps, guided walks and other buddy-type schemes.

6 Exercise at home if you can't get out. Cultural practices mean that some women find it difficult to go to a gym. In this case, experts recommend buying an exercise bike.

7 Take up yoga. According to a 2005 study by the Preventative Medicine Institute, women who do yoga have higher self-esteem and a lower incidence of eating disorders than those who get sweaty doing aerobics. Yoga puts you in closer touch with your body, so you have more a positive attitude to your body, become less preoccupied with appearance, and are more disposed to eat healthily.

8 Do some housework. It burns 100–150 calories an hour and provides an excellent psychological workout. There's something very satisfying about putting every object in its place and removing the dust.

9 Don't overdo it. Addiction to exercise can cause injury, loss of relationships and unsatisfactory work performance. Research among athletes has shown that psychological distress may result from high volumes of training.

10 Have fun. Recent evidence shows that people exercising in a competitive setting report less favourable emotional responses than those who exercise in a non-competitive setting.

HELPING YOUR BODY TO FEEL GOOD

The state of your body is crucial to your happiness. If it's not feeling good, neither will you. Exercise is a great way to feel better, but you have to find the kind of exercise that suits you best. If you really don't know what to do, start with walking (see page 159), then gradually experiment with other activities, such as dancing, swimming or running, until you find what you like.

Remember the following points:

- Take exercise regularly.
- Exercise outside if you can.
- Extend your exercise regime as you get fitter.

Now decide on the exercise you will take during the coming weeks.

I will

_____

_____

_____

_____

_____

_____

_____

_____

_____

_____

_____

14

Happiness Is Pet-shaped

The four-legged wonder drug

Pets do wonders for our physical and mental well-being. They provide their owners with unconditional love and loyalty, and in return we experience the pleasure of caring for an animal, feel needed and enjoy the opportunities it provides for play and amusement. Even simply watching your pet can promote relaxation.

Relationships with animals are largely free of the psychological games inherent in human relationships. Pets don't have mood swings or meltdowns, and they never talk back. They live in the moment and encourage us to do the same. They are great levellers, transcending racial, cultural, age and social barriers. Increasingly, pets are an important resource for those who live alone or work from home. Indeed, for many people pets are like children, arousing similar attachments and emotions.

According to Dr June McNicholas, a research psychologist who has examined the link between human health and animal companionship, pets allow us to have 'risk-free' relationships. They also provide a sense of worth outside the world of work. As McNicholas observes, it is important to know you are loved for who you are, not just because you are rich, beautiful and famous. No wonder a pet is the ultimate accessory for so many celebrities!

Of course, some of the attraction between man and beast may be primal and evolutionary. In the early days of human existence animals probably helped us with hunting. Now their presence in our homes harks back to that link with nature. Physiological tests have shown that stroking and petting animals can improve our general health, and in cases of serious illness pets may also stimulate the survival instinct by reminding patients that they are needed.

'I'd been away on business and returned home late to an empty house. Suddenly my two cats arrived from nowhere and gave me lots of affection. It felt good to have been missed.'
Slough volunteer

Connection to the wider world

Pets are a form of social capital. They help us to develop empathy and broaden our focus beyond ourselves, making us feel connected to a larger world. Dogs facilitate the establishment of trust between total strangers, and even cats and goldfish can provide an excuse to make a friendly connection with our neighbours.

Studies have shown that when dogs and cats visit a care facility, there is more laughter and interaction among residents than during any other entertainment or 'therapy'. In an in-patient setting the presence of animals encourages people to socialize, while a pet can also give an older person who lives alone a new lease on life.

Pets and children

Children see animals as their peers and can identify better with them than with human beings. It requires maturity to read and interpret human body language, while with animals what you see is what you get.

Contact with pets develops nurturing behaviour. Studies report that children who live in homes in which a pet is considered a member of the family are more empathetic than those in ones without pets. That ability to empathize eventually carries over into children's relationships with people. Meanwhile, animals can open a channel of emotionally safe, non-threatening communication.

Children's self-esteem is enhanced by owning a pet, and later they tend to be more involved in activities such as sports, hobbies and chores.

What type of pet is best?

It really doesn't matter what animal you choose as a pet. Cat, dog, parakeet, goldfish… they all provide the same therapeutic benefit. The important thing is to choose an animal that interests you and that suits your personality, living space and lifestyle. Otherwise it will just be an additional source of stress.

'I'm looking after a baby bird that fell from its nest. I found some moss and put it in a box with some water and so far he is doing really well. It's satisfying to know that he could survive thanks to me looking after him.'
Slough volunteer

Pets on the ward

The use of animals in hospitals is not a new idea. As far back as the 1790s the Quakers created a retreat for the mentally ill, where patients communed with farm animals. This was felt to be more helpful than the harsh treatment often meted out to those with psychiatric problems.

Nowadays some hospitals have formal programmes that use dogs, cats and rabbits to visit depressed and anxious patients. Sometimes the animals are also offered to patients in stroke units who may be embarrassed about speaking to people because their speech is impaired, but will chat to a dog. Mental health units report that having a dog visit the ward is an important normalization factor. Similarly, taking a one for a walk makes people feel they are part of the real world.

The effect of pets on nursing-home patients has been well documented over the years. Researchers discovered the patients were more alert and smiled more when the animals were present, while those who were physically aggressive calmed down and allowed people to be near them.

Animals are also used in out-patient programmes for people who have been physically or sexually abused. Staff are not allowed to touch the clients, but they offer them an animal to hold and hug. This can make a world of difference to individuals who have never had positive, appropriate physical contact. No wonder some psychologists call pets 'silent therapists'.

WHY DO PET OWNERS LIVE LONGER?

- Just by their presence, pets make their owners feel optimistic and less stressed, which lowers blood pressure and cholesterol levels, raises chances of survival after a heart attack, and reduces loneliness and depression.
- Among a sample of patients hospitalized in coronary care units for angina or heart attack, those who owned pets were more likely to be alive a year later than those who did not. In fact, having a pet was found to boost survival more than having a spouse or friends.
- Pets make us feel less nervous because they don't judge us. Research has also shown that people perform better in tests when their pet is in the room. In fact, they are more relaxed if they are allowed to pet even an animal they have never met before.
- Just looking at animals promotes relaxation. It has been found that watching tropical fish in an aquarium in a dentist's waiting room works as well as hypnosis for patients nervous about their treatment.
- Dog ownership helps people to cope in the early stages of bereavement. It provides the normality of social contact with other dog walkers, alleviates empty-house syndrome and allows them to air their grief out loud to a 'safe' companion.

'Happiness is a warm puppy.'
Charles Schultz, American creator of Peanuts *cartoon strip*

Pets in prison

In the USA the Prison Pet Partnership Program has been a model for the rehabilitation of female offenders. It helps inmates learn how to train, groom and board dogs within the prison walls, and has been highly successful. The prisoners are allowed to keep the dogs with them until the animals are ready to be placed, and warders have noted dramatic changes in the prisoners' behaviour. They benefit from having the responsibility of taking care of something. It also gives them a chance to be gentle and show their more compassionate side.

Prisons involved in this are having fewer disciplinary problems with their inmates than pet-less prisons. And so far the programme has placed over 700 dogs among children and adults with disabilities, and in families as pets.

Happy Holidays

'If our lives are dominated by a search for
happiness, then perhaps few activities reveal as
much about the dynamics of this quest – in all its
ardour and paradoxes – as our travels. They
express, however inarticulately, an understanding of
what life might be about outside the constraints of
work and the struggle for survival.'

Alain de Botton, The Art of Travel *(2003)*

DO WE REALLY LIKE TRAVEL?

- Half of all Britons find that getting ready to go away on holiday is more stressful than commuting or being at work.
- Last-minute pre-holiday panics, such as checking tickets, finding passports and locking the house, make 64 per cent of us uptight.
- Four in 10 holiday-makers say they find the idea of a long flight stressful.
- Women find getting away on holiday more stressful than men.
- A recent survey revealed that would-be travellers from the West Midlands are Britain's most nervous, while Londoners are the most laid-back.

Travel can be a source of great joy, broadening our experience of other lives and cultures, making us more adventurous and empathetic, and allowing us the chance to be caught up in flow activities (see page 37).

According to psychologists, there are seven socio-psychological benefits of travel. They are:

1 Exploration and evaluation of self
2 Relaxation
3 Escape from a perceived mundane environment
4 Prestige
5 Regression to a childlike, playful state
6 Enhancement of kinship relationships
7 Facilitation of social interaction.

A holiday brings an individual back to a state of equilibrium. We are taken away from the daily working routine and offered social and climatic conditions (sun and warmth), movement, sporting activities, closeness to nature, increased libido, participation in outdoor activities, discovery and change, self-indulgence and reward.

Holidays provide special opportunities for emotional connection, to pass on family traditions and teach values. We also get the chance to think about our life away from the usual daily distractions. 'Journeys are the midwives of thought,' says Alain de Botton. 'Few places are more conducive to internal conversations than a moving plane, ship, or train.'

'Talking to a friend, I recalled a sailing holiday I had spent with my son and four friends sailing around the Greek islands. We had with us the story of Ulysses and took turns to read it aloud as we sailed around Ithaca and imagined the magic of the myth. It was a special time and I'm grateful for such memories.'
Slough volunteer

A study by David Gilbert and Junaida Abdullah found that people waiting to go on holiday are much happier with their life as a whole, experience fewer negative or unpleasant feelings, and enjoy an overall net positive effect. The holiday-makers also reported being happier with their family, financial situation and health than a non-holiday-taking group.

A successful holiday can relieve anxiety and produce real joy as we reconnect with lovers, friends and family. One of the great – often overlooked – benefits of a holiday is simply getting more sleep. Sleeping longer and better (paying off your accumulated sleep debt, see pages 149 and 151) will make anyone feel happier and more alive. So don't feel guilty about lie-ins and siestas. That's what holidays are for.

But holidays can also be a social minefield. Who to take? Who to avoid? What to wear? An exciting change can turn into a source of enormous pressure, forcing some people to face the emptiness of their life and admit (at least to themselves) that they have no one to go with.

Meanwhile, others may find relationships with friends and lovers strained to near breaking point by character traits they'd never noticed before. According to a 2003 holiday compatibility survey, two-thirds of respondents said their companions were inconsiderate, while half rated them boring.

Most of us are simply not used to spending 24 hours a day with our loved ones, so tolerance can be sorely stretched. There may also be a sense of disappointment that we can never escape from our own thoughts, even though we might be far removed from our usual situation.

Why are holidays so stressful?

Instead of switching off and relaxing on a sunny beach, many people spend their holiday worrying about work. They are haunted by images of overflowing in-trays, important meetings they have missed and ambitious colleagues using their absence to gain favour with the boss.

In an era of downsizing and cost cutting, few people are able to pass their workload to colleagues while they are away. Instead, they have to 'earn' their annual leave by working extra-long hours in the weeks before and after the holiday. In fact, one out of three men and one out of six women in full-time employment do not go on holiday because they believe they are too busy.

Even when we do find the time and energy to get away, many of us leave behind our mobile numbers, or take work with us – both of which defeat the object of a holiday – namely, to relax and take a break from the daily grind.

How to holiday with a clear conscience

With proper planning, it is possible to avoid most of the pitfalls outlined above and have a truly restful holiday.

- Make a list well in advance of all the work things that need to be done, and drop or delegate anything non-urgent. Try to give yourself an easy week before and after your break.
- Don't reschedule anything for after the holiday unless you really have to.

Do it before or just forget it. And, importantly, agree your plan with your boss and colleagues so that they know what you will and will not be doing, and what they might have to look after while you're away.

- Don't leave all the holiday preparations to one family member (Mum). Encourage teamwork and allow the children to help plan and pack.
- If you're going away with your extended family, get together and brainstorm long before the holiday happens. Are there potential clashes? Will other siblings feel left out? How much time will you spend together each day? What will you do about finances?

'We are inundated with advice on where to travel to; we hear little of why and how we should go.'
Alain de Botton, The Art of Travel (2003)

What kind of holiday is right for you?

The idea of a holiday is to relax, switch off from everyday life and do something new and different. For some people relaxation might involve trekking in the Himalayas; for others it could mean lying on a beach with a cocktail. You need to be aware of what you want from a holiday. There is simply no point in going to a beautiful and remote self-catering villa in the Italian countryside if you don't want to drive or cook while you're away.

Ask yourself these key questions:

- How far am I prepared to travel to my destination?
- How much holiday entitlement do I and my family have?
- Do I want to be somewhere lively or quiet?
- Do I need facilities for children/elderly relatives/disabled people?
- How much money do I want to spend? If your budget is tight, there are still many holidays you can take, such as youth hostelling or staying in B&Bs, which won't cost a fortune.
- What do I actually want to do on holiday? Play golf? Visit historical sites? Spend time on the beach? Go shopping?
- Can I compromise and adjust my holiday ideals? Realistically, an art gallery in Florence is not going to be the best place for a toddler.
- Do I want to meet people? A mate? Be on my own? Successful solo travelling requires creative ingenuity, and remember that single supplements can often add around 30 per cent to the cost of a holiday.
- Do I want an all-inclusive holiday offering hassle-free relaxation, or a self-catering apartment or villa?

- Am I choosing heavy-travel days, such as bank holidays, for my journey?
- Do I want the satisfaction of learning something new, such as skiing or white-water rafting?
- Do I want to lie back and relax in a state of bliss while a team of therapists polishes and pampers me on a spa break?
- Is sunshine important?
- Do I want to drive while I'm away?
- What do the rest of the family want and will they be happy?
- What kind of food do I want to eat?
- Can I get over my fear of flying? If you have a serious, deep-rooted flying phobia, you could try attending one of the fear-of-flying courses held at various airports around the country.
- Would I prefer to visit many places during my trip rather than stay in a single destination?
- Do I want to be by the sea?
- Am I happy to be with other tourists, or would I rather be off the beaten track with few other British people?
- Do I want to take moral support? Inviting friends to join your family holiday can be a great way to enliven tired rituals, and help you see things with fresh eyes.

And if all else fails...

You can always fake it. This is called taking a 'balcony holiday'. You stay in, don't answer the phone, and do exactly what you want for two weeks. Apparently, 3 million Italians do not take a holiday, but pretend they do in order to seem sociable and popular. In reality, they barricade themselves in at home with adequate supplies and spend their time watching television and videos. Some holiday refuseniks go to quite extraordinary lengths to keep up the pretence. A quarter take their plants to a neighbour and buy sunlamps or self-tanning creams; 13 per cent go as far as purchasing souvenirs on the Internet from their pretend holiday spots. Some even manage to have postcards sent from the places they have not been to.

'I wouldn't criticize anyone for having nice holidays. There's this idea that consumerism is bad when it means going to Las Vegas to play poker or to Ibiza to drink lager. But in terms of good experiences, it's all equally valid.'
Richard Reeves, BBC happiness expert

How to Be Happy

Happiness and Community

HOW FRIENDLY IS BRITAIN?

- In 2001 a government survey showed that 34 per cent of people saw or spoke to friends less than once a week.
- 42 per cent knew fewer than five people they could turn to in a crisis.
- People under the age of 30 are the least neighbourly, and the least likely to be involved in their community.
- Scotland is the most neighbourly area of the UK.
- More than 13 million people count their neighbours as close friends.
- More than a quarter of all households in Britain consist of one person living alone.
- Joining a social group cuts in half your odds of dying next year.

Have you ever organized a street party? Mentored a child? Sung in a choir? Do you support your local shops or make a guilty dash to the out-of-town supermarket in your car? Do you even know your neighbours' names? Chances are, if you live in a large urban city, that you don't.

Although we all know the importance of social connectedness, many of us are less involved in our communities than ever before. The main culprits are the 'me culture' of individualism, the long-hours culture of work, and television. Changes in family structure also mean that more of us are living alone, while suburban sprawl has fractured the traditional neighbourhood where everyone knows everyone. 'Sometimes the way streets and environments are designed, it's quite an effort for people to come together,' says social entrepreneur Andrew Mawson, an adviser on the BBC programme. 'Scale really does affect things.'

The word 'community' means friends and neighbours, and the places where you live, shop and work. As you interact with this environment, do you find it friendly or intimidating? Do you have a shared sense of history? Research shows that people who live near where they grew up, close to parents and old friends, have a network of social support not found in more 'mobile' communities.

BBC happiness expert Richard Stevens argues that the culprit most responsible for increasing alienation from our communities is the car. 'We now tend to drive to shopping malls or city centres where we are surrounded by strangers, rather than mixing with and connecting with friends and acquaintances in local communities as we did in the past.'

Community gives us a sense of belonging, and we need to belong to understand our community. MORI's 2004 survey 'Understanding Life Satisfaction and Trust' found that what gives us pleasure is living in a place we don't want to move out of, and feeling safe in our surroundings. Joining groups, participating, volunteering, going to the theatre... all these community activities score high on the pleasure scale, and through them comes trust in others.

No man is an island

The good news is we can all be part of a wider, interpersonal group, whether it's a shared community, an ethnic or religious group or a political party. (In ancient Greece the word 'politics' actually meant being involved in something that went beyond personal and family welfare.)

'A lot of our society is very much into "me, me, me" and "my little world", thinking "If I feel better everything will be wonderful",' says Andrew Mawson. 'But actually, I don't think that's true. I find that as people become involved with others and do things together, they come to care about them. So they do some good for others and improve their own world at the same time. Happiness is actually about "us, us, us".'

We all need meaning in our lives

Positive psychologist Martin Seligman has identified three distinct components of happiness:

- The pleasant life (a glass of wine)
- The good life (work, romance, hobbies)
- The meaningful life (using personal strengths in the service of something larger than you, such as politics, religion, community action).

Of the three roads to a happy, satisfied life, Seligman believes that the meaningful life gives us most long-term joy. If we fill our life with transitory pleasures, sooner or later most people find themselves looking in the mirror and asking, 'Is this all there is?'

We want to feel that we matter. That we *can* make a difference.

In a now classic exercise that Seligman calls 'Philanthropy versus Fun', he persuaded his psychology students to engage in one pleasurable activity and one philanthropic activity, then write about both. The results, he claims, were life-changing.

The afterglow of the fun activity (watching a film, eating ice cream) paled in comparison with the effects of the kind action (volunteering at a soup kitchen, helping at the school fair). The reason, Seligman suggests, is that kindness is a gratification. 'It calls on your strengths to rise to an occasion and meet a challenge. Kindness is not accompanied by a separate stream of positive emotion, like joy; rather, it consists in total engagement and in the loss of self-consciousness. Time stops.' In other words, it's a classic flow activity (see page 37).

Helping others makes us feel good

Volunteering in a good cause gives us as much happiness as doubling our income. Those who do so even live longer. In a study conducted by Peggy Thoits and Lyndi Hewitt of Vanderbilt University in Nashville, Tennessee, happy people were found to be more likely to sign up for voluntary work. But it was also found that the volunteers became happier, and the more voluntary work they did, the happier they got.

When we feel happy we are more willing to help others. In study after study, a mood-boosting experience (finding money, passing an exam, recalling a happy event) makes people more likely to do a kindness, such as donating money, picking up someone's dropped papers and volunteering time. Psychologists call it the 'feel-good, do-good phenomenon'.

And doing good also makes us feel good. We establish deep interpersonal relationships and empathy for others, and also have the perfect opportunity to practise flow activities – those things we enjoy and that really take us out of ourself.

Scientists agree that being kind to others triggers a cascade of positive effects. It makes us feel generous and capable, and gives us a greater sense of connection with others. And when we do a good deed, we are helping more than just the recipient: we are helping everybody.

Of course it feels good to be on the giving end, but psychologist Jonathan Haidt suggests that people witnessing others performing good deeds also benefit; they experience an emotion called 'elevation'. He explains that we get this feeling when we see people behave honourably or act heroically, or when we witness someone show gratitude or help someone else. And when you feel elevated it makes you more open and considerate, and more loving towards humanity.

'I'm doing good deeds for others that take little effort or expense, such as giving neighbours lifts into town and giving cold drinks to the guys looking after our communal garden, yet reap rewards previously unimagined. Kindness brings out the best in people and I feel good about myself.'
Slough volunteer

Neighbourliness is good for democracy

Although we are more tolerant of one another than previous generations were, we trust one another less. Living without trust and without social connections is no fun, as indicated by many surveys about happiness. But it also has serious social implications. If we don't have traditional community spirit and neighbourliness, we may become a nation of strangers. In his important book *Bowling Alone*, Robert D. Putnam charts the painful deterioration over the past two decades of the organized ways in which American people relate to one another. At one time they went bowling together after work and participated in the PTA, churches, unions or political parties. Now all these habits have disintegrated.

Putnam warns that our stock of social capital – the very fabric of our connections with each other – has plummeted, impoverishing our lives and communities. This is reflected, he argues, in critical ways: higher crime rates, lower educational performance, more teenage pregnancies, child suicides, low-birth-weight babies and infant mortality.

He draws on evidence, including nearly 500,000 interviews over the last quarter century, to show that we sign fewer petitions, belong to fewer organizations that meet, know our neighbours less, meet with friends less frequently, and even socialize with our families less often.

In the mid-1970s the average American attended a club meeting every month, but by 1998 that rate of attendance had been cut by nearly 60 per cent. Today Americans spend about 35 per cent less time visiting friends than they did 30 years ago, and families have dinner together only two-thirds as often as they did a generation ago. They're even bowling alone.

In his book Putnam argues passionately for the importance of civic engagement if we want a society that is happy, well educated, healthy and safe. As he observes, 'A society characterized by general reciprocity is more efficient than a distrustful society... trustworthiness lubricates social life. Frequent interaction among a diverse set of people tends to produce a norm of generalized reciprocity.' Indeed, his book has inspired a whole grass-roots movement, with websites such as www.bowlingalone.com and www.bettertogether.org

How to Be Happy

teaching Americans the tools and strategies to reconnect with others.

So far the USA is much further ahead in civic engagement than the UK, which has no equivalent grass-roots movement to Bowling Alone, but the success of *Making Slough Happy* might just change all that...

Individualistic versus collective societies

Most Western countries are individualistic societies, where personal rights, such as the right to privacy and personal freedom, prevail. Self-fulfilment (at almost any cost) is the ultimate goal. In collectivist societies (the majority of Asian countries) group interests prevail. Loyalty is paramount. Collectivism fosters strong relationships, where everyone takes responsibility for fellow members of their group.

It is difficult to imagine a harder existence than life on the streets or in the slums of Calcutta or even working as a prostitute there. Yet despite the poverty and squalor they face, people there are much happier than you might imagine. Psychologist Ed Diener interviewed 83 people from these three groups and measured their life satisfaction using a scale on which a score of 2 is considered neutral. Overall, they averaged 1.93 – not great, but creditable when compared with a control group of middle-class students in the city who scored 2.43. Most interesting is that the slum dwellers, the happiest of the three disadvantaged groups, scored 2.23, which is not significantly different from the students' score.

Diener thinks that social relationships are partly responsible for this result. He points out that all three deprived groups got high satisfaction ratings in specific areas, such as family (2.5) and friends (2.4). But slum dwellers did particularly well, perhaps because they have more access to the social support provided by the extended family, an important part of Indian culture. In America and the UK, for example, the homeless don't have this social support, and often, despite their better material conditions than the slum dwellers, they are less happy.

How can we make a difference?

There are lots of things you can do to help others, and help yourself in the process. Here are a few ideas.

Community action
'At the heart of every person is a passion,' says *Making Slough Happy* adviser Andrew Mawson. 'The question is, can we discover it?'

Mawson believes in discovering and fostering the passions of individuals and communities. People have the most extraordinary hobbies and skills that can be channelled into small businesses or ambitious community projects.

A United Reformed Church minister for the past 20 years, Mawson is also a leading social entrepreneur. Under his direction the Bromley-by-Bow Centre in east London has become the UK's first integrated healthy-living centre. Housed in a former church, it includes a health centre, a children's nursery, a church, seven social enterprises (including a horticultural business, a furniture business and a restaurant), a 3-acre park, and a 'communiversity' with 400 students. Around 125 activities a week take place on site. 'It is a place where people can take responsibility for their future and be neighbourly,' says Mawson. The centre has been responsible for helping found a £200 million housing company, and a regeneration company that now runs a £100 million programme at what will be the heart of the 2012 Olympic site.

Creating the centre has been a 21-year project, as Mawson recalls cheerfully. 'We started out with £400 in the bank and 12 old people sitting in a run-down church in the middle of a group of challenged East End estates, where 50 languages and dialects are spoken.' The centre, which each week attracts over 2000 paying visitors from across the UK, now has 140 staff (69 per cent of whom come from the surrounding estates).

In 1998 Mawson co-founded the Community Action Network (CAN) with Adele Blakebrough and Helen Taylor Thompson. This charity supports social entrepreneurs from every field of social change in a wide range of projects, from recycling to mental health, and helps them develop sustainable ways of working based on clear business principles. 'People genuinely get healthier when you help them set up their own business. They take responsibility for their future. They then walk differently, dress differently, and you can tell their life is coming together.'

At CAN's mezzanine office at London Bridge you'll find 40 charities operating ('It's like a trading floor for the social sector'). And this social enterprise no longer needs grants. 'It now has a replicable business model and is sustainable,' says Mawson.

The real aim of CAN is to lay the foundation stones of a more entrepreneurial culture in public service because, as Mawson puts it, 'We're fed up with all the yatter from theorists and politicians who've never done it themselves. It's not about old-fashioned liberal ideas about poverty where we all get poor together. The voluntary sector should be about delivering high-quality public services. We've done it through developing very practical projects – learning by doing rather than talking.'

And it means getting real about money. 'I've listened to liberal academics pontificating about "money doesn't matter". But in my experience the poor need to get wealthier. They don't need my charity; they need enterprise skills to move on in their lives and look after their kids.'

How to Be Happy

The Slough community experience

In *Making Slough Happy*, Andrew Mawson worked with five dedicated volunteers to create a concert in the town square to mark Slough's Happiest Day. Musicians from every community were invited to perform, from Punjabi dancers and Caribbean steel-drummers to a jazz band and a local rap artist. Then volunteers, who had spent the summer learning a special song written by BBC happiness expert Brett Kahr, took to the stage to perform Slough's happiness anthem 'We're Going to Change the World'.

The results were profoundly positive, as one volunteer recalled: 'I used to feel really intimidated walking across the town square, but now that we've performed a concert in it, I feel like we own it. Seeing different acts, and different cultures, all up there performing together, was amazing. I'm quite shy but I just got up and did the conga, I was grabbing people. Thanks to the happiness project I've met people I never would have known and we're definitely going to stay in touch.'

As well as the concert, Andrew and his volunteers created a huge smiling-face mural made from 2000 photographs of Slough, taken by local people, which was unveiled in the town square. According to Andrew, 'This huge image was made up of little images of people, activities, local landmarks, the real life of Slough. To politicians who say, "It's all about the big picture", I'd say, "Only if you understand the little pictures".'

'I really enjoyed doing the experimental night photography for the collage with a local artist. It was exciting, educational and enlightening.'
Slough volunteer

How you can get involved

Andrew hopes that other towns and communities will be inspired to create their own photomontage. It could be a unique way of branding your city, he says. 'You could display the images in a health centre, a school, a shop, a gallery, and create a whole tourist business that guides people round the town seeing where the photo subjects actually are. Or why not publish a book of the images? You could also display the montage in the library, so in 100 years' time others will be able to see the life of the town.

'My message is that in any community there's a hidden life going on. If you want to get under the stereotypes, look for the hidden life. And you'll only get into the hidden life by embedding yourself and beginning to get into the gossip networks. That way you'll meet people, such as the older volunteers who have taken their music and movement workshops into old people's homes, or the young steel-drummers making fantastic music.'

Slough of the future?

In the final workshop session, Richard Stevens and his team helped the volunteers to set up community facilitation groups that would continue after the project had finished. A 'Happiness Group' agreed an agenda to promote happiness practices in their community. Another group decided to take responsibility for improving the local environment, starting by cleaning up the roundabout near the town centre. Two other groups took on the promotion of fair-trade practices in local supermarkets and the encouragement of youth activities.

Volunteering

These days volunteering can take any form, from clearing canals to delivering meals on wheels. According to the government's 2003 Citizenship Survey, there are already 26 million people engaged in some kind of informal volunteering in England and Wales, while another 11 million of us want to help but just don't know how.

The corporate sector is also getting more actively involved, or at least encouraging its employees to do so through volunteering and payroll giving – for which small and medium-sized businesses are awarded a £500 grant. Even blue-chip companies have moved away from simply giving money to charity. Now they also encourage staff to take time off and volunteer, knowing that the experience will help teams to bond and bring new skills that are transferable to their role in the company (see www.employeevolunteering.org.uk).

LETS schemes

Local Exchange Trading Systems (LETS) are local, non-profit networks for trading all kinds of goods and services without money. LETS members earn credits by doing, for example, child care or computer work for other members of the network, and can spend them on food, hiring equipment or getting the house decorated. The credits they earn are interest-free and direct exchange is not necessary.

LETS work by producing their own directories of members' offers and requests – goods, services and items for hire or sale. Members use the directory to contact other members and arrange to trade. There is no obligation to trade if it does not suit either party.

Members pay by writing a LETS cheque for the amount of LETS units agreed between the two people trading. LETS cheques are sent to the bookkeeper, who adjusts both members' accounts – one will be plus x units and the other will be minus x units. It is common to have payments partly in LETS units and partly in cash, especially where there is a cash cost for materials to be used on the job, such as paint for decorating or fuel for a car journey.

There are lots of good reasons for using the LETS scheme. Individuals can use, and often pass on, their skills. For some, trading may provide a welcome opportunity to practise skills. For others, it may have an impact on how they feel about themselves. Individuals can purchase goods and services that they might not otherwise be able to afford. LETS build new communities and encourage trading at a local level.

HOW TO BE HAPPIER WITH YOUR COMMUNITY

Social capital is built up through hundreds of actions, big and small, that we take every day. We can all do more than we think.

- Organize a social gathering to welcome a new neighbour.
- Attend town council meetings.
- Use your vote in local and national elections.
- Join an amateur dramatics group (see www.amdram.co.uk); it's an ideal place for community action.
- Sing in a choir or play in an amateur music ensemble (see www.makingmusic.org.uk). These are exhilarating ways of blending your skills with those of others and experiencing 'flow'. You don't actually have a music skill? See www.hotcourses.co.uk for classes in everything from drumming to the didgeridoo.
- Form a tool-lending library to share ladders, drills and suchlike with neighbours.
- Join the British Trust for Conservation Volunteers. Founded in 1959, the charity helps over 130,000 volunteers take hands-on action each year to improve the rural and urban environment. It also runs the People's Places Award Scheme in England, which helps less advantaged communities to create or improve green spaces (see www.btcv.org).
- Start or join a carpool.
- Plan a walking tour of a local historic area and invite others to come along.
- Offer to help in your child's classroom, chaperone a school trip or volunteer to supervise a breakfast or after-school club.
- Support your local shops.
- Donate blood.
- Start a community garden or form a group to clean up a local park or cemetery.

- Arrange to shadow someone from a different ethnic or religious group, then invite them to shadow you.
- Attend your children's sports days, plays and concerts. Get to know their teachers.
- Attend PTA meetings.
- Join or start a babysitting cooperative.
- Persuade a local restaurant to have a designated 'meet new people' table.
- Take dance lessons with a friend.
- Fight to keep essential local services, such as your post office, police station, school, etc.
- Hold a neighbourhood barbecue.
- Ask neighbours for help, and reciprocate when needed.
- Say hello to strangers.
- Contact TimeBank (see www.timebank.org.uk) to find out where you can give your time and skills.
- Find out more about the work of social entrepreneurs and the Community Action Network (see www.can-online.org.uk)
- Join or start a book club or a group to discuss local issues.
- Build a neighbourhood playground.
- Turn off the TV and talk with neighbours, friends or family.

'You suddenly feel really powerful as an individual when you've worked on something like the Slough Project. Having taken on board love thy neighbour, investing in community and investing in people, you just want to go out there and stop the next person you meet and ask what they do for a living or how their day's been. The real world doesn't operate like that, but I hope that when this programme is screened, people don't just look on it as a documentary, or as Slough going on telly to prove it's not as awful as people think. What they need to do is look at the heart of this programme and realize there was a real message behind it.'
Slough volunteer

How to Be Happy

Smile and Feel Better

STATISTICS ON SMILING
- It takes only 16 muscles to smile, 28 to frown.
- Women smile more than men.
- There are 18 different kinds of smile used in a variety of social situations.
- Even 'faking' a smile can lead to feeling happier.
- Babies smile in the womb proving that people are born with this ability. Even babies who are born blind smile.
- A newborn baby shows a preference for a smiling face over a non-smiling face.
- Babies reserve special smiles (Duchenne smiles of joy and happiness) for their loved ones.
- In clinical tests, participants shown a child's smile experienced the same level of stimulation as they would have had from eating 2000 chocolate bars or receiving £16,000 in cash.
- A smiling person is judged to be more pleasant, attractive, sincere, sociable, and competent than a non-smiling person.
- The reason life always looks brighter from behind a smile is because a smile helps to change perceptions, attitudes and beliefs.
- Scots are among the most likely in Britain to return a smile.

'Every time you smile at someone, it is an action of love, a gift to that person, a beautiful thing.'
Mother Teresa of Calcutta, charity worker

Human beings need smiles. Indeed, the happiness a smile expresses is probably the first emotion to be recognized by babies, and their smile in response to a cheerful face is innate rather than learnt. Our tendency to smile when we're happy is built into the wiring of our neurosystem and our facial musculature. And we don't just smile with the mouth; the eyes also convey pleasure, and are an important feature of a genuine smile.

A full-on, radiant smile is a wonderful thing and can reveal our innermost personality. However, there are times when we don't feel in the mood, such as when posing for a photograph, dealing with someone we don't like, or listening to our boss telling his favourite joke for the hundredth time. On those occasions we use a fake smile that stretches the mouth but never reaches the eyes. Think of Hollywood stars at film premieres: are those smiles on the red carpet fake or real?

Different types of smile

It's hard not to respond positively to someone who is smiling, but the warmth of our response depends on what type of smile we receive.

The Duchenne smile (named after the eighteenth-century French physiologist Guillaume Duchenne, who first described it) is genuine. It is the ultimate non-Botox smile! The corners of the mouth turn up, there is a gleam in the eyes and the skin around them crinkles up. The muscles that do this are very difficult to control voluntarily, so this type of smile is linked to genuine feelings of happiness, which are activated in the left-hand part of the brain that creates positive emotions. Babies smile like this when they see their mother.

Quite the opposite is the Pan-American smile (named after the forced grin of flight attendants), which involves mouth muscles and little else. It is thought to be more related to the rictus that lower primates display when frightened than to happiness. This is the 'fake' smile.

Research carried out by psychologist Dacher Keltner found that when people are shown a picture of a Duchenne smile, even if only briefly, it makes them smile in return, as well as making them feel 'calmer and more relaxed'. As part of his research Keltner and LeeAnne Harker of the University of California at Berkeley analysed the smiles of women in a 1960s college yearbook and found that half were Duchenne smilers. They contacted all the women at ages 27, 43 and 52 and asked about their marriage and life satisfaction. It turned out that from their senior-year smile alone it was possible to predict what these women would say. Duchenne women (who were no prettier than their peers) were more likely to be married and stay married, and to experience more personal well-being over the next 30 years. The indicator of happiness came down to a crinkling of the eyes.

'A smile costs nothing, but gives much. Some people are too tired to give you a smile, so give them one of yours. No one needs a smile as much as he who has none to give.'
Samson Raphael Hirsch, nineteenth-century German Jewish theologian

Who's fooling?

In a recent study of 15,000 participants 77 per cent of women rated themselves highly intuitive, while only 58 per cent of men did. Despite this, women were found to be more likely than men to fall for the fake smile.

Overall, men spotted 72 per cent of the genuine smiles and women detected 71 per cent. But men were significantly better at spotting fake smiles among the opposite sex, correctly detecting 76 per cent, while women detected 67 per cent.

Smiling and friendship

Smiling is the first step in making friends and can communicate more than any number of words. Unsurprisingly, research has found that people are more likely to speak to someone who has smiled at them. In addition, smiling actually makes you feel happier because of the feel-good chemicals it releases. Think about how you feel when someone smiles at you, and try to give that feeling to someone else.

Unfortunately, there are people who literally can't smile, and it is a loss that they take very hard. It arises from a medical condition called Moebius syndrome, which causes facial paralysis. This prevents sufferers from showing any positive emotion on their face, so they react to the friendliest conversation completely deadpan. As a result, they have enormous difficulty in making and keeping friends.

'Smiling makes you and others feel better and it makes you look younger!'
Marie Helvin, American-born British model

SMILING IN WRITING

It can be very difficult to gauge someone's emotions when communicating by email or text message. The written word is notoriously easy to misinterpret, so some people use smileys (emoticons) to help get their message across. Tilt your head to the left to read these commonly used ones:

:-) Smiling   :-D Laughing   :* Kissing   :-o Shocked   :-! A smoker
:'-(Crying   :-x Lips are sealed   :-(Sad   8-I Surprised   #-) Hungover

---

SLOUGH'S SMILE CAMPAIGN

During the *Making Slough Happy* project, Richard Reeves set about persuading the citizens of Slough to cheer up. 'We tried to get a ripple effect going by persuading one person to smile, then another, and another.' Armed with a megaphone, he walked around Asda supermarket, getting people on the cheese counter to smile more, talk to fellow customers and even dance down the aisles. 'Everyone agreed it was better when people smiled more, which raises the question: why don't we? It turns out to be fear – fear of being seen as a loony or a pervert. So there's a self-fulfilling prophecy about this, where the less people smile the odder it seems when they do.

'One bloke I spoke to said, "I wouldn't smile at anyone round here, mate, or you'd get a smack in the mouth!" But I found that as soon as people get past their shyness and inhibitions, they're fine. So what you need is to give an artificial stimulant to people, to intervene to get the process started. Certainly you can liven up the atmosphere of a supermarket just by getting people to open up their faces to one another, rather than going round heads down, seeing people as obstacles to their own progress. So why not get traffic wardens and police officers to smile? It's quite a small thing, but cumulatively it's one of the key factors in the social climate for a community or a town. And we want to try to change the weather in Slough to make it a funnier place by the way people interact with one another.'

How did the Slough volunteers get on?

One of the volunteers set herself the task of smiling at people in the street, saying hello and then engaging in a short conversation. After one smile exercise she went back to her office to continue her work and there was a knock at the door: it was the stranger she had spoken to. He handed her a poem he had just written about her: 'I met a girl with a heart of jam/Nice and sweet – a real rare treat/Quite makes your heart miss a beat.'

Another volunteer also had a happy experience. 'I've been smiling and saying hello to people quite a lot throughout my life, but when I got lost on a recent car journey I went one further. I thought, "Let's talk to a stranger. Let's see who looks nice on this housing estate." I saw a lovely guy standing there and I thought, "I'll chat him up!" So I did and he was great fun. He knew the place I was trying to find and we had a laugh. It was silly and fun!'

How
to Be
Happy

Laughter: the Sound of Happiness

'Laughter is the shortest distance between two people.'
Victor Borge, Danish-born American entertainer and humorist

FANCY THAT

- In a 2005 survey 45 per cent of people admitted to having a total sense of humour failure first thing in the morning.
- Having 100–200 belly laughs a day will burn off 500 calories, and it tones your stomach.
- The amount of time we spend chuckling is three times less than in the 1950s (six minutes a day as opposed to 18 minutes).
- Londoners laugh more than people anywhere else in Britain (17 times a day compared with the national average of 14).
- Older men who have a sense of humour and low hostility experience fewer flu-like symptoms.
- In conversation, speakers are more likely to laugh than listeners.
- Women laugh most in the presence of men they find attractive.
- Laughter revs up your immune system, lowers blood pressure and enhances cardiovascular and respiratory functions.
- Single women aged 18–24 are the happiest people in the UK and the Welsh are the unhappiest people, with only 11 laughs a day. The happiest couples (aged 25–34) are found in Bristol.
- The 'ha-ha' of human laughter is similar to the simian 'pant-pant' when apes wrestle and chase. Laughter is basically the sound of laboured breathing.

We love people who make us laugh. Humour is a social lubricant that can help to forge relationships and strengthen existing ones, as well as reducing the biological effects of stress. Laughing is a natural painkiller because it raises levels of the feel-good chemicals serotonin and endorphins. A good laugh is definitely good for your health and medical researchers have found that laughter exercises the upper body, too. After laughing we feel a physical glow that relaxes muscle tension, massages the lungs, restores breathing and expands the circulation. Laughter also inspires the immune system to create white T-cells, commonly called 'happy cells', which help prevent infection.

According to research by Robert Provine, a psychologist at the University of Maryland, laughing is 30 times more likely to occur in a group situation than a solitary one. This is because laughter is largely a tool of communication – a wordless bond that we use to send disarming cues to other people. It helps us hold a listener's attention and offer – or seek – encouragement to go on.

Whether or not what we say is genuinely funny, any reciprocal laughter from the listener serves as a powerful reward. It flatters the speaker, which can be especially useful if the tone of the conversation becomes flirtatious. Men tend to do more of the performing and make more jokes while it's women who do more of the laughing. For example, wives often laugh at their husband's jokes, even if they aren't funny. The women are not judging his skills as a stand-up comedian; rather they want to express pleasure at his desire to 'connect' with them.

Why is laughter good for us?

Like sleep, laughter is safe and pleasant. It promotes connectedness, the most important of all the building blocks of happiness. It is also very handy in awkward social situations, allowing us to tackle complicated or taboo issues in a non-threatening way. Humour also promotes creativity, sometimes making the noisiest workplaces among the most productive ones.

Scientists have shown that laughter produces healthy neurotransmitters (hormones fired between nerve cells) that produce and perpetuate the feelings of happiness and joy. In fact, laughter is something of a wonder drug. It jogs the muscles, provides an internal massage for all the organs and tissues, oxygenates the blood and gets the lymph flowing. Dynamic laughter (big belly laughs) gives your diaphragm and abdominals quite an aerobic workout.

Research has shown that laughter increases the blood flow to the heart by 22 per cent because it causes the endothelium – the tissue that forms the inner lining of blood vessels – to expand. It is therefore conceivable that laughing may be important to maintain a healthy endothelium and reduce the risk of cardiovascular disease.

Laughter can decrease stress

Psychologists describe people prone to frequent bouts of stress as Type H personalities – hostile, hurried and humourless. They are too busy to have fun. For these people laughter is the perfect solution. Lee Berk, professor of pathology and anatomy at Loma Linda University in California, set up a study of 10 volunteers and drew samples of their blood before, during and after they watched a one-hour comedy video. He found that laughter decreased stress chemicals, particularly cortisol, the primary stress hormone.

In a follow-up study in 2001 he tracked two groups of cardiac patients for a year after a heart attack. One group watched 30 minutes of comedy a day in addition to having medical therapy; the other received medical care alone. At the end of the year the group prescribed laughter had lower blood pressure, lower stress hormone levels, fewer episodes of arhythmia, and fewer repeat heart attacks. Berks felt that laughter was a form of internal jogging. It gets the lungs moving and the blood circulating, so its effects are beneficial.

Laughter can reduce pain

As laughing raises levels of serotonin and endorphins, it is a natural painkiller. In 1979 Dr Norman Cousins (the modern 'father of laughter therapy') wrote a book called *Anatomy of an Illness*, describing how he used laughter to help heal him of a painful spinal disease called ankylosing spondylitis. He discovered that 10 minutes of genuine belly laughter had an anaesthetic effect on him and gave him at least two hours of pain-free sleep. His prescription of Marx Brothers movies and cartoons both raised his spirits and relieved his pain.

Laughter can help us through grief

Pychologist Dacher Keltner studied people who have little reason to laugh: namely, those whose spouses had died six months previously. Most psychologists consider a period of sadness or anger after a traumatic event to be normal and healthy, and positive emotions soon after the death of a spouse to be inappropriate. But Keltner wasn't so sure.

He interviewed mourners and noted their tendency to laugh or smile through their sadness just weeks after a loved one's death. He then discovered that those who had displayed more positive emotions showed less depression and anxiety 2–4 years later. As a result, Keltner now thinks that humour can transform the sadness of a tragedy; that laughter is something that enables people to separate themselves from their grief and that it is a healthy mechanism which allows you to distance yourself from an event in order that you can engage in healthier, more social, emotions.

Tickling and giggling

Although we all dread getting the giggles during an important meeting, laughter can provide a lot of subversive fun, especially when it spreads to the person next to you. Tickling is another two-way pleasure that is essentially non-verbal. Babies especially love being tickled by their parents, who take pleasure in the bonding that results.

It may be no coincidence that the most ticklish parts of the body are also the most vulnerable: stomach, throat and groin. During childhood games we are often taught by our parents to keep those areas safe and to pull away if the touch is too intense. This may also explain why we lose our taste for being tickled as we get older.

Laughter clubs

The Indian physician Dr Madan Kataria, convinced of the therapeutic effects of laughter, started his first laughter club in Bombay in 1995. At first he told funny stories, but when he ran out of source material, he began to incorporate yoga stretches, and then tried encouraging people to laugh for no reason at all.

There are now 1800 laughter clubs in India. They start at 6 a.m. and people simply laugh their heads off. Not everyone is automatically rolling in the aisles of course, but Kataria says there's nothing wrong with faking laughter. Besides, your body doesn't know the difference.

At his clubs, which are free, laughter instructors start things off by encouraging people to go for a 'ho-ho' or 'ha-ha' chant, or even the 'lion laugh', which involves sticking out your tongue and flapping your hands by your ears. Kataria believes that laughter can't solve your problems, but it can dissolve them.

His formula for laughing yoga clubs has been hugely successful. There are now 700 clubs outside India, from New York and Finland to the Philippines. Every year on World Laughter Day (celebrated on the first Sunday in May) 10,000 Danes gather in Copenhagen for the world's largest mass laugh-in.

In the USA there are therapeutic laughter groups, and even a website (www.worldlaughtertour.com) offering training for 'certified laughter leaders', who set up clubs in hospitals and nursing homes to bring patients together and get them laughing. And there are a number of similar British groups. United Mind (www.unitedmind.co.uk), a holistic therapy centre in St Albans, is just one.

LAUGHTER: THE SOUND OF HAPPINESS

The laughter workshop takes the principles of Dr Madan Kataria's laughter yoga into the workplace, where they aim to tackle stress. They also run the Laughter Club International of St Albans, which meets on the second Sunday of every month for a free laughter class. Others laughter clubs include ones in:

Bristol (www.bristollaughterclub.com),
London (www.laughteryoga.co.uk),
Manchester (www.writelaugh.co.uk),
Solihull (www.understandyou.com).

The international site of Dr Madan Kataria's laughter yoga can be found at www.laughteryoga.org and has links to sites worldwide.

The British actor John Cleese, who attended a session at Kataria's club in Bombay, was so impressed by the good humour he felt for his fellow man that he called it a 'force for democracy'. One of the *Making Slough Happy* volunteers tried out the technique in a local supermarket: 'I saw a group of staff I vaguely knew. They looked so serious that I went up and said, "The usual Monday morning feeling?" Some nodded, so I said a good laugh would help. I demonstrated the forced laughter that we did at the laughter clinic and it worked! Soon they were all laughing and saying they were going to try it out.'

Another volunteer told us: 'I have been having a laugh at least once a day. The way I have achieved this is by turning frustration into laughter. My computer at work is the bane of my life. So now, instead of getting upset about it, I make a bet to see how long it lasts until it crashes. And it really makes me laugh.'

HOW TO BRING MORE LAUGHTER INTO YOUR LIFE

- Learn one really great joke.
- Start a laughter club with your friends.
- Keep a library of comedy videos and watch them on stressful days.
- Share humour: when you hear a funny story, pass it on and laugh all over again.
- Put a favourite cartoon on your fridge door, and stick smiley faces on your dashboard, mirror and computer to remind you to lighten up.
- Don't take life too seriously.
- Take up a new hobby – ice skating, salsa dancing, underwater aerobics – because first attempts at anything new can reduce you to hysterical laughter.
- Allow yourself one day when you don't watch or listen to serious news first thing. Instead listen to a talk show, comedy station or a CD of stand-up comedy.

19

Spiritual Happiness

HOW POPULAR IS RELIGION?

- Some 41 million Britons (72 per cent of the population) regard themselves as Christian.
- Around 42 per cent of the British public considers themselves 'a religious person'.
- A third of Muslims, a quarter of Sikhs and a fifth of Hindus in Britain were under 16 in 2001.
- Only 7 per cent of adults in England and Wales go to church on an average Sunday.
- 91 per cent of people in the USA say they believe in God.
- 29 per cent of Britons think the world would be a more peaceful place if people didn't believe in God.
- 19 per cent of Britons say they would die for their God or religious beliefs (compared to 71 per cent of Americans).
- People with no religion are the most likely to be living together outside marriage. Muslims, Sikhs and Hindus are least likely to cohabit.
- The highest levels of religious belief are generally found in the poorest countries.

Recent studies have shown that people who follow a religion are generally more satisfied and have more positive emotions about their life. They also have a lower suicide rate and live longer. No wonder, then, that scientists are increasingly keen to study links between religion and mental health.

Religion's benefits broadly divide into four factors: social support, spiritual support, a sense of purpose and meaning, and the avoidance of risky and stressful behaviours. Doing good works through acts of charity provides another sense of connection to community. Often religion can help us feel more included in society, and it can give us a sense of being united and a feeling of continuity in life.

How to Be Happy

Believers say that their faith can relieve stress in difficult times, such as illness, divorce and bereavement. They also generally have a lower level of anxiety about their own death because of their belief in an afterlife. In addition, faith can also be a powerful buffer against the effects of social and economic deprivation. It helps us to think beyond our own selfish interests.

Religion can also make us more compassionate, and the results of our compassion can make us feel better too. Clinical psychologist Lorne Ladner has studied Buddhism's capacity to foster happiness and observes, 'A person might emulate the Buddha by imagining he's breathing in the suffering of others and breathing out energy to heal them. You literally breathe in sadness and exhale joy. This doesn't magically alleviate people's suffering, but the practice does help a person develop a strong sense of compassion, and compassion has been linked to happiness.'

However, some researchers question professions of happiness by the devout, wondering if they feel obliged to say they're happy because they don't want to appear lacking in faith.

'We sat in the beautiful garden of the tiny Methodist church where my son is getting married and talked about the deeper things and feelings in our lives that had been triggered by the morning's church service. Despite our different backgrounds, we believe the best things in life are free – and that resonates with all human beings.'
Slough volunteer

Maybe it's the social life

The word 'religion' derives from the Latin *religio*, meaning 'to bind together', and this is what organized religion tends to do to its followers. As we know from earlier chapters, being connected to others is an important ingredient for happiness, so it comes as no surprise to learn that religious people are generally happier than those who aren't. However, the friendships that people form in traditional places of worship are based on more than belief in their God. In most cases people are drawn to particular communities of worship because they are familiar with their rituals and agree with their values.

Psychology professor Ara Norenzayan from the University of British Columbia believes that social networking is the reason for religious people's increased levels of happiness rather than the actual practising of the religion itself. Worshipping as a community reduces many people's sense of isolation (especially among the poor, the ill, the uneducated, the unmarried, the elderly and ethnic minorities), and increases happiness by creating an atmosphere of reciprocal support. However, researchers have found that people who attend church for non-spiritual reasons, such as wanting to make friends or gain in social importance, tend to have poorer mental health than those who go primarily because of their faith. This suggests that faith is necessary for the benefits to be felt.

'I am a Muslim and Muslims are very community-orientated. Family is everything, so we already understand much of the ethos of happiness that is in the manifesto.'
Slough volunteer

Religion keeps you healthy

In addition to increasing happiness, religion also benefits health. Patients with high levels of spirituality have a significantly slower progression of cognitive decline in illnesses such as Alzheimer's disease. Spirituality appears to demonstrate that the brain, acting through its connections with the neuroendocrine system, can have important effects on health.

In addition, many religions ban forms of behaviour that would be self-destructive, such as taking drugs. Believers are also less likely to divorce, a high source of stress and unhappiness, unless they are in a mixed-faith marriage.

'As a Sikh my religion is the most important thing in my life. It gives me absolute faith, generosity of spirit and the support of my community when I go to the temple.'
Slough volunteer

Religion is a code

The strictures of religion can be a huge relief for some people. Psychologist Barry Schwartz believes that one of the benefits of observance is that it frees people from having to make certain decisions for themselves. Behaviour and morality are codified, so they can simply follow their religion's teaching on, say, abortion or euthanasia, and thus avoid a difficult debate.

However, some studies have shown that religion can have a negative effect on believers because those who are religious also tend to be more prone to prejudice and less tolerant of groups from different ethnic or religious back-grounds. Votes on gay marriage, for example, suggest that some religious people do not favour the happiness of others if it directly contradicts their idea of what their religion allows.

Ara Norenzayan has made a three-year study of the links between religion, violence and intolerance, and found the results disturbing. It seems that the more intense people's religious commitment, the more intolerant they are towards others who think or behave differently. Norenzayan points to the present-day connection between religion and terrorism, and notes that religious people are also more likely to support wars. This he puts down to people wanting to maintain group boundaries.

Graveyard therapy

During the TV series BBC happiness expert Richard Stevens organized a meditation session at a local graveyard. His aim was to make the volunteers more aware of the reality of death so that they would no longer settle for a predictably mundane existence. People who have had a near-death experience or survived serious illness, he says, often acquire a new, more positive attitude to life. He therefore wanted the volunteers to contemplate the whole subject of death in order to make the experience of living more vivid and exciting.

'The graveyard therapy session was probably one of the most powerful, potent and persuasive sessions I've ever participated in. Little did I expect to get so much out of sitting at a young boy's grave for 45 minutes. It made me think about how wonderful life actually is and that every month, minute, millisecond is there to be enjoyed.'
Slough volunteer

Other forms of spirituality

Of course, religion is not the only source of spiritual happiness. Faith in a framework of, say, humanism or pure science can provide benefits similar to those experienced by religious people. Equally, fulfilled and loving relationships can offer a spiritual dimension to life.

One of the most popular forms of spirituality is meditation, which can in fact be practised with or without a religious context. Meditation is a form of mind–body medicine. It can clear your head and raise your consciousness, increase creativity, improve memory and learning ability, and promote inner calm. The muscles, nervous system and endocrine system have a kind of 'memory' that stores the hurts, fears and sadness that we experience throughout the day. Meditation helps dissipate this.

Alpha brainwaves, which are the type associated with relaxation, increase during meditation. There is also a rise in the level of melatonin, the hormone associated with better sleep. The end result is that meditation makes us healthier and happier. In fact, big companies such as Apple already schedule a 30-minute daily meditation break for their employees.

How does meditation work?

Meditation reverses the negative effects of stress by lowering the cortisol and adrenalin that build up when you are under daily stress. As a result, worries diminish and problems don't loom as large. Neuroscientists have found that meditators shift their brain activity to different areas of the cortex: brainwaves in the stress-prone right frontal cortex move to the calmer left frontal cortex. There is also less activity in the amygdala, where the brain processes fear.

The feeling induced by meditation has been described as 'bliss', but the benefit is much greater than that. Meditation contributes to an overall feeling of happiness by making those who practise it feel more in control of their life.

Of course, there are many kinds of meditation, and different methods are suited to different people. Some of the major ones are associated with the religious teachings of Zen, Sufism and figures such as Gurdjieff. Many will have encountered meditation through yoga. Others will have heard of the transcendental form. The important thing to understand is that there many 'paths' of meditation: the teaching of it may be approached through the intellect, the emotions, the body or action.

Transcendental meditation (TM)

Perhaps the most widely known form of meditation, TM is based on ancient Vedic philosophy and is the method often used in scientific research studies. TM, which seeks to induce less active thinking processes and create a state of 'restful alertness', was founded by the Maharishi Mahesh Yogi (the guru to the Beatles). Apart from its calming effects, it is believed to have a beneficial effect upon risk factors for cardiovascular disease, including high cholesterol, high blood pressure and even tobacco use.

A US study conducted in 2005 found that people practising transcendental meditation had 30 per cent fewer deaths from heart disease and 49 per cent fewer from cancer. Overall, the group studied had a 23 per cent lower risk of premature death from all causes.

How to meditate

Meditation may be done sitting, lying or standing – whichever position you find most comfortable – but the mind is more likely to wander or go to sleep if you lie down. The key thing is to set aside 20 minutes every day at a time when you are unlikely to be disturbed. It could be first thing in the morning, the middle of the day or the evening.

The primary aim is to stop all thoughts as much as possible, so first make sure you are comfortable. If you are seated, sit up straight with your lower back supported, and your head centred above your shoulders. Legs may be crossed.

Begin by relaxing your muscles, breathing deeply from your diaphragm (you should feel the lower part of your lungs filling up with air as first your tummy region, then your chest and upper chest, fill up with air). Breathe out in the reverse order, letting out the air first from the top of your chest then down through to your tummy region. Your heartbeat will automatically slow with each exhalation.

Try not to think about problems. Just focus on your breathing, counting breaths in and out (this teaches you to do one thing at a time). Alternatively, you can use a particular sound, such as 'om', saying it silently in time with your breathing. If thoughts keep intruding, use your imagination to visualize a colour or a calming scene: hear the sounds of birds or waterfalls. Imagine all the stress and problems draining out of you. Imagine golden light flowing down.

It may take a while to ease into a soothing meditative state of mind, but as the minutes pass you will find yourself becoming calmer. In this state you may find that ideas, answers to questions or solutions to problems just pop into your head. You can stop to write them down, but in the early days of learning to meditate it might be better to wait until later.

You may be surprised at how quickly you can feel the benefits of meditation. Calmness and clear-headedness soon become apparent, but even less obvious improvements, such as a lowered heart rate, can be measured (you'll need a heart-rate monitor for this).

Case study

One of the *Making Slough Happy* volunteers was very sceptical about being introduced to Zen meditation, but he was pleasantly surprised.

'We had a Zen session with Richard Stevens in the grounds of a beautiful mansion. He asked us to sit quietly by a small lake in pairs, relax, put on a blindfold and inhale the scent of jasmine. Then we had to take off the blindfold, look at the surroundings again, and try to empty our minds. It was wonderful to feel so in tune with everything. Then Richard asked us to walk slowly to a small gazebo, still taking in the nature around us. While doing this, thoughts began to come back into my mind, but I managed to blank them out again. It was a good experience and I felt I must do it more often.' .

Using a similar approach, Richard also took a group of volunteers camping in the rain, encouraging them to become aware through their senses of the richness of the sights, sounds and smells around them.

> 'I'm considering trying to discover more about the "inner" me. I'd like to revisit the Japanese garden at Capel Manor to recapture the "feelings" and philosophy of Zen gardens and the philosophy of Buddhism. I think that I may be able to learn more about "life" and "now" via the teachings of Buddhism.'
> Slough volunteer

The power of the retreat

If you find meditating alone too difficult, you could try visiting a retreat. Type the word 'retreat' into an Internet search engine and an astonishing number of options appear: Christian, Buddhist, Zen, Sufi, New Age. In an increasingly stressful world, more of us are visiting retreats in an attempt to stay sane. According to the British Retreat Association the desire to find peace and solitude has never been so strong.

Retreats have even been the subject of a TV documentary. The BBC series *The Monastery* examined the effect of the cloistered life on five different men, including one who had been connected with terrorism in his youth and another who was involved in a sex chatline. The experience of spending 40 days and nights in a Benedictine monastery had a profound effect on them, and all five men changed their lives dramatically as a result. The series proved remarkably popular and attracted 2.5 million viewers.

Richard Stevens has strong views about people's inability to switch off. He believes that we're doing too much – that we don't allow enough time for being totally present in the here and now. 'Even when people are relaxing,' he says, 'they're often engaged in low-level activity, such as watching telly or reading a newspaper, which frankly doesn't give them a lot in terms of physical or mental satisfaction.'

SEARCHING FOR INNER DIRECTION

What makes many people happy is having a sense of meaningfulness in life. You can't create this to order, but you can do things that make it more likely you will move in the right direction. For the *Making Slough Happy* workshop sessions, Stevens and his team devised this exercise to encourage the volunteers to reflect on what they wanted their lives to be about. Try doing it to help you focus on what's important to you and find ways of getting more direction and fulfilment in your life. Ask yourself:

- What kind of person would I really like to be?
- How would I like to feel?
- What's really important to me?
- What direction am I going in now?
- What direction would I like to be going in?

And complete the following sentences:
- In 20 years' time I'd like to be _____
- In the next year I'd like to be _____
- In the next month I'd like to be _____
- The most important of these is _____

- In the next two weeks I could take the following steps to this goal:

_____
_____
_____

Talking to others, reflecting, meditating and reading help some people to find new directions. Think about what's really important to you.

Building a vision of how you'd like things to be in the future gives your mind a new map that can help you create what you want in your life.

In the next weeks, how are you going to work towards finding direction in your life?

I will

_____
_____

20

Happy Ageing

BLOOMING OLD AGE

- Life expectancy is 80.5 years for British women, and 75.9 years for men.
- Seven in 10 women aged over 85 live alone compared to just four in 10 men.
- In 2001 people aged over 60 outnumbered children for the first time ever in the UK.
- In 2002 there were 19.8 million people over 50 in the UK. This figure is expected to climb to 27 million by 2031.
- By 2025 there will be more over-60s than there will be under-25s.
- The number of workers aged over 60 is set to double in the next two decades as people increasingly feel too young to retire.
- Those aged over 65 are more likely than any other group to own their homes outright.
- The over-65s spend more time watching television, reading and listening to music or the radio than those in the 50–64 age range.
- The over-50s are the most likely group to be providing unpaid care for elderly relatives or neighbours.

Thanks to improvements in living conditions and health care, Western populations are living longer and spending perhaps a third of their lives as elderly people. But the good news is that the UK is a long way from turning into a nation of Victor Meldrews. The image of crotchety old people who complain about everything no longer fits reality. Increasingly, people have a second life after they retire from their main job but before they believe themselves to be old. So someone in their mid-50s in Britain today feels only as old as a 40-year-old in 1900.

We all know the joke that 50 is the new 40, but increasingly, researchers suggest, the best way to define age is not according to how many years you have lived, but how many more you can expect before you die. They define this as the difference between 'retrospective age' and 'prospective age'.

'The secret of a happy life is to accept change gracefully.'
James Stewart, American actor

Getting happier as we get older

In surveys people over 70 are on average just as happy as the young, and actually rate themselves more satisfied with their lives overall. This is referred to as the 'paradox of ageing' because the problems associated with age make it hard to understand how the elderly could really be more satisfied.

In a study conducted by psychologist Laura Carstensen of Stanford University in California, she gave pagers to 184 people between the ages of 18 and 94 and paged them five times a day for a week, asking them to fill out an emotions questionnaire each time. The older people reported positive emotions just as often as the younger ones, but they reported negative emotions much less frequently. This may be because they are more realistic about the goals they set, only going for those they can achieve. And Carstensen thinks that, with time running out, older people have learnt to regulate their emotions, focusing on things that make them happy and letting go of those that don't. 'People realize not only what they have, but also that what they have cannot last for ever,' she says. 'A goodbye kiss to a spouse at the age of 85, for example, may elicit far more differentiated and complex emotional responses than a similar kiss to a spouse at the age of 20.'

Research has also shown that older people do slightly better in terms of pleasure. Through trial and error they have learnt how to live in ways that maximize pleasure and minimize displeasure.

A major study of 60,000 adults from 40 nations divides happiness into three components: life satisfaction, pleasant affect and unpleasant affect. Life satisfaction goes up slightly with age, pleasant affect declines slightly and negative affect does not change. What does change is the intensity of emotions. Both 'feeling on top of the world' and being 'in the depths of despair' become less common with age and experience. That said, elderly people derive much of their happiness from the same source as younger people: namely, connection with family and friends.

'In the cool of the evening my wife and I walked together into a brilliant setting sun, its light fracturing the water into a thousand diamonds. The sheer peace was a positive joy. I felt an enhanced sense of gratitude for life and the fact that we are still able to share it after all the years we have spent together.'
Slough volunteer

Work can make you happy

People in their 60s are the happiest at work, according to a recent survey by the Employers Forum on Age (EFA).

Some 93 per cent of those aged 60–69 said they felt happy on most work-days, and four out of 10 were happy to work until 70 – more than in any other age group. Meanwhile, 74 per cent of over-50s said they liked to keep up with new technology – only 5 per cent less than among teenagers.

In comparison, workers between the ages of 20 and 49 were most likely to say they lacked interesting challenges, and 30-somethings were least happy with their work–life balance.

A positive ageing workforce

Recent reports on the government's pension strategy have stated that we will all end up having to work until we are 70 in order to pay for our old age. But this may not be as bad as it sounds. Recent research shows that most of us are not against the idea at all:

- 71 per cent of Britons actually want to continue to work after 65.
- 90 per cent of us are opposed to a mandatory retirement age.

Many people see retirement as an opportunity to do more with life, not just a time to sit back and relax:

- 56 per cent of Britons think retirement is an opportunity for a whole new chapter in life.
- Only 26 per cent of us never want to work again after retirement.
- Only 28 per cent see retirement as a time for rest and relaxation.

The employment rate for people aged 55–64 is more than 55 per cent in Britain, compared with 39 per cent in Germany, 36 per cent in France and 30 per cent in Italy.

There are clear health and psychological benefits to working later in life. In addition, the role of the family is changing, and older people consider it increasingly important to be self-reliant in later life. It therefore makes sense to find ways of retaining and motivating workers, and to offer flexibility, training and development irrespective of age.

Careers in which it is easy to work past the age of 65 include retailing, management, public relations, farming, politics, writing, entertaining and journalism. Of course, if you are self-employed you can work till you drop.

Happy childhood, happy old age?

According to a pioneering experiment conducted by Alzheimer's expert David Snowdon at a convent in Mankato, Minnesota, experiencing lots of positive emotion in early life seems to help us live longer. The nuns' longevity – they boast seven centenarians and many others well on their way to that age – is surely in no small part attributable to their impeccable lifestyle. They do not drink or smoke, they live quietly and communally, they are spiritual and calm, and they eat healthily and in moderation. Nevertheless, small differences between individual nuns seem to reveal the key to a healthy mind in later life.

Some of the nuns have suffered from Alzheimer's disease, but many have avoided any kind of dementia or senility. The latter include Sister Matthia, who was mentally fit and active from her birth in 1894 to the day she died peacefully in her sleep aged 104. A post-mortem revealed that her brain showed no signs of excessive ageing. But in some other remarkable instances Snowdon has found nuns who showed no outward signs of senility in life, yet had brains that looked as if they were ravaged by dementia.

How did Sister Matthia and the others cheat time? Snowdon's study, which includes an annual barrage of mental agility tests, has found several common denominators. The right amount of the B vitamin folate (folic acid – found in lentils, spinach, green beans and wholemeal bread) is one, and verbal ability early in life is another. Even more important, though, are the positive emotions each experienced early in life, which were revealed in autobiographical essays the nuns wrote at the time of taking their vows. Activities such as crosswords, knitting and exercising also helped to prevent senility. And faith, or the positive attitude that comes from it, may also have contributed.

Are you clever enough to be happy?

A happy old age is what many people spend their lives preparing for, aiming for financial security and good health. But one thing people need not worry about, it seems, is how clever they are. A study of more than 400 pensioners reveals that cognitive ability is unrelated to happiness in old age.

The research, conducted by Alan Gow and colleagues at the University of Edinburgh, looked at a group of 416 people born in 1921, who underwent intelligence tests at the ages of 11 and 79. At the age of 80, the group was also sent a 'satisfaction with life' questionnaire, which had them assess their current level of happiness.

'We found no association between levels of mental ability and reported happiness, which is quite surprising because intelligence is highly valued in our society,' says Gow. 'Neither childhood IQ, IQ at 80 or any change in IQ over a lifetime appear to have any bearing on how satisfied you are with how your life has turned out. Maybe all that is necessary is that you have the ability to carry out your daily tasks.'

The best is yet to come

The latest research demonstrates that happiness is U-shaped, meaning that people begin and end life at their happiest, experiencing a dip around the age of 40. All the evidence therefore suggests that we are most likely to get happier as we get older. According to BBC evangelist Richard Reeves, the happiest people in Britain seem to be those who retired with enough money to make them feel comfortably off, who are healthy and do not want to move from their current home.

Significantly, too, the older generation seems to enjoy happier marriages, something that researchers have put down to the fact that they 'married at a time when people held more pragmatic views about marriage, support for marriage was stronger, and couples were more committed to the norm of lifelong marriage'.

An inspiration to us all

An older couple aged 83 and 75 were the most extraordinary of the Slough volunteers. The wife had trained as a ballerina at Sadler's Wells, but the Second World War interrupted her professional training. After the war, she studied music and movement and trained as a teacher and counsellor (she also became director for 12 years of a branch of the Samaritans).

For many years the couple organized clown workshops and music and movement in hospices and day centres. They also ran holiday courses in Slough and Spain 'based on the journey of life' (one course helping older people to celebrate retirement was called 'The Lion in Winter').

Now the couple run music and movement workshops for the old and infirm. As the husband explained, 'It's a group in which nothing is "silly" and there are no rules apart from mutual consideration. Each person in turn dances or moves to express what they are feeling, and my role is to follow that feeling with a piano improvisation that reflects the emotions that the person is expressing.'

The couple attribute their well-being to keeping active, socializing with family and the wider community, and, of course, love. It is a second marriage for both of them (their blended family includes his four children, her two sons and 18 grandchildren) and they never forget how precious their relationship is. In 1997 the husband underwent heart-bypass surgery, and in 1999 they both survived a terrible car crash.

Four times a year now they arrange a dance to celebrate the solstice and equinox, which have ancient Celtic significance and are closely connected to nature. During filming, we saw them celebrate the summer solstice with family and friends. They sat and sang in the garden, discussed the importance of the solstice, created artwork and poems, then took it in turns to do a dance to improvised music. It was a magical and unforgettable evening.

The husband later said, 'It reawakened in me a sense that there was still something we could do that was useful – perhaps helping folk to understand and make the best of growing older.'

'Be happy while ye'er leevin,
for ye'er a lang time deed.'
Scottish motto

10 WAYS TO IMPROVE WELL-BEING AS YOU GET OLDER

Eating well and taking regular exercise can add years to your active life, but having a positive attitude is the most important thing. Any of the ideas listed below will help you stay fit and happy as you get older, but always consult an expert or doctor before commencing strenuous exercise or diets you aren't used to.

1   Keep up with friends. A 2005 study by the University of Adelaide in Australia found that a strong network of friends and confidants significantly improves chances of survival in older people.

2   Count your blessings. Looking at the glass as half empty can obscure good feelings and lead to dwelling on small annoyances. Write down three good things that happen each day. For each item, ask, 'What did I have to do with it?'

3   Stock up on antioxidants. Vitamin C, vitamin E and beta-carotene, found in foods such as tomatoes, squash and carrots, protect cells from the effects of oxidation.

4   Enjoy being outdoors but make sure you use a daily sunscreen (SPF15 is recommended) on any exposed skin – even in winter. Harmful UV rays speed up the ageing process. Although people with olive and dark skin commonly age between five and 10 years more slowly than those with fair complexions and blue eyes, sunscreen is crucial for everyone.

5   Eat lots of fish. Saltwater varieties (salmon, tuna, cod and halibut) are highest in omega-3 fatty acids, which help keep the skin in good condition and also improve memory and mental skills.

6   Keep active. Gardening, amateur dramatics, playing with your grandchildren… they all count. To beat the bulge, try to do a minimum of four 20-minute sessions of cardiovascular exercise a week.

7   Pump iron to maintain bone density, increase muscle mass and fight osteoporosis. Lift a manageable weight, such as a bag of sugar, 10–12 times, and do this at least once a day.

8   Drink 8–10 glasses of water a day. Water decreases inflammation, helps you metabolize fat and flushes waste out of the body's cells.

9   Make love. In a 10-year study involving 3500 people, Dr David Weeks, a neuropsychologist at the Royal Edinburgh Hospital and author of *Secrets of the Superyoung*, found that men and women who have sex four or five times a week look more than 10 years younger than the average person, who has sex twice a week. Dr Weeks believes that the pleasure derived from sex is a crucial factor in preserving youth. 'It makes us happy and produces chemicals [endorphins and oxytocin] telling us so.'

10 Have a good laugh at least once a day!

Part 3

What Next?

Further Help

The aim of *How to Be Happy* is, of course, to boost your personal well-being. Our experts' Happiness Manifesto offers some remarkably successful ways to make more of friends, family and work. It is the first step in a journey towards making the most of your life.

But sometimes we can't get happier until we address the underlying source of our problems. By now you may have identified more complex, long-term issues that you want to resolve – from difficulties in your marriage to feeling tired all the time and unable to make decisions. Everyone gets low occasionally, but if you feel down a lot of the time you may be depressed. Depression is an illness and there are some good treatments that can help you feel better.

One of the most effective solutions is to talk to a qualified professional who can give you the space – and privacy – to explore these feelings. Counselling and therapy are often seen as the last refuge of the desperate, when in fact they should be seen as an investment in your own psychological well-being – in much the same way as physiotherapy is used to address physical problems. (According to the Mental Health Foundation, one in four people will suffer from some form of mental health problem during the course of a year.)

If you would like to follow up the issues raised in this book, there are a number of avenues open to you. The following information explains some of the main therapies on offer, how you should choose a therapist and what you can expect.

Talking therapies are the most widespread forms of therapy, and are used to treat conditions such as depression, anxiety and stress. In some cases they may be used in combination with antidepressants. Treatment usually consists of regular sessions (often weekly, but sometimes more frequently) between the therapist and patient(s).

These therapies often take one of three forms – counselling, cognitive behavioural therapy (CBT) or psychodynamic psychotherapy – and involve talking about your problems and possible solutions to them with a trained therapist. To fully realize the potential of these therapies, it is important that a client has a good relationship with the therapist and feels confident enough to talk openly and honestly.

Counselling

The aim of counselling is to provide one-on-one, non-judgemental support, and a forum in which you can talk through your problems with someone who is taking the

time to listen properly. Unlike CBT and psychodynamic therapy, counselling is usually used as a direct response to a specific event, such as bereavement, illness or unemployment. A course often runs for a limited period in weekly 50-minute sessions, and counsellors can have a wide range of training. There is also no legal necessity for them to be registered with a professional body.

How can I find a counsellor?

Counselling can often be accessed through your GP, through a voluntary organization, or sometimes through the workplace. Alternatively, lots of people see private counsellors, often through someone's personal recommendation.

Your GP will assess whether the method used (often limited to six or 12 sessions) is suitable, and will refer you elsewhere if not. If there's no practice counsellor, GPs may refer clients to a counselling agency, or to a private counsellor. Counselling psychologists (whose training is similar to that of many counsellors) or psychotherapists may also work as counsellors within a GP practice. They will be able to explain their professional background to you.

The GP or the practice counsellor can also help you decide whether it would be better for you to see a different mental health professional, such as a clinical psychologist, a psychotherapist, a psychiatrist or a member of the local Community Mental Health Team (CMHT).

Private counsellors. You can find advertisements for private counsellors in Yellow Pages, GP practices, alternative health clinics, libraries or online. Most will clearly state their professional credentials, and you should not be reluctant to ask about these or to verify them with the professional body concerned (see page 212).

Voluntary organizations. Otherwise known as charities, voluntary organizations rely heavily on donations and grants to help subsidize their work. Most voluntary-sector counselling organizations operate a sliding scale of fees, or offer 'affordable' counselling. Some voluntary organizations that are not devoted solely to counselling may also offer help on a particular issue, such as domestic violence.

Workplace counselling. Some employers operate an Employee Assistance Programme (EAP). EAPs employ their own counsellors, who usually have their own consulting rooms. As a rule, the counselling is free to clients because their workplace pays the EAP. It usually runs to six or 12 sessions. This can be useful for someone trying out counselling, who might decide to pursue something more open-ended afterwards. In other cases, a few sessions may be helpful in addressing an immediate problem. Many EAPs also offer telephone counselling.

What should I look for?

The British Association for Counselling and Psychotherapy (BACP, see page 212) is the umbrella organization for counselling. Most counsellors are registered with it, and many are accredited by it, but this is not yet a legal requirement. The profession is now working towards a voluntary agreement on minimum standards, ahead of statutory regulations that are due to be in place by 2008. At present, accreditation by the BACP is a guarantee that the counsellor has done a thorough training and has many hours of counselling experience. The BACP's *Resources Directory* lists counsellors by geographical area.

Non-BACP counsellors may well have undergone reputable training and be very experienced, but it's important to check this out with them, particularly if you look for a counsellor through an advertisement.

The BACP also lists counselling organizations. These are professional bodies, and sometimes training institutions, that will also be able to refer you to a suitable counsellor in your area, possibly after an assessment meeting.

Cognitive behavioural therapy

CBT works on the assumption that your feelings and behaviour can be changed if your thinking patterns are changed. Your past experiences and coping mechanisms may be having an adverse effect on your current life, so CBT aims to replace these with new, more useful techniques, correcting the learnt misconceptions. The therapy analyses destructive or unhelpful thought patterns and encourages you to practise new behaviour, which means that CBT can be used to treat a range of illnesses, from anxiety, panic and depression to eating disorders. Therapy may include keeping a journal of your negative thoughts, role playing, or trying a new approach to a part of your everyday life. A course of therapy may consist of up to 16 weekly sessions, and there can often be a long waiting list for it.

Psychodynamic psychotherapy

Like classic Freudian psychoanalysis, psychodynamic therapy is based on the idea of the unconscious mind, and sees thoughts, feelings and behaviours as manifestations of this inner drive. It encourages you to explore your feelings while trying to understand past influences, such as childhood and relationships. However, unlike psychoanalysis, psychodynamic therapy places a stronger emphasis on the role of the client as an active participant in the therapy. A course of therapy usually takes 20 weekly, one-hour sessions, but can continue for much longer. The aim is for the client to become more aware of how past experiences and current behaviours are linked. It is best suited to people who are actively interested in this form of self-exploration.

Other approaches

Within the three main strands of therapy described above there are a number of additional alternatives, some of which are described below.

Behavioural therapy encourages people to learn new ways of dealing with problems through gradual changes to their behaviour. Treatment usually involves clients keeping a diary to record their activities and progress as they are slowly exposed to feared situations. It is particularly effective in treating phobias and anxiety.

Family and relationship counselling can help. It can be useful for counselling to be held with a couple or family rather than one-on-one. The therapist encourages dialogue between the participants to help improve communication skills. Counselling in a group also allows the therapist to understand each individual's problems within the wider context of their family group.

Group therapy enables people with similar problems, such as self-harm, to be counselled together and this can often be rewarding. The style can differ, taking in any of the main forms of therapy but in a group setting. Those taking part can share experiences and insights, offer support to each other and discover new ways of coping with their problems.

Humanist therapy sees a person's interpersonal environment as a source of their emotional problems, so therapy is intended to act as a support and reinforcement of a person's sense of self-worth.

Psychoanalysis can be an intensive and long-term form of therapy in which a therapist encourages clients to explore whatever comes to mind and make links between events and feelings from earlier parts of their life.

Finding the right therapy and therapist for you

If you are having treatment under the NHS you may not have much choice in your therapist, or, indeed, the therapy on offer. However, if you choose to pay for treatment, there are several key considerations. First, is the treatment you want available in your area? Counselling is widely accessible from a number of different sources, including GPs' surgeries, but psychodynamic psychotherapy and CBT are less widespread. The type of therapy you opt for often comes down to how comfortable you are with it; there is no single 'best' approach to treating depression. The key is to find a therapy and a therapist you are comfortable with.

Whatever approach you choose, do make sure your therapist is properly accredited and has ongoing training. It is both sensible (and expected) to ask about his or her training, experience or approach, and do not be afraid to try a number of different therapists before settling on one.

Alternative or complementary therapies

If talking therapy is not what you want right now, you could always try one of the many types of alternative therapies. Most have a wide range of applications, and some have a good success rate with emotional and mental problems. Aromatherapy, exercise, hypnotherapy, meditation and yoga have all been shown to have some effect in reducing stress, tension and anxiety, and in alleviating mental distress. There are numerous other alternative or complementary therapies and approaches to trying to improve your mood and happiness levels. Some are outlined below, or for further information visit your local library or consult the Internet.

Acupuncture can have a positive effect for some people diagnosed with schizophrenia. **Applied relaxation** uses a therapist to teach a method of relaxation that can be practised at home daily to relieve muscle tension and stress. This can also be used alongside other treatments and therapies. You can improve your **diet** – research into nutritional and dietary medicine has demonstrated that food sensitivities may cause psychiatric symptoms, while a lack of folic acid has been associated with depression and schizophrenia. In addition, supplementing certain amino acids has been shown to relieve depression. **Herbalism** provides many herbs used to treat emotional problems; among these are St John's Wort (hypericum) which has been linked to the relief of mild to moderately severe depression. **Homeopathy** has been shown to help people with severe mental health problems to recover if used over long periods and if used alongside conventional antipsychotic medication. **Massage** has been shown to reduce levels of anxiety, stress and depression in some people. **Neurolinguistic programming (NLP)** is based on the idea that life experiences inform the way you see the world. Clients are helped to change their behaviour to improve communication and happiness. **Reflexology** has been shown to aid relaxation, relieve stress and restore energy. It can also help to reduce the side effects of psychotropic medication (drugs to treat mental problems), and can moderate the highs and lows of mood swings.

Useful Addresses

COMMUNITY ACTION

Action Earth
CSV Environment
St Peter's College
College Road
Saltley
Birmingham B8 3TE
Tel: 0121 328 7455
Website: www.actionearth.org.uk

Community Action Network
1st Floor
Downstream Building
1 London Bridge
London SE1 9BG
Tel: 020 7785 6204
Website: www.can-online.org.uk
A national charity developing 750 social enterprises across the UK.

Community Service Volunteers (CSV)
237 Pentonville Road
London N1 9NJ
Tel: 020 7278 6601 (switchboard)
   020 7643 1385 (Retired and Senior
   Volunteer Programme – RSVP)
Website: www.csv.org.uk
The UK's largest volunteer and training organization, working with 129,000 volunteers. If short of time, volunteer for CSV 'Make a Difference Day' every October.

Do It
3rd Floor
2–3 Upper Street
Islington
London N1 0PQ
Tel: 020 7226 8008
Website: www.do-it.org.uk
A government-sponsored scheme to promote voluntary work both in the UK and overseas.

Employee volunteering scheme
(organized through CSV)
Tel: 020 7643 1427
Website: www.csv.org.uk

Full-time volunteering
(organized through CSV)
Tel: 0800 374 991
Website: www.csv.org.uk
Offers opportunities within the UK for 4–12 months.

Mentoring and Befriending Foundation
1st Floor
Charles House
Albert Street
Eccles
Manchester M30 0PW
Tel: 0161 787 8600
Website: www.mandbf.org.uk

National Council for Voluntary Organizations
Regent's Wharf
8 All Saints Street
London N1 9RL
Tel: 020 7713 6161
Website: www.ncvo-vol.org.uk
Works with and for the voluntary sector in England by providing information, advice and support, and by representing the views of the sector to government and policy-makers.

New Economics Foundation
3 Jonathan Street
London SE11 5NH
Tel: 020 7820 6300
Website: www.neweconomics.org

The Scarman Trust
Kemp House
152–160 City Road
London EC1V 2NP
Tel: 020 7689 6366
Website: www.thescarmantrust.org

Student Volunteering England
Oxford House
Derbyshire Street
London E2 6HG
Tel: 0800 0182 146
Website: www.studentvolunteering.org.uk
Offers an enormous range of projects, including work with children, young people, ex-offenders, the homeless, people with disabilities, older people, animals and the environment.

Volunteering England
Branches in London and Birmingham
Tel: 0845 305 6979
Website: www.volunteering.org.uk
Works across the voluntary, public and private sectors to raise the profile of volunteering as a powerful force for change.

Weekend volunteering in London/ Go London
Tel: 020 7643 1341
Website: www.csv.org.uk/Volunteer/ Part-time/GO

DIET

The following organizations all report on research conducted into the links between diet and health.

Action Against Allergy
PO Box 278
Twickenham
Middlesex TW1 4QQ
Tel: 020 8892 2711
Website: www.actionagainstallergy.co.uk

Allergy UK/British Allergy Foundation
Deepdene House
30 Bellegrove Road
Welling
Kent DA16 3YP
Tel: 020 8303 8525
Website: www.allergyuk.org

Brain Bio Centre
Carters Yard
London SW18 4JR
Tel: 020 8871 9261
Website: www.mentalhealthproject.com
Directed by leading nutritionist and psychologist Patrick Holford, this clinic specializes in helping people with mental health concerns, from depression to memory loss, using optimum nutrition principles.

British Association of Nutritional Therapists
27 Old Gloucester Street
London WC1N 3XX
Tel: 08706 061284
Website: www.bant.org.uk

British Society for Allergy Environmental and Nutritional Medicine
PO Box 7
Knighton
Powys LD7 1WT
Tel: 01547 550 378
Website: www.bsaenm.org

Depression Alliance
35 Westminster Bridge Road
London SE1 7JB
Tel: 0845 123 2320
Website: www.depressionalliance.org

Eating Disorders Association (EDA)
103 Prince of Wales Road
Norwich NR1 1DW
Tel: 0870 770 3256
Website: www.edauk.com

Food and Behaviour Research
PO Box 6066
Nairn
Scotland IV12 4YN
Tel: 01667 456972
Website: www.fabresearch.org

The Food and Mood Project
PO Box Lewes
East Sussex BN7 2GN
Tel: 01273 478108
Website: www.foodandmood.org
A web-based, user-led, dietary self-help service that provides resources for individuals and groups. Backed by Mind, the UK's leading mental health charity, it is led by former nutritional therapist Amanda Geary and founded on her first-hand experience of recovering from ill-health using dietary self-help.

Foods Matter
5 Lawn Road
London NW3 2XS
Tel: 020 7722 2866
Website: www.foodsmatter.com

Hyperactive Children's Support Group
71 Whyke Lane
Chichester
West Sussex PO19 7PD
Tel: 01243 551313
Website: www.hacsg.org.uk

Manic Depression Fellowship
Castle Works
21 St George's Road
London SE1 6ES
Tel: 08456 340 540
Website: www.mdf.org.uk

Mind
15–19 Broadway
London E15 4BQ
Tel: 020 8519 2122
Website: www.mind.org.uk

Restorative Health Company Limited
Outalong
Lower Broad Oak Road
West Hill
Ottery St Mary
Devon EX11 1XH
Tel: 01404 815992
Website: www.rehealth.com

Schizophrenia Association of Great Britain
Bryn Hyfryd
The Crescent
Bangor
Gwynedd LL57 2AG
Tel: 01248 354048
Website: www.sagb.co.uk

PETS

Pets as Therapy
3 Grange Farm Cottages
Wycombe Road
Saunderton
Princes Risborough
Bucks HP27 9NS
Tel: 0870 240 1239
Website: www.petsastherapy.org
A national charity founded in 1983, PAT provides therapeutic visits to hospitals, hospices, nursing and care homes, special needs schools and a variety of other venues by volunteers with their own friendly dogs and cats (all temperament-tested and vaccinated). More than 4000 dogs and 90 cats visit 100,000 people every week.

Battersea Dogs Home
4 Battersea Park Road
London SW8 4AA
Tel: 020 7622 3626
Website: www.dogshome.org
If it's impractical for you to look after a pet of your own, Battersea Dogs Home has a volunteer scheme that allows members of the public to become 'socializers', visiting and playing with the animals.

MENTAL HEALTH

Mental Health Foundation
Sea Containers House
20 Upper Ground
London SE1 9QB
Tel: 020 7803 1100
Website: www.mentalhealth.org.uk

OR

Mental Health Foundation
Merchants House
30 George Square
Glasgow G2 1EG
Tel: 0141 572 0125
Website: www.mentalhealth.org.uk

Mind
15–19 Broadway,
London E15 4BQ
Tel: 020 8519 2122
Website: www.mind.org.uk

NHS
The website: www.besttreatments.co.uk has information on therapies and treatments available through the NHS.

COUNSELLING
Although there is no legal requirement for counsellors to be registered, there are several bodies with which they can be registered. These include:

Association of Counsellors and Psychotherapists in Primary Care
Queensway House
Queensway
Bognor Regis
West Sussex PO21 1QT
Tel: 01243 870701
Website: www.cpc-online.co.uk

British Association for Counselling and Psychotherapy (BACP)
BACP House
35–37 Albert Street
Rugby
Warks CV21 2SG
Tel: 0870 443 5252
Website: www.bacp.co.uk

Counselling Ltd
39 Warwick Road
Atherton
Manchester M46 9TA
Tel: 01942 894 885
Website: www.counselling.ltd.uk

Institute for Counselling and Personal Development Trust
Interpoint
20–24 York Street
Belfast BT15 1AQ
Tel: 02890 330 996
Email: icpd@btconnect.com

RELATIONSHIP COUNSELLING
Couple Psychotherapy Service
(deals with intense marital conflict)
Tel: 0870 902 4878
Website: www.couplepsychotherapy.co.uk
This is a confidential answering service. If you leave a message with your name and telephone number, a therapist will return your call within one working day.

Relate
(short-term counselling)
11 Little Church Street
Rugby
Warks CV21 3AW
Tel: 01788 573241
Helpline: 0845 130 4010
(9.30–4.30, Mon–Fri)
Website: www.relate.org.uk

Tavistock Centre for Couple Relationships
(deals with serious marital conflict)
120 Belsize Lane
London NW3 5BA
Tel: 020 7447 3724
Website: www.tccr.org.uk

COGNITIVE BEHAVIOURAL THERAPY
British Psychological Society
St Andrews House
48 Princess Road East
Leicester LE1 7DR
Tel: 0116 254 9568
Website: www.bps.org.uk

British Association for Behavioural and Cognitive Psychotherapies (BABCP)
Globe Centre
PO Box 9
Accrington
Lancs BB5 2GD
Tel: 01254 875277
Website: www.babcp.com

PSYCHODYNAMIC PSYCHOTHERAPY
British Confederation of Psychotherapists (BCP)
37 Mapesbury Road
London NW2 4HJ
Tel: 020 8830 5173
Website: www.bcp.org.uk

United Kingdom Council for Psychotherapy (UKCP)
167–169 Great Portland Street
London W1W 5PF
Tel: 020 7436 3002
Website: www.psychotherapy.org.uk

SPIRITUAL HELP

For more information on Transcendental Meditation, contact:

Transcendental Meditation
Website: www.t-m.org.uk
National telephone enquiries:
08705 143733

Yoga and Meditation
For a listing of retreat centres and holidays search:
Website: www.yogaholidays.net

Retreat Association
The Central Hall
256 Bermondsey Street
London SE1 3UH
Tel: 020 7357 7736 or
        0845 456 1429
Website: www.retreats.org.uk
A Christian organization, founded in 1913, to give women factory workers a break. It has more than 200 centres throughout the UK.

Sources and Notes

All references are in order of mention within each chapter.

The following books are referred to in full on first mention. Thereafter they are abbreviated thus:
AH – *Authentic Happiness: Using the New Positive Psychology to Realise Your potential for Lasting Fulfillment*, Martin P. Seligman
Flow – *Flow: The Classic Work on How to Achieve Happiness*, Mihaly Csikszentmihalyi
Happiness – *Happiness: Lessons from a New Science*, Richard Layard
MHP – *Making Happy People: The Nature of Happiness and Its Origins in Childhood*, Paul Martin
RC – *The Relationship Cure: A 5-step Guide to Strengthening Your Marriage, Family and Friendships*, John M. Gottman

Happiness Manifesto: More information can be obtained from the New Economics Foundation, which has also published a well-being manifesto for government and policy-makers.

CHAPTER 1: What Is Happiness?
• A study by Professor Andrew Oswald at the University of Warwick looked at 9000 families in Britain throughout the 1990s, observing the impact on those who enjoyed substantial windfalls. It found that a windfall of less than £1 million is unlikely to have a lasting effect on a person's happiness.
• 'The Biology of Joy', Michael D. Lemonick, *Time* magazine, 17 January 2005
• 'The New Science of Happiness', Claudia Wallis, *Time* magazine, 17 January 2005
• 'Emotion in the Body Mapped by the Mind', M. Bradley, *News in Science*, ABC Science Online, 22 September 2000
• *Happiness: Lessons from a New Science*, Richard Layard (Allen Lane, 2005)
• 'Endorphins Q&A', Nathaniel Altman, www.healingsprings.com
• *Making Happy People: The Nature of Happiness and Its Origins in Childhood*, Paul Martin (Fourth Estate, 2005)
• 'Happy', Dorothy Rowe, *Observer*, 10 December 2000
• *Authentic Happiness*, Martin P. Seligman (Nicholas Brealey Publishing, 2003)
• 'Dr Feelgood on the Science of Happiness: The Power of Optimism', Dr Nick Baylis, *The Times*, 23 April 2005
• 'The Family Report 2003: Choosing Happiness', Kate Stanley, Laura Edwards & Becky Hatch (commissioned by Lever Fabergé). A survey of 1500 men and women aged 20–40 across Britain
• 'The Secrets of Happiness', David G. Myers, *Psychology Today*, 1992 (see also www.davidmyers.org)
• World Database of Happiness, 'Distributional Findings in Nations', R. Veenhoven, Erasmus University, Rotterdam, 2005
• 'The Pleasure Seekers', Helen Phillips, *New Scientist*, 11 October 2003

CHAPTER 2: Are You Happy?
• Survey of 1000 people by advertising agency Publicis, April 2005
• Suicide and job satisfaction statistics from 'Happiness and Economic Performance', Andrew J. Oswald, *Economic Journal*, April 1997
• *AH*
• *The Optimistic Child*, Martin Seligman (Houghton Mifflin, 1995)
• 'Happy', Dorothy Rowe, *Observer*, 10 December 2000
• *Britain on the Couch: Why We're Unhappier than We Were in the 1950s – Despite Being Richer*, Oliver James (Arrow, 1998)
• 'The Power of Optimism', Dr Nick Baylis, *The Times*, 23 April 2005
• 'The Secrets of Happiness', David G. Myers, *Psychology Today*, July 1992

CHAPTER 3: The Science of Happiness
• *AH*
• 'The Biology of Joy', Michael D. Lemonick, *Time* magazine, 17 January 2005
• 'Happy Days', Alison Stein Weliner & David Adox, *Psychology Today*, May/June 2000
• Seligman interview – How to be Happy, Ian Sample, *Guardian*, 19 November 2003
• Focus: Think Happy (Seligman), John Elliott, *Sunday Times*, 23 November 2003
• *Flow: The Classic Work on How to Achieve Happiness*, Mihaly Csikszentmihalyi (Rider, 2002)
• 'Our Bias Towards Past, Present or Future', Dr Nick Baylis, *The Times*, 10 April 2004
• '11 Steps to a Better Brain', Kate Douglas & Alison George, *New Scientist*, 28 May 2005

CHAPTER 4: The Friends Maintenance Programme
• 'What Are Friends For?', Jenni Russell, *Guardian*, 24 January 2005
• *MHP*
• 'It's Friends not Family Who'll Help You Live Longer', Jenny Hope, *Daily Mail*, 16 June 2005
• 'Fewer Friendships at Work', *Manchester Evening News*, 28 May 2004 Survey of 500 UK staff by recruitment firm Pertemps
• 'Too Little Friendship?', Andrew Oswald, *Sunday Times*, April 2004
• 'Friends Reunited', Lindsay Baker (and quoting Philip Hodson), *Guardian*, 20 March 2005 (© Guardian Newspapers Limited)
• 'Let's Say It Loud: We're Single... and Proud', Liz Hoggard, *Observer*, 1 February 2004
• 'Very Happy People', by Martin Seligman & Ed Diener, *Psychological Science*, Vol. 13, 2002, pp. 81–84
• *Flow*
• 'The Funny Thing about Laughter', *Time* magazine, 17 January 2005
• *The Pursuit of Happiness*, David G. Myers (Avon Books, 1993), abridged in *Psychology Today*, July/August 1993
• 'Let Your Hands Talk', John Naish, *The Times*, 14 May 2005
• 'Oxytocin increases trust in humans', M. Karsfeld and E. Fehr, *Nature*, Vol. 435, 2 June 2005
• 'Acting Chirpy Makes You Happy', Bob Beale, *News in Science*, ABC Science Online, 24 February 2003

CHAPTER 5: Can't Buy Me Happiness
• 'Money and Happiness', Polly Toynbee, *Guardian*, 7 March 2003
• 'The True Cost of Living', Gerard Seenan, *Guardian*, 26 April 2005
• Cadbury happiness survey of 1050 adults in the UK, led by psychologist Dr Dylan Evans, 2002
• 'Now It's the Northerners Who Can't Stop Flashing Their Cash', Carol Midgely, *The Times*, 28 April 2005
• *MHP*
• 'Happiness? Who Needs It? Not the Poor Employee, It Would Seem. But Contented Workers Do Make for Better Companies', Simon Caulkin, *Observer* 10 April, 2005
• Prudential Insurance Company report, 2005
• *Gaming Magazine*, 17 April 2002

• Money, Sex and Happiness: An Empirical Study, David G. Blanchflower, Andrew J. Oswald, *Scandinavian Journal of Economics*, 2004
• 'Britain's Diet: Chocolate and Credit', Lucy Ward & Rupert Jones, *Guardian*, 9 June 2005
• 'Annual Cost of a Child's Toys', Polly Curtis, *Guardian*, 10 June 2005
• 'Seven Deadly Sins', *Daily Mail*, 18 June 2005
• 'Happiness Fights off Colds', Hazel Morris, *New Scientist*, 28 July 2003
• 'Reasons to Be Cheerful', Bob Holmes, Kurt Kleiner, Kate Douglas and Michael Bond (using material from Robert Frank and Andrew Oswald), *New Scientist*, 4 October 2003
• 'The Real Truth about Money', Gregg Easterbrook, *Time* magazine, 17 January 2005
• *How Not to Buy Happiness*, Robert H. Frank (Daedalus, 2004)
• 'Now It's a Fact: Money Doesn't Buy Happiness', Matthew Herper, *Forbes* magazine, 23 September 2004
• 'Happiness and Economic Performance', Andrew J. Oswald, *Economic Journal*, Vol. 107, November 1997
• 'The Pursuit of Happiness', Michael Bond (using material from H. Roy Kaplan), *New Scientist*, 4 October 2003
• National Bureau of Economic Research, Cambridge, Massachusetts, USA
• *MHP*
• 'To Do or To Have? That is the Question', Leaf Van Boven and Thomas Gilovich, *Journal of Personality & Social Psychology*, Vol. 85, 2004

CHAPTER 6: Happy at Work?
• 'The Joy of Work', Nick Isles, Work Foundation survey of over 1000 people in June 2004
• 'Employee Positive Emotion and Favourable Outcomes at the Workplace', B. Straw, R. Sutton & L. Pelled (1994), *Organization Science* 5, pp. 51–71
• *Happiness*
• *MHP*
• 'Money, Sex and Happiness: An Empirical Study', David G. Blanchflower Dartmouth College, Hanover, USA, and Andrew J. Oswald, Warwick University, using recent data on a sample of 16,000 adult Americans. This showed that commuting to and from work produced the lowest levels of psychological well-being.
• 'Working Too Hard Piles on the Pounds', Jenny Hope, *Daily Mail*, 14 May 2005
• *Happy Mondays: Putting the Pleasure Back into Work*, Richard Reeves (Momentum, 2001)
• 'The Rewards of Work', Nick Baylis, *The Times*, 30 April 2005
• 'Work It Out', Jenni Russell, *Guardian*, 26 January 2005
• 'Flexible Working and Thinking', Sean Coughlan, *Guardian*, 21 May 2005
• 'Would You Prefer This... or This?', Ben Summerskill, *Observer*, 20 April 2003

• A study by MORI on work–life balance in 2003 for the DTI showed over four in 10 (43 per cent) thought that working shorter hours would negatively affect their job security, and even larger proportions thought a range of flexible arrangements would affect their career prospects.
• 'What Workers Want', Open University Survey compiled by Professor Andrew Oswald (www.open2.net/economics/workers/workhap.html#)
• 'Happy at Work?', MORI survey conducted for Equal Opportunities Commission, 1 November 2004
• 'Diversity Matters', MORI survey conducted for the *Guardian* and TMP Worldwide, 13 October 2003
• 'Small Is Beautiful for UK Workforce', Johann Tasker, *Personnel Today*, 5 October 2004
• *Flow*
• 'Happiness Is More Important Than Financial Success', *Personnel Today*, 14 October 2004
• UK commute 'longest in Europe', BBC News, 22 July 2003
• 'Cake Doesn't Cut It in UK Workplace', online recruitment magazine, 1 October 2004 (www.onrec.com)
• Hairdressers 'happiest at work', BBC News, 4 March 2004
• Long hours a 'national disgrace', BBC News, 4 February 2002
• 'Long Hours Can Work for All', Tim Randles, employment lawyer, Laytons, BBC News, 24 February 2005
• Britons 'dissatisfied and dull at work', Alan Jones, *Manchester Evening News*, 3 March 2005
• 'How to Ride the Work/Life Seesaw', Sarah Jagger (www.Channel4.com/4money)
• Working 'a joy' for most Britons, *Manchester Evening News*, 29 July 2004
• '11 Steps to a Better Brain', Kate Douglas & Alison George, *New Scientist*, 28 May 2005
• 'Working in a Dead-end Job Can Endanger Your Health', Dan Parkinson, *Daily Mail*, 8 June 2005

CHAPTER 7: Love Makes the World Go Round
• 'Social Allergies in Romantic Relationships', *Personal Relationships*, Vol. 12, No. 2, June 2005 pp. 273–95. This study, led by Michael Cunningham at Louisville University, Kentucky, on behalf of the US government's health research arm, charted the end of 160 relationships and looked at the causes. It also examined links between bad habits and relationship success or failure in another 274 individuals.
• *The Relationship Cure: A 5-step Guide to Strengthening Your Marriage, Family and Friendships*, John M. Gottman (Three Rivers Press, 2002)
• 'If You Don't Understand the Emotions This Woman Is Showing You Must Be a Man', Roger Dobson, *Independent on Sunday*, 5 June 2005
• Re-examining adaptation and the set point model of happiness: reactions to

changes in marital status, by Richard E. Lucas, Andrew E. Clark, Yannis Georgellis, Ed Diener, *Journal of Personality and Social Psychology*, Vol. 84, p. 527, March 2003
• Figures compiled in 2005 by the Government Actuary's Department show the number of couples who get married in England and Wales is set to fall by 10 per cent in the next 25 years. They also predict that cohabiting couples will virtually double from 2 million to 3.8 million within 25 years. The number of people who have never married is also expected to rise by 2031.
• In 2003 the Cabinet Office released figures quantifying major life events in terms of annual salary equivalents: losing job = minus £276,000; getting married = plus £72,000; getting separated = minus £132,000; death of spouse = minus £168,000.
• 'Money, Sex and Happiness: An Empirical Study', David G. Blanchflower Dartmouth College, Hanover, USA, and Andrew J. Oswald, Warwick University, using recent data on a sample of 16,000 adult Americans.
• *Happiness*
• *AH*
• *Flow*
• 'Is There a Hitch?', Joel Stein, *Time* magazine, 17 January 2003
• *The Sex Inspectors Master Class*, Tracey Cox and Michael Alvear (Michael Joseph, 2005)
• 'Truly, Deeply, Madly', John Naish, *The Times*, 4 June 2005
• 'Work in Progress', Alice Wignall, *Guardian*, 31 May 2005
• Based on data from 10,641 adults in the 1996 national survey of mental health in Australia, psychologist Dr David de Vaus from La Trobe University in Melbourne reported in 2002 that both men and women are happier if they are married.
• 'Marriage Makes You a Bit Happier – for a While', *News in Science*, ABC Science Online, 17 March 2003
• 'Lone Danger', Jill Phillip, *Observer*, 28 May 2004
• Marriage and happiness survey from *Happiness: Facts and Myths*, Michael Eysenck (Psychology Press, 1990)

CHAPTER 8: Sexual Happiness
• 'Global Sex Survey', Durex, 2004. More than 350,000 people from 41 countries took part in the world's largest ever survey of sexual attitudes and behaviour.
• 'It's Little Things That Wreck Romance', Roger Dobson & Lois Rogers, 15 May 2005
• 'Endorphins Q&A', Nathaniel Altman, www.healingsprings.com, 26 June 2002
• 'Semen Makes Women Happy', Raj Persaud, *New Scientist*, 26 June 2002
• 'Sniffing Out Mr Right', Emma Gold, *Independent on Sunday*, 29 May 2005
• 'Low Libido – or Is Your Man Simply Bad in Bed?', Michelle Kirsch, *The Times*, 2 June 2005

• *Supersex*, Tracey Cox (Dorling Kindersley, 2002)
• *Pocket Supersex*, Tracey Cox (Dorling Kindersley, 2004)
• *The Sex Inspectors Master Class*, Tracey Cox and Michael Alvear (Michael Joseph, 2005)

CHAPTER 9: Happier Families
• The family facts are taken from the 2001 Census, Office of National Statistics; *Expenditure and Food Survey*, Office of National Statistics, June 2005; *Living in Britain 2002*, Office of National Statistics, 2004.
• 'What Kind of Parent Are You?', Paul Martin, *Guardian*, 23 February 2005
• *Happiness*
• *MHP*
• *RC*
• www.natashakerr.co.uk
• *AH*

CHAPTER 10: How to Make Happy Children
• 'What Kind of Parent Are You?', Paul Martin, *Guardian*, 23 February 2005
• *Happiness*
• *MHP*
• 'Why Children Need Three Portions of Play a Day', (using material by Doug Cole), *Daily Mail*, 28 May 2005
• 'Children's Attitudes Towards Parenting', a study of 256 middle and secondary state schools, conducted by the National Family & Parenting Institute, 2000
• *RC*
• 'The Importance of Resilience', Christine Gorman, *Time* magazine, 17 January 2005
• *AH*

CHAPTER 11: Eat Yourself Happy
• 'ONUK Survey', Institute for Optimum Nutrition, 2004 (www.ion.ac.uk)
• Busy Britons 'eating on the move', BBC News, 23 January 2004
• 'The Time of Our Lives', Adrian Turpin, *Independent*, 28 May 2005
• *Optimum Nutrition Cookbook*, Patrick Holford & Judy Ridgway (Piatkus Books, 2000)
• 'Low-carb State of Mind', Brenda Goodman, *Psychology Today*, 4 June 2004
• *The Food and Mood Handbook*, Amanda Geary (Thorsons, 2001)
• *Potatoes Not Prozac*, Kathleen DesMaisons (Pocket Books, 2001)
• *MIND Guide to Food and Mood*, Amanda Geary (MIND, 2004)
• *Flow*, 'The joy of tasting', ch. 5, p. 113
• 'Food and Mood', Carol Ottley, *Nursing Standard*, Vol. 15, 27 September 2000
• 'Comparison of Nutrient Intake among Depressed and Non-depressed Individuals', L. Christensen & S. Somers, *International Journal of Eating Disorders*, Vol. 20, issue 1, 1996
• 'Alterations in Mood after Changing to a Low-fat Diet', A.S. Wells et al, *British Journal of Nutrition*, Vol. 79, issue 1, pp. 23–30, 1998
• Study led by Alexandra Richardson

at Oxford University's Laboratory of Physiology, reported in US journal *Pediatrics*, May 2005
• 'Why It's Time We Faced Fats', Felicity Lawrence, *Guardian*, 5 May 2005
• 'Dietary Folate and Depressive Symptoms Are Associated in Middle-aged Finnish Men', T. Tolmunen et al, *Journal of Nutrition*, Vol. 133, issue 10, October 2003
• Ice cream research by Unilever, 2005, using ice cream made by Walls, which it owns
• 'Omega-3 Fatty Acids in Bipolar Disorder: A Preliminary Double-blind, Placebo-controlled Trial', A.L. Stoll et al, *Archives of General Psychiatry*, 56, pp. 407–12, 1999

CHAPTER 12: Being Happy Makes You Healthy
• Heart health facts from British Heart Foundation and the British Cardiac Patients Association
• 'The Biology of Joy', Michael D. Lemonick, *Time* magazine, 17 January 2005
• 'Doctors Who Are Happy to Make More Accurate Liver Diagnosis', Rosenzweig & Young, 1991
• Survey by advertising agency Publicis, April 2005
• Study conducted by University College, London, published online in *Proceedings of the National Academy of Sciences (PNAS)*, 18 April 2005
• 'Happiness Helps People Stay Healthy', Shaoni Bhattacharya, *New Scientist*, 18 April 2005
• 'Happiness: Nature's Tonic for a Healthier Life', David Adam, *Guardian*, 19 April 2005
• 'The Nun Study', D. Danner, D. Snowdon & W. Friesen, *Journal of Personality and Social Psychology*, 80, pp. 804–13, 2001
• *Counting Sheep: The Science and Pleasures of Sleep and Dreams*, Paul Martin (Flamingo, 2003)
• '11 Steps to a Better Brain', Kate Douglas & Alison George, *New Scientist*, 28 May 2005
• 'World Values Survey', MORI, 1997, in *The Good Life*, by Robert M. Worcester (DEMOS, 1998)
• *AH*
• *MHP*
• 'Sick? But I'm Just Not the Type', Jerome Burn, *Independent*, 14 June 2004 'Can Stress Help You Stay Healthy and Live Longer?', Julie Wheldon, *Daily Mail*, 9 May 2005
• 'The Stress Buster', Harriet Griffey, *Guardian*, 10 May 2005
• 'Smile to Keep the Doctor Away', Jerome Burn, *The Times*, 22 April 2005
• 'Why Texting Harms Your IQ', Michael Horsnell, *The Times*, 22 April 2005
• Facts about alcohol and drugs taken from 'Tobacco, Alcohol, Drugs and Mental Health, 2000', Office of National Statistics; 'British Crime Survey 2003/04'; 'General Household Survey, 2003/04', Office of National Statistics

• 'Survey on the Food Mood of the Nation', Sara McCluskey, eating disorders consultant for the Priory Group, 23 August 2003
• 'Young Free and Fat – A Case Study', New Economics Foundation, 2003
• 'National Diet and Nutrition Survey', Office of National Statistics, 24 January 2004
• 'The Paths to Pleasure', *Time* magazine, 17 January 2004
• 'Food and Mood', Carol Ottley, *Nursing Standard*, Vol. 15, 27 September 2000
• 'For 20 Years Dr Ruut Veenhoven Has Been Obsessed with Our Well-being', Dr Feelgood, *Independent*, 3 January 2005
• 'Ecstasy – Once Used always Depressed?', Lynn Taurah & Dr Chris Chandler at British Psychological Society Annual Conference, 15 March 2002
• 'Prevalence of Mental Disorders by Smoking, Drinking and Cannabis Use among Children Aged 11–15 Years', Office of National Statistics, 1999
• 'The Joy of Work', Nick Isles, Work Foundation, June 2004 – a survey of over 1000 people
• 'Warnings Go Up in Smoke', Dr Thomas Stuttaford, *The Times*, 2 June 2005
• 'Addiction Is a Brain Disease, and It Matters', Alan I. Leshner, *Science*, Vol. 278, 3 October 1997

CHAPTER 13: Exercise: Why a Pedometer Beats a Vibrator
• 'World Values Survey', MORI, 1997, in *The Good Life*, by Robert M. Worcester (DEMOS, 1998)
• '11 Steps to a Better Brain', Kate Douglas & Alison George, *New Scientist*, 28 May 2005
• 'Endorphins Q&A', Nathaniel Altman, www.healingsprings.com
• 'The Influence of Exercise on Mental Health', Daniel M. Landers, *PCPFS*
• *Research Digest*, Series 2, p. 10, 2002
• *The Mind Guide to Physical Activity*, Trudi Grant (MIND, 2001)
• SMILE (Standard Medical Intervention and Long-term Exercise) involved 156 patients aged between 50 and 77, who had a major depressive disorder, *Journal of Ageing and Physical Activity*, January 2001.
• 'You're Sitting Pretty', John Naish, *The Times*, 21 May 2005
• 'We Lose Power at 30', John Naish, *The Times*, 16 April 2005
• 'People Think a Bigger Belly Is a Sign of Wealth', James Meikle, *Guardian*, 16 May 2005
• Walking statistics supplied by Sport England (www.sportengland.org)

CHAPTER 14: Happiness Is Pet-shaped
• 'The Pet Connection: Pets As a Conduit for Social Capital', Lisa Wood, Bille Giles-Corti & Max Bulsara, *Social Science & Medicine*, Vol. 61, Issue 6, September 2005
• 'What Pets Bring to the Party', Sara Song, *Time* magazine, 17 January 2005

Pet owners feel less afraid of being a victim of crime when walking with a dog or sharing a residence with a dog (Serpel, 1990).

CHAPTER 15: Happy Holidays
• *The Art of Travel*, Alain de Botton (Penguin, 2003)
• 'Good Companion or Bad Karma?', Rob Penn, *The Times*, 25 June 2005
• Reprinted by permission of Sage Publications from 'A Study of the Impact of the Expectation of a Holiday on an Individual's Sense of Well-being', D. Gilbert & J. Abdullah, *Journal of Vacation Marketing*, Vol. 8, issue 4, pp. 352–61, September 2002 (© Sage Publications 2002)
• 'An Exploratory Study of the Relationship between Healthy Living and Travel Behaviour', A. Zaher & A. Hallob, thesis, 1999
• 'No Holiday Cash? Hide at Home', *Saturday Telegraph*, 21 May 2005
• 'Beating Holiday Stress', Linda Whittern, *Guardian*
• 'This Summer, I Shall Mostly Be Taking a Balcony Holiday...', Liz Hoggard, *Observer*, 10 August 2003
• '33 per cent of workers refuse to take all their holiday', *Daily Mail*, 15 July 2005

CHAPTER 16: Happiness and Community
• *MHP*
• 'For the Good Neighbour Policy, Look Northwards', Kirsty Scott, *Guardian*, 10 June 2005
• 'Life Satisfaction Report 2003', Nick Donovan & David Halpern for the Cabinet Office. 'It has been estimated in the USA that going to monthly club meetings, monthly volunteering, monthly entertaining or bi-weekly church attendance each have the happiness equivalent of a doubling of money income.'
• '33 per cent of workers refuse to take all their holiday', *Daily Mail*, 15 July 2005
• 'Laid-back Britain Tolerates Everything Except the State', John Elliott, *Sunday Times*, 10 April 2005
• 'World Values Survey 2005' compiled using research from the London School of Economics
• *Bowling Alone*, Robert D. Putnam (Simon & Schuster, 2001) www.bowlingalone.com
• 'Reasons to Be Cheerful', Bob Holmes *et al* (using material from Ed Diener), *New Scientist*, 4 October 2003
• *AH*
• *Flow*
• 'The Biology of Joy', Michael D. Lemonick, *Time* magazine, 17 January 2005

CHAPTER 17: Smile and Feel Better
• Facts about smiling taken from www.raisingkids.co.uk
• 'One Smile Can Make You Feel

a Million Dollars', Alastair Jamieson, *Scotsman*, 4 March 2005
• 'Laughter Is Still the Best Medicine', Dr Robert Holden, *Daily Express*, November 2004
• 'Smile, It's Good for You', BUPA health information, www.bupa.co.uk
• 'The Funny Thing about Laughter', Jeffrey Kluger, *Time* magazine, 17 January 2005
• *AH*
• 'Face Facts: Female Intuition is a Myth', Jayne Atherton, *Metro*, 12 April 2005

CHAPTER 18: Laughter: the Sound of Happiness
• 'Laughter Survey' conducted on 1000 adults around Britain by holiday firm Ocean Village, May 2005
• 'Laughing Matters: Humour and Health', Yori Gidron, University of Southampton, September 2004
• Laughter 'boosts blood vessels', BBC News, 7 March 2005
• 'Laughter Is Still the Best Medicine', Dr Robert Holden, *Daily Express*, November 2004
• 'The Funny Thing about Laughter', Jeffrey Kluger, *Time* magazine, 17 January 2005
• 'Highest Functions of Brain Produce Lowest Form of Wit', David Adam, *Guardian*, 23 May 2005
• 'Perhaps Laughter Is the Best Medicine', Mary Beth Janssen, *Conscious Choice* magazine, April 2004

CHAPTER 19: Spiritual Happiness
• Facts about religion taken from 'Focus on Religion', using the 2001 Census, Office of National Statistics
• Of the dozens of studies that have looked at religion and happiness, the vast majority have found a positive link. Harold Koenig at Duke University Medical Center in Durham, North Carolina, uncovered 100 papers on the subject, 79 of which showed that people who get involved in a religion are happier or more satisfied with their lives, or have more positive emotions than others.
• 'Reasons to Be Cheerful', Bob Holmes et al, *New Scientist*, 4 October 2003
• 'The Power to Uplift', *Time* magazine, 17 January 2005
• MORI Survey of 1230 British adults interviewed throughout Britain 1997
• 'Laid-back Britain Tolerates Everything Except the State', John Elliott, *Sunday Times*, 10 April 2005
• 'World Values Survey 2005' compiled using research from the London School of Economics
• *Happiness: Facts and Myths*, Michael W. Eysenck, (Psychology Press, 1990)
• *MHP*
• 'Does Religion Cause Violence? New UBC Study Finds Correlation between Social Aspect of Religion and Intolerance', Jesse Marchand, *Ubyssey College Magazine*, University of British Columbia, 23 November 2004
• *RC*
• *AH*

• *The Paradox of Choice: Why More Is Less*, Barry Schwartz (Ecco, 2004)
• 'The Benefits of Meditation', Colin Allen, *Psychology Today*, 24 April 2003
• 'The Biology of Joy', Michael D. Lemonick, *Time* magazine, 17 January 2005
• 'Meditation Leads to Longer Life', David Adam, *Guardian*, 2 May 2005
• 'Buddhist Leader to Teach in Anchorage', Debra McKinney, *Anchorage Daily News*, 21 April 2005
• 'Meditation', Johnny Adams, Lee-Benner Institute online newsletter, issue 44, www.theantiagingdoctor.com
• 'Silence Is Golden', Kate Kellaway, *Observer*, 12 June 2005

CHAPTER 20: Happy Ageing
• Facts about ageing taken from 'Focus on Older People', Office of National Statistics, 2001
• 'New Approach to Ageing', study led by Dr Sergei Scherbov of the Vienna Institute of Demography, 2005
• 'Reasons to Be Cheerful', Bob Holmes et al, (using material from Laura Carstensen) *New Scientist*, 4 October 2003
• '11 Steps to a Better Brain', Kate Douglas & Alison George, *New Scientist*, 28 May 2005
• 'The Future of Retirement', survey conducted for HSBC, 2005
• Over-60s 'too young to retire', Alan Jones, *Manchester Evening News*, 16 March 2005
• City & Guilds survey of 1200 people, 2005
• *MHP*
• *AH*
• 'Well-being over Time in Britain and the USA', David G. Blanchflower, Dartmouth College, Hanover, USA, & Andrew J. Oswald, Warwick University, *Journal of Public Economics*, 2004
• 'Intelligence is irrelevant to a happy old age', Gala Vince (using material from Alan Gow), *New Scientist*, 15 July 2005
• 'Marital Happiness, Marital Duration, and the U-Shaped Curve: Evidence from a Five-wave Panel Study', John Van Laningham, David R. Johnson, and Paul Amato, *Social Forces*, 78, 2001
• *Secrets of the Superyoung*, Dr David Weeks (Berkley Publishing Group, 1999)

Further Help
All information sourced from Mental Health Foundation; Mind; BUPA; NHS.

SLOUGH FACTS AND FIGURES

Here's a quick summary of facts about Slough to give you an idea of why the town was chosen for the TV series *Making Slough Happy*.

Founded 1186

Population 119,000 (2001 Census)

Location Berkshire, southeast England, about 25 miles from London. (Slough used to belong to the county of Buckinghamshire until the county boundaries were realigned in 1979, making the town part of Berkshire.)

Boroughs 14 in total – Langley St Mary's, Foxborough, Kedermister, Colnbrook with Poyle, Cippenham, Central, Wexham Lea, Chalvey, Stoke, Farnham, Britwell, Baylis, Upton and Haymill

Total businesses 3800, and the town is ranked as the 14th Best Place in Britain for business

Total jobs 78,000, including 30,000 daily commuters from other areas

Unemployment 3 per cent

Total homes Approximately 44,000

Local MP Fiona MacTaggart, Labour

Community Ethnically diverse, with 36 per cent of the population from ethnic minority backgrounds, including Pakistani, Indian, Afro-Caribbean, Polish, Ukrainian, Chinese and Italian

Education 38 schools, East Berkshire College and Thames Valley University are all located in the town.

Intelligence Records state that the highest concentration of educated people in the UK is in Slough

Health The residents of Slough enjoy health that is well above the national average, with the percentage of people deemed to have long-term illness below national figures. Their good health may be connected to the town's hard-water supply, which has been proven to reduce the risk of cardiovascular disease.

Parks 42 different parks set over 600 acres

Sports teams Slough Town FC; Slough Jets ice hockey team

Famous for The trading estate (the world's first), which was used as the location for the hit BBC2 comedy *The Office*. It remains the largest trading estate in Europe that is still under single ownership.

Oldest building St Lawrence's Church in Upton. The remaining walls and tower date back to Norman times.

Landmark The Montem Mound in Chalvey was the initiation site for new boys attending nearby Eton College, and was constructed during Norman times.

Culture Slough has an active arts and music scene, and frequently hosts festivals and community events at the West Wing Arts Centre. In July 2004 some 6000 people attended the 'Dance in the Park' festival to watch a range of dance performances by local young people.

Royal visits Queen Victoria made her first ever train journey from Slough railway station on 13 June 1842. Elizabeth II has visited twice – once during her 1953 Coronation year and again during the 2002 Jubilee Celebrations.

Famous residents Tracey Ullman, actress; Sir William Herschel (1738–1822), Astronomer Royal, who discovered the planet Uranus.

Links for further information

www.sloughmuseum.co.uk

www.slough.gov.uk

A SHORT HISTORY OF SLOUGH

Slough has a long history that dates back a thousand years to Saxon times. Its name was first recorded in 1444, and probably derives from the medieval word 'sloh', meaning a 'muddy, boggy place'. For many years the chief occupation in the area was farming, and the town's proximity to the river Thames meant that produce could be easily transported.

At the start of the coaching era in the eighteenth century Slough was transformed from a quiet hamlet to a thriving market town with a range of shops and services. The high-street inns served as welcome rest stops for travellers between London and Bath. However, the real catalyst for change was the London to Bristol railway, which passed through Slough. A station was built there in 1838 and the trains made it easier for people to move to the town in search of work: indeed, by 1851 the population had doubled.

When the First World War began in 1914, it kick-started Slough's second phase of industrial growth after masses of broken war vehicles were taken to the town for repair. What was initially known as 'The Dump' eventually became the world's first trading estate, and by 1927 around 65 firms were based there, including Black & Decker, Citroën Cars and Gillette.

During the years of the Depression (1929–34) the trading estate flourished, and thousands of unemployed people, particularly from Wales and Tyneside, flocked to Slough in search of work. Several new housing estates were built to accommodate them and the town boomed.

Further expansion and building followed the Second World War, when many Londoners and refugees from Poland, Ukraine and Hungary moved to Slough, attracted by the prospect of cheap rent and good work opportunities. Later influxes came from Commonwealth countries, such as India, Pakistan and the West Indies, and these were followed by new arrivals from Kenya and Uganda.

Industry, of course, does not always have an attractive face, and the poet John Betjeman lamented the loss of Slough's market-town charms in terms that rankle with local residents to this day.

How
to Be
Happy

'Come friendly bombs and fall on Slough
It isn't fit for humans now,
There isn't grass to graze a cow
Swarm over, Death!'
John Betjeman, 'Slough' (1937)

SLOUGH TODAY

Walk down Slough High Street today and you will quickly see that it has an eclectic fusion of different cultures. Pakistanis, Indians and Afro-Caribbeans constitute the town's largest ethnic groups and run many of the local businesses. They have all established their own community institutions and contributed greatly to Slough's vibrant arts scene.

Industry continues to boom and capitalize on the town's excellent location only a few miles from the world's busiest international airport at Heathrow. The trading estate is currently home to over 400 businesses, and many major international concerns, such as O_2 and Honda, have chosen Slough as their headquarters. It is a town for our times.

Appendix

How to work out your scores for the questions in the Happiness Questionnaire on pages 24–28

Although this scoring may seem complicated, it's worthwhile! Work through the instructions given below for calculating and interpreting your scores on each of the six questions. You will be calculating each score separately first, and then you can, if you want, work out your overall happiness score.

For purposes of comparison, the average scores of the *Making Slough Happy* volunteers as they were at the *beginning* of the happiness project are noted below for each question.

Life satisfaction
Question 1: Your score is the figure you gave yourself out of 10. Our Slough volunteers averaged 6.5 on this question before the project began.

This question has been asked in many countries, and the average results from a selection of them are as follows: Switzerland 8.4, Ireland 7.9, US 7.7, China 7.3, Turkey 6.4, Hungary 6.0, Romania 5.9, Russia 5.4, Bulgaria 5.0.

General happiness level
Question 2: Work up from the base of the list of feelings to find your score, using 1 for extremely unhappy to 10 for extremely happy. The Slough volunteers got an average score here of 6.5.
Question 3: Make sure your three percentages add up to 100. Compare the percentages you awarded yourself with the average percentages for the Slough volunteers: happy 41% of the time; unhappy 24% of the time; neutral 35% of the time.

Satisfaction with various aspects of your life
Question 4: Compare the scores you awarded yourself with the following figures for the Slough volunteers.

Work	6.2
Home	6.4
Leisure	6.0
Relationship	6.8
Family	7.0
Community	4.9
Environment	4.8
Diet	5.3
Exercise level	4.7
Yourself generally	6.0

Slough questionnaire
Question 5: Score yourself as follows:
1. Add up your scores on the following 15 statements: 1, 3, 6, 7, 9, 11, 13, 15, 17, 19, 22, 24, 27, 29, 30. This gives your positive (P) score.

2. Add up your scores on the other 15 statements: 2, 4, 5, 8, 10, 12, 14, 16, 18, 20, 21, 23, 25, 26, 28. This gives your negative (N) score.

3. Subtract your N score from your P score (i.e. P minus N). The result can range from -135 to +135.

4. Add 135 to your score to give a figure between 0 and 270. This is your 'raw' happiness score.

5. Look up your 'raw' happiness score on the Slough Questionnaire conversion table (see opposite, above). Your final happiness score for question 5 is the number in the column next to it (given on a scale of 100). On this 100 scale, the average score for the Slough volunteers at the beginning of the project was 62. How does your score compare?

Affectometer (mood scale)
Question 6: This is a scale that measures how positive or negative you are feeling. As such, it is likely to be more sensitive and changeable than the other scores above. It provided us with a very useful barometer of the mood in the Slough group at any particular time.

Score yourself as follows:
1. Add up your scores for the following 11 feelings: 1, 3, 7, 9, 11, 12, 14, 16, 19, 21, 22. This gives your positive affect (P) score.

2. Add your scores on the other 11 feelings: 2, 4, 5, 6, 8, 10, 13, 15, 17, 18, 20. This is your negative affect (N) score.

3. Subtract your N score from your P score (i.e. P minus N). The result can range from -99 to +99.

4. Add 99 to this result to arrive at a figure of up to 198. This is your 'raw' Affectometer score.

5. Look up this 'raw' score on the Affectometer conversion table (see opposite, below). The converted score in the column next to your 'raw' score is your final Affect (A)/mood scale score. The average A score for the Slough volunteers was 52.

Overall happiness measure
You can get an overall indication of your level of happiness by combining your scores on five of the questions (1, 2, 4, 5 and 6) as follows (question 3 provides an interesting comparison but is not included in calculating your overall happiness score):

1. Multiply by 10 each score on questions 1 and 2 to give scores between 10 and 100.

2. Add together all 10 subscores for question 4 to give a score between 1 and 100.

3. Add together the three scores you got from steps 1 and 2. Then add this total to your final happiness score from question 5 (Slough Questionnaire) and your final A score from question 6 (Affectometer). The figure you get now represents your combined total score for questions 1, 2, 4, 5 and 6.

4. Divide this combined total score by 5. This is your overall happiness score. The Slough volunteers averaged 60 on this.

SLOUGH QUESTIONNAIRE CONVERSION TABLE

Raw Score	Converted Score	Raw Score	Converted Score	Raw Score	Converted Score	Raw Score	Converted Score	Raw Score	Converted Score
1	0	55	20	109	40	163	60	217	80
2	1	56	21	110	41	164	61	218	81
3	1	57	21	111	41	165	61	219	81
4	1	58	21	112	41	166	61	220	81
5	2	59	22	113	42	167	62	221	82
6	2	60	22	114	42	168	62	222	82
7	3	61	23	115	43	169	63	223	83
8	3	62	23	116	43	170	63	224	83
9	3	63	23	117	43	171	63	225	83
10	4	64	24	118	44	172	64	226	84
11	4	65	24	119	44	173	64	227	84
12	4	66	24	120	44	174	64	228	84
13	5	67	25	121	45	175	65	229	85
14	5	68	25	122	45	176	65	230	85
15	6	69	26	123	46	177	66	231	86
16	6	70	26	124	46	178	66	232	86
17	6	71	26	125	46	179	66	233	86
18	7	72	27	126	47	180	67	234	87
19	7	73	27	127	47	181	67	235	87
20	7	74	27	128	47	182	67	236	87
21	8	75	28	129	48	183	68	237	88
22	8	76	28	130	48	184	68	238	88
23	9	77	29	131	49	185	69	239	89
24	9	78	29	132	49	186	69	240	89
25	9	79	29	133	49	187	69	241	89
26	10	80	30	134	50	188	70	242	90
27	10	81	30	135	50	189	70	243	90
28	10	82	30	136	50	190	70	244	90
29	11	83	31	137	51	191	71	245	91
30	11	84	31	138	51	192	71	246	91
31	11	85	31	139	51	193	71	247	91
32	12	86	32	140	52	194	72	248	92
33	12	87	32	141	52	195	72	249	92
34	13	88	33	142	53	196	73	250	93
35	13	89	33	143	53	197	73	251	93
36	13	90	33	144	53	198	73	252	93
37	14	91	34	145	54	199	74	253	94
38	14	92	34	146	54	200	74	254	94
39	14	93	34	147	54	201	74	255	94
40	15	94	35	148	55	202	75	256	95
41	15	95	35	149	55	203	75	257	95
42	16	96	36	150	56	204	76	258	96
43	16	97	36	151	56	205	76	259	96
44	16	98	36	152	56	206	76	260	96
45	17	99	37	153	57	207	77	261	97
46	17	100	37	154	57	208	77	262	97
47	17	101	37	155	57	209	77	263	97
48	18	102	38	156	58	210	78	264	98
49	18	103	38	157	58	211	78	265	98
50	19	104	39	158	59	212	79	266	99
51	19	105	39	159	59	213	79	267	99
52	19	106	39	160	59	214	79	268	99
53	20	107	40	161	60	215	80	269	100
54	20	108	40	162	60	216	80	270	100

AFFECTOMETER CONVERSION TABLE

Raw Score	Converted Score	Raw Score	Converted Score	Raw Score	Converted Score	Raw Score	Converted Score
1	1	51	26	101	51	151	76
2	1	52	26	102	52	152	77
3	2	53	27	103	52	153	77
4	2	54	27	104	53	154	78
5	3	55	28	105	53	155	78
6	3	56	28	106	54	156	79
7	4	57	29	107	54	157	79
8	4	58	29	108	55	158	80
9	5	59	30	109	55	159	80
10	5	60	30	110	56	160	81
11	6	61	31	111	56	161	81
12	6	62	31	112	57	162	82
13	7	63	32	113	57	163	82
14	7	64	32	114	58	164	83
15	8	65	33	115	58	165	83
16	8	66	33	116	59	166	84
17	9	67	34	117	59	167	84
18	9	68	34	118	60	168	85
19	10	69	35	119	60	169	85
20	10	70	35	120	61	170	86
21	11	71	36	121	61	171	86
22	11	72	36	122	62	172	87
23	12	73	37	123	62	173	87
24	12	74	37	124	63	174	88
25	13	75	38	125	63	175	88
26	13	76	38	126	64	176	89
27	14	77	39	127	64	177	89
28	14	78	39	128	65	178	90
29	15	79	40	129	65	179	90
30	15	80	40	130	66	180	91
31	16	81	41	131	66	181	91
32	16	82	41	132	67	182	92
33	17	83	42	133	67	183	92
34	17	84	42	134	68	184	93
35	18	85	43	135	68	185	93
36	18	86	43	136	69	186	94
37	19	87	44	137	69	187	94
38	19	88	44	138	70	188	95
39	20	89	45	139	70	189	95
40	20	90	45	140	71	190	96
41	21	91	46	141	71	191	96
42	21	92	46	142	72	192	97
43	22	93	47	143	72	193	97
44	22	94	47	144	73	194	98
45	23	95	48	145	73	195	98
46	23	96	48	146	74	196	99
47	24	97	49	147	74	197	99
48	24	98	49	148	75	198	100
49	25	99	50	149	75		
50	25	100	50	150	76		

.67

-, 68

... friendships 62
... marriage 56, 90
... and satisfaction levels 17, 36, 199
and smoking 152
and work 73
ageing see older people
Ainsworth, Mary 92
alcohol 151, 152–3, 156
alternative therapies 210
Alzheimer's disease 143, 192, 201
ambition 42, 45
anxiety 35, 148, 155, 158, 159, 164
anxious lovers 92, 93
applied relaxation 210
Argyle, Michael 17
authoritarian parents 124f5
authoritative parents 124, 125
autotelic personalities 73
avoidant lovers 92, 93

babies, and smiling 181, 182
Bacon, Sir Francis 50
'balcony' holidays 170
Balding, Angela 157
behavioural therapy 209
Bentham, Jeremy 66
Bergman, Ingrid 143
Berk, Lee 187
beta-endorphin 157
Betjeman, John 218–19
biodanza 41–2, 111
Blakebrough, Adele 11, 176
Blumenthal, James 157
body language 82
Borge, Victor 185
Bowlby, Dr John 92, 124
the brain
    activity patterns 18
    and ageing 201
    creating new habit pathways 45
    and exercise 157–8
    and food 128, 129–32, 136
    and laughter 186
    and loving relationships 91–2
    and meditation 194
    plasticity 22
    and sex 104–5
    and sleep 149
    and smiling 181, 182
Buddhism 191
Burns, George 117

caffeine 135, 151
Camus, Albert 74
CAN (Community Action Network) 11, 176, 180
cannabis 152, 153
carbohydrates 130, 131, 136
career breaks 89
Carlyle, Thomas 85
Carnegie, Dale 53
Carstensen, Laura 199
CBT (cognitive behaviour therapy) 206, 208, 209
changing ways of thinking 32–3
Chapman, Philippa 10–11, 74, 78, 79, 80
child-rearing practices 17

childcare 41, 83
childhood ambitions 42
children 71, 95, 118–27
    attitudes to parents 120
    birth of and sexual happiness 107
    and education 123–4
    and exercise 157
    facts about 118
    and family relationships 118, 119
    fostering resilience in 122–3
    and parenting styles 124–5
    and pets 163–4
    and play 120, 126
    and quality time 121
    setting loving boundaries 121
    and sleep 151
Churchill, Winston 112
Citizenship Survey (2003) 178
civic engagement 174–5
Cleese, John 189
Cole, Doug 120
collective societies 175
communication 61, 100
    and laughter 186
    and stress 154
    taking time to talk 12
community 171–80
    action 175–8
    and democracy 174–5
    facts about 171
    and meaning in life 172–3
    and social capital 174, 179–80
    and social support 171, 175
    and voluntary work 30, 76, 173–4, 178, 179
comparing yourself with others 32, 43
complementary therapies 210
Connolly, Billy 103
Corlett, Linda 23
cortisol 144
counselling 206–8
counting your blessings 12, 18, 35, 44, 204
couscous, spicy mackerel with 140
Coward, Noël 72
Cox, Tracey 105, 107, 108
creativity 20, 30, 186
Crisp, Quentin 119
Cosby, Bill 125
Csikszentmihalyi, Mihaly 37, 39, 55, 61, 72, 88, 135

dancing 17, 41–2, 111, 203
Davidson, Richard 148
de Botton, Alain 166, 167, 169
depression 16, 20, 21, 35, 64, 65, 143
    and cannabis 153
    in children 126
    and diet 129, 130, 136
    exercise as an antidepressant 155, 156, 158, 159
    and pets 164
    and physical health 146
    treatments for 206
    and work 74, 75
diabetes 146
Dickens, Charles 67
Diener, Ed 32, 55, 69, 70
diet see eating
Dietrich, Marlene 52
disabilities and serious illnesses 21–2, 147

divorce 94, 95, 99, 112, 192
dogs 160, 165
dopamine 18, 132
downshifting 89
drug abuse 152, 153, 156
Duchenne smiles 181, 182

eating 128–42, 204
    as an art form 135
    diet and mental health 128, 130, 132–4, 136, 210
    facts about food 128
    family mealtimes 127
    food and the brain 128, 129–32, 136
    food diaries 134–5
    good mood foods 132–4
    recipes 138–42
education 123–4
email 183
Emmons, Robert 146, 154
endorphins 104, 131, 155, 156, 186
Epicurus 51
exercise 12, 16, 155–61
    and the brain 157–8
    and children 127
    facts about 155
    moderate 159
    and older people 156–7, 204
    and pain relief 157
    walking 159, 160
experiencing self 41
extended families 113–15
eye contact 61, 82, 111

fake smiles 182, 183
families 112–17
    arguments and feuds 114
    extended 113–15
    facts about family life 112
    and friendships 55, 56–7
    siblings 116–17
    strengthening family ties 115
family and relationship counselling 209
fat in the diet 132
Ferguson, Will, Happiness TM 20
fish 136, 204
    salmon and monkfish kebabs 139
    spicy mackerel with couscous 140
flexitime 88–9
flow activities 37–40
    and children 120
    and community 179
    eating 135
    and family life 113
    and friendships 52
    and holidays 167
    and kindness 173
    and work 72, 73, 88
flying, fear of 170
food see eating
Frank, Robert 63, 67
Franklin, Benjamin 111
Freud, Sigmund 42, 76
friendships 12, 50–62
    best friends 58
    cross-generational 62
    defining 51
    facts about 50
    and families 56–7
    freedom in 51–2
    ladder of needs 57

How to Be Happy

and life expectancy 54
maintenance of 58–9
need for 54–5
and older people 204
and play 52
and the power of touch 53–4
and religion 191
and smiling 182
and social skills 53, 55
ways to be a better friend 60–2
and work 50, 56, 77

gardening 47, 158, 159, 160, 204
garlic 137
genes and happiness 16, 21, 22
Gervais, Ricky 147
Gilbert, David 167
glucose 129–30
Goldmeier, Dr David 105
Gottman, John, The Relationship Cure
    57, 96, 97, 99, 108
Gow, Alan 202
GPs (general practitioners), and
    counselling 207
`gratitude party' 48
graveyard therapy 193
grief, and laughter 187
group therapy 209

habits, couples and most hated habits
    98
happiness, defining 15
Happiness Manifesto 7–8, 12–13, 56,
    153, 206
hardship, coping with 46
Harker, LeeAnne and Keltner 182
health 143–54
    and alcohol/drugs 152–3
    and exercise 146, 155, 156
    facts about 143
    and friendships 50, 51, 54
    and happiness 145, 146–7
    and laughter 186
    and meditation 194, 195
    and optimism 30, 144, 145
    and pets 162–3
    and religion 192
    and sleep 149–51
    and work 144
    see also mental health
healthy eating 129–35, 136–7
heart disease 57, 143, 145, 146,
    147, 165
    and laughter 187
hedonistic treadmill 21, 64
Helvin, Marie 183
Henry, Jane 23
herbalism 210
herbs for happiness 134
Hirsch, Samuel Raphael 182
hobbies 46, 72
Hodson, Philip 55
holidays 166–70
    `balcony' holidays 170
    choosing the right holiday
        169–70
    and stress 166, 168
    and work 168–9
Holmes, Kelly 123
homeopathy 210
homosexuality 90
hospitals, animals in 164
housework 39, 158, 160
humanist therapy 209
humanistic psychologists 38
Huxley, Aldous, Brave New World 20

immigrants 16
immune system 144, 147
India
    laughter clubs 188, 189

life satisfaction in 175
individualism culture 171, 175
indulgent parents 125
intelligence, and old age 201–2
intolerance, and religion 193

Jourard, Sidney 54
junk food 136

Kahneman, Daniel 22
Kahr, Brett 9–10, 35, 42, 97, 107,
    177
    on children 121
    on family life 114
    and friendships 51, 56, 59
Kaplan, Dr H. Roy 70
Kataria, Dr Madan 189
Keller, Helen 30
Keltner, Dacher 182, 187
kidney dialysis patients 22
kindness 12, 48, 173–4

Ladner, Lorne 191
laughter 12, 50, 52, 185–9
    clubs 188–9
Layard, Richard 65, 123
LETS (Local Exchange Trading Systems)
    178–9
life expectancy 54, 145, 198
listening 100, 101, 102
living alone 55, 171
lottery winners 21, 67, 70
love 90–102
    building a relationship `bank'
        96–7
    choosing a happy partner 92–3
    facts on the British love life 90
    handling conflict 97–8
    and romantic illusions 91
low self-esteem 31–2
low-carbohydrate diets 130
Lucas, Dr Richard 94

McNicholas, Dr June 163
marriage 90, 99–101, 182
    age of 56, 90
    and family life 112
    and happiness 17, 93–4
    and older people 202
    and sex 103, 104
Martin, Paul 120, 123, 124, 151
Maslow, Abraham 38
massage 54, 210
Maurois, André 110
Mawson, Andrew 11, 171, 172,
    175–6, 177
maximizers 33, 34
medal-winners 17
meditation 193–6
men
    and alcohol 152
    and exercise 155
    and friendships 50, 56, 57
    and holidays 166, 168
    and laughter 185
    and loving relationships 90, 91–2,
        93, 95
    and money 63
    and retreats 196
    and sex 103, 105, 110
    single 94–5
    and smiling 182, 183
mental health 35, 36, 143
    and cannabis 153
    and diet 128, 130, 132–4, 136,
        210
    and exercise 155, 156, 158
    and friendships 51
    and money 65, 71
    and pets 162–3
    and religion 190–1, 192

and sex 104
    see also depression
minerals in food 133
Moebius syndrome 183
The Monastery (BBC series) 196
money 16, 36, 42, 63–71
    facts about 63, 71
    income levels 63–4, 67, 70
    and lottery winners 21, 67, 70
    and the politics of happiness 65–6
    and reference anxiety 68–9
    and status 68
    wealth and happiness 16, 17, 29,
        67–8, 69
    and work 67, 73, 76
Morton, Samantha 123
Mother Teresa 181
Mullan, Nevia 23, 45
music 17, 46
Muslims 190, 192
myths about happiness 20

negative feelings 43, 44–5, 87–8
neighbourliness see community
neurolinguistic programming (NLP) 210
noradrenalin 132
Norenzayan, Ara 191–2
nuns 134, 201

obesity 74, 146, 155
older people 198–204
    and exercise 156–7, 160, 203
    and happiness 16, 36, 199–200
    and sex 105, 204
    and work 198, 200–1
Ono, Yoko 35
optimism 30, 43, 144, 145
    pretending 46
Oswald, Andrew 68, 70, 71
oysters 137

pain relief
    and exercise 157
    and laughter 187
paraplegics 22, 147
parenting styles 124–5
pedometers 159
pessimism 30, 43, 44–5
    and health 143, 154
pets 17, 160, 162–5
play 52, 120, 126
pleasure 18–19, 29, 43
politics
    and community 172
    of happiness 65–6
positive psychology 22, 35, 36, 38
positive thinking 43, 44
poverty 63, 175, 176
power-napping 150, 151
prisoners, and pets 165
protein-rich foods 131, 132, 136
Provine, Robert 186
Pryce-Jones, Jessica 10–11, 46, 100
    and work 74, 75, 78, 79, 80, 87
psychoanalysis 209
psychodynamic therapy 208, 209
Putnam, Robert D. 174
putting unwelcome thoughts out of
    mind 148

questionnaires
    happiness 23–8
    work 84–5

recipes
    baked aubergines 142
    lemon and dill turkey escalopes
        138
    spicy mackerel with couscous 140
    salmon and monkfish kebabs 139
    vegetarian chilli 141

...self 41
...ricted Environmental
...mulation Therapy) 151
...eats 196
Reynolds, Arthur 122
Rogers, Carl 38

sadness 18, 19
satisfaction 17, 29, 32, 36
satisficers 33, 34
schizophrenia
    and cannabis 153
    and exercise 156, 158
Schultz, Charles 165
Schwartz, Barry 33, 192
science of happiness 35–48
seasonal affective disorder (SAD)
    156
secure lovers 92, 93
securely attached children 119
self-absorption 60
self-employment 89, 201
self-esteem 31–2, 46
    and exercise 156, 158, 160
    and pets 164
Seligman, Martin 31, 32, 38
    on children 127
    on components of happiness
        172–3
    on emotional types 92
    on friendships 55
    on gratification activities 43
    on health 147
    on loving relationships 100, 101
    on money 69
    on pessimism 154
    and positive psychology 35
    on signature strengths 36–7
serotonin 129, 131, 136, 147, 156,
    186
'set point' of happiness 21–2, 95
sexual happiness 71, 103–11
    and affairs 109
    and the brain 104–5
    and exercise 156
    facts about sex 103
    mismatched desire 106–7
    and role confusion 107
    ways to have a better sex life
        108–9
Shaw, George Bernard 6
Shields, Brooke 48
shift work 149
shopping 71
short cuts to happiness 43
siblings 116–17, 127
signature strengths 36–7, 87, 88,
    100
    of children 126
Sikhs 190, 192
single people 93, 94–5
sleep 108, 127, 149, 149–51, 156
    and holidays 167–8
    power-napping 150, 151
Slough
    facts and figures 217
    short history 218
    today 219
Slough Project 7–8, 32, 35

and alcohol 153
and childhood dreams 42
and children 125
and community 175, 177–8, 180
and exercise 156, 157, 158, 161
and families 115, 116
and flow 38, 39, 40
and friendships 52, 55, 56, 59
'gratitude party' 48
Happiest Day 177
and the Happiness Manifesto 7–8,
    13
happiness questionnaire 26–7
happiness workshops 47
and health 144, 146, 147
and laughter 189
and loving relationships 94, 102
and money 69
and negative feelings 44–5
and pets 163, 164
and sex 107, 110, 111
Smile Campaign 184
and spiritual happiness 191, 192,
    195
and touch 54
and work 74, 78, 79, 80–1
smiling 181–4
smoking 152, 154
Snowdon, David 201
social capital 163, 174, 179–80
social skills 53, 55
Spain, Nancy 121
spiritual happiness 190–7
Steinem, Gloria 94
Steptoe, Professor Andrew 144
Stevens, Richard 9, 18, 54
    and community 172, 178
    and dancing 41
    and diet 137
    and exercise 156
    and friendship 61
    and graveyard therapy 193
    and the ingredients of happiness
        19
    and kindness 48
    and loving relationships 93, 100,
        102
    and maximizers/satisficers 33
    and money 64
    and parenting 122
    and putting unwelcome thoughts
        out of mind 148
    and the science of happiness 38,
        39, 42, 43, 47, 48
    and sex 111
    and spiritual happiness 196, 197
    and touch 53–4
    and work 80–1
Stevenson, Robert Louis 19
Stewart, James 199
strangers 12
stress management 146
    'good' stress 147–8
stress relief 46
    and holidays 166, 168
    and laughter 187, 189
    and meditation 194
    and religion 191
stress-related illness 143
suffering 20
suicide 29, 71, 143
sunscreens 204

taking good care of yourself exercise
    47–8
television viewing 12, 46, 115
    and children 127, 151
text messaging 183
therapy 206–10
Thompson, Helen Taylor 11, 176
tickling 188

time
    past, present and future 31
    taking control of 46
touch, and friendships 53–4
transcendental meditation (TM) 104
treats 12
tryptophan 131–2, 136, 151
Tunes (Slough engineering company)
    74, 79
twelve steps to happiness 46–7
Type H personalities 187

unemployment 76
uninvolved parents 125

very happy people 32, 53
VHF (visual, hearing, feeling) 81–2
vitamins 133, 137, 204
voluntary work 30, 76, 173–4, 178,
    179

walking 159, 160
Watters, Ethan, Urban Tribes 56–7
Weeks, Dr David 106, 204
Werner, Emmy 122
widows 95
women
    and alcohol 152
    and exercise 155, 160
    and friendships 50, 56, 57
    and holidays 166, 168
    and laughter 185
    and loving relationships 95
    and money 63, 67
    and sex 90, 103, 104, 105, 110
    single 94, 185
    and smiling 182, 183
    and work 77, 82
work 72–89
    bad jobs 74, 75–6
    and body language 82
    and career breaks 89
    commuting to 6, 73, 86
    facts about 73
    and flexitime 88–9
    and flow 72, 73
    and friendships 50, 56, 77
    happiness at 75, 77–80
    'happy' professions 86–7
    and health 144
    and holidays 168–9
    job satisfaction 72, 73, 76–7,
        80–1, 84
    long hours of 55, 74, 82–3
    and money 67, 73, 76, 85
    and older people 198, 200–1
    and personal relationships 72
    and the politics of happiness 65
    questionnaire 84–5
    relationships with colleagues 78,
        80, 81–2
    shift work 149
    and signature strengths 87
    and stress 143
    unpaid/voluntary 72, 76
work and happiness 29
work–life balance 82–3, 85, 151, 200
workplace counselling 207

yoga 160, 194
    laughing yoga clubs 188–9
young offenders, and exercise 156
young people 71, 90

Zen meditation 196
Zimbardo, Philip 31

How to Be Happy